Ms. Anna L. Wilson
2523 Pickett Rd.
Durham, NC 27705-5606

US FOREIGN POLICY ON
TRANSITIONAL JUSTICE

US FOREIGN POLICY ON TRANSITIONAL JUSTICE

ANNIE R. BIRD

OXFORD
UNIVERSITY PRESS

OXFORD
UNIVERSITY PRESS

Oxford University Press is a department of the University of
Oxford. It furthers the University's objective of excellence in research,
scholarship, and education by publishing worldwide.

Oxford   New York
Auckland   Cape Town   Dar es Salaam   Hong Kong   Karachi
Kuala Lumpur   Madrid   Melbourne   Mexico City   Nairobi
New Delhi   Shanghai   Taipei   Toronto

With offices in
Argentina   Austria   Brazil   Chile   Czech Republic   France   Greece
Guatemala   Hungary   Italy   Japan   Poland   Portugal   Singapore
South Korea   Switzerland   Thailand   Turkey   Ukraine   Vietnam

Oxford is a registered trademark of Oxford University Press
in the UK and certain other countries.

Published in the United States of America by
Oxford University Press
198 Madison Avenue, New York, NY 10016

© Oxford University Press 2015

Library of Congress Cataloging-in-Publication Data
Bird, Annie R.
US foreign policy on transitional justice / Annie R. Bird.
pages cm
Includes bibliographical references and index.
ISBN 978-0-19-933841-2 (hardcover : alk. paper)   1. Transitional justice—Government policy—United
States.   2. United States—Foreign relations.   3. Transitional justice—Cambodia.   4. Truth commissions—
Cambodia.   5. Transitional justice—Liberia.   6. Truth commissions—Liberia.
7. Transitional justice—Colombia.   8. Truth commissions—Colombia.   I. Title.   II. Title: United States foreign
policy on transitional justice.
JC580.B57 2015
327.73—dc23
2014032892

Dr. Annie Bird authored this work in her private capacity before beginning employment with the U.S. government and
does not advise on policy for the countries referenced. The views and analysis presented do not necessarily reflect U.S.
government policy views on conflict situations, peace negotiations or transitional justice agreements.

9 8 7 6 5 4 3 2 1
Printed in the United States of America
on acid-free paper

For Mom and Yuuki

CONTENTS

ACKNOWLEDGMENTS

Three UC Berkeley professors—Eric Stover, David Cohen, and Rita Maran—inspired my interest and lasting commitment to human rights over a decade ago. I am forever grateful.

The research for this book was undertaken at the London School of Economics and supported by a Marshall Scholarship. Chris Brown provided helpful supervision along the way, and Jens Meierhenrich and Kieran McEvoy served as thoughtful PhD examiners. Erik Voeten provided guidance while I was a visiting researcher at Georgetown University. Leslie Vinjamuri and other members of the London Transitional Justice Network afforded a supportive transitional justice community in London. Financial support for fieldwork was generously provided by the Marshall Commission, LSE's International Relations department, and the Abbey Santander Group.

I benefited from the valuable insights of nearly 200 people who agreed to be interviewed for my research. US war crimes ambassadors, embassy officials, and many others in Washington helped me understand the landscape of US transitional justice policy. Officials at the Extraordinary Chambers in the Courts of Cambodia, the Special Court for Sierra Leone, the Liberian Truth and Reconciliation Commission, the Colombian Justice and Peace Unit and National Commission for Reparations and Reconciliation, and the courts in The Hague helped me understand their experiences in working with the US government. Academic experts, along with staff from numerous international organizations, NGOs, local civil society groups, and media outlets provided a more complete picture and thoughtful analysis on the topic. This book would not have been possible without these interviewees, and those who helped connect me to them.

Kirsten Ainley encouraged me to get the research published. Angela Chnapko at Oxford University Press showed enthusiasm for the project from the start. Cindy Huang helped get me to the finish line. Special thanks to David Bosco, Par Engstrom, Eric Wiebelhaus-Brahm, John Ciorciari, Beth van Schaack, Jaya Ramji-Nogales, Erik Voeten, Ruti Teitel, Thierry Cruvelier, Roger Duthie, Peter Winn, Andy Loomis, Charlie Brown, Chandra Sriram, and Lara Nettlefield for their important feedback on all or parts of the manuscript.

My gratitude for the moral support of friends and family cannot be overstated. My London friends helped get me through my PhD—Gillian Cameron, Lila Caballero-Sosa, Mariana Escobar, Alia Mossallam, Maja Rasmussen, Filippo Dionigi, Yaniv Voller, Simon Bastow, Vaho Vakhtangidze, Stephane Derone, Joyce Baz, and Rachel Katzman. Old friends in California provided steady long-distance support, and new friends in Washington kept me motivated through the revision process. Yuuki Shinomiya kept me going through the highs and lows of writing with food, encouragement, and calm. My mother, Maiu Bird, never wavered in her support for me or this book.

LIST OF ABBREVIATIONS

AUC   United Self-Defense Forces of Colombia
CNRR   National Commission for Reparations and Reconciliation
DOD   US Department of Defense
DOJ   US Department of Justice
ECCC   Extraordinary Chambers in the Courts of Cambodia
ICC   International Criminal Court
ICGL   International Contact Group on Liberia
ICTJ   International Center for Transitional Justice
ICTR   International Criminal Tribunal for Rwanda
ICTY   International Criminal Tribunal for the Former Yugo-slavia
IMT   International Military Tribunal
JPL   Justice and Peace Law
JPU   Justice and Peace Unit
NGO   nongovernmental organization
NSC   National Security Council
RGC   Royal Government of Cambodia
SCSL   Special Court for Sierra Leone
TRC   Truth and Reconciliation Commission
UNSC   United Nations Security Council
USAID US Agency for International Development
USUN   US Mission to the United Nations

US FOREIGN POLICY ON
TRANSITIONAL JUSTICE

Introduction

Nearly 70 years have passed since the historic Nuremberg trials prosecuted the leadership of Nazi Germany. Of the Allied powers, the United States took the lead in establishing an international military tribunal, staffing it with expert lawyers, and funding it. Another 12 trials of Nazi leaders were prosecuted by the United States alone.[1] Nuremberg—and the legacy it left about the importance of accountability for war crimes, crimes against humanity, and genocide—would not have happened without US support. Yet this support was not inevitable, nor was it unaffected by specific visions of what this justice should look like or the impact of other US interests.

This book sheds light on these ambiguities in US foreign policy. Since the Cold War ended, the United States has played a pivotal role in "transitional justice"—a term often used to describe a society's attempts to address a legacy of large-scale past abuses, often through measures like trials, truth commissions, and reparations.[2] In a range of measures established around the globe, the United States has been a key driver of transitional justice, providing crucial political backing, as well as key technical and financial assistance. Among the handful of donors most active in transitional justice, US assistance far surpasses the others.[3] The United States exercises significant influence on domestic and international decisions to establish transitional justice measures, their design, and how they are carried out.

US involvement in transitional justice, as in other areas of its foreign policy, is multifaceted and complex. By "opening the black box" of US foreign policy, this book shows how the diverse interests and constantly evolving priorities of presidential administrations, Congress, the State Department, and other federal agencies shape US involvement in transitional justice. What we discover is that, despite multiple influences, a distinctive US approach to the field is evident.

Understanding the US approach to transitional justice is important because it has significantly influenced how societies address past abuse. Surprisingly, however, studies of US involvement in transitional justice are almost nonexistent. What literature there is tends to critique US involvement in excessively broad terms,[4] or has assessed details of the US role in a single mechanism, with a great deal of attention on the International Criminal Court.[5] No study thus far has analyzed the US approach to transitional justice in a systematic, cross-cutting manner. This study aims to address this gap.

This book argues that US foreign policy on transitional justice is characterized by a distinctive approach that is symbolic, retributive, and strategic. The symbolic feature helps explain how and why the United States supports transitional justice. The retributive feature highlights a particular model of transitional justice that the United States promotes. The strategic feature explains fluctuations in US support for the field. Together, these themes shed light on how an influential, international actor like the United States approaches a new policy area and how this approach can shape an emerging international norm like transitional justice.

The United States supports transitional justice first and foremost because of the powerful symbolic role that "justice" plays in American society. Trials, in particular, are seen as an enactment of justice by making sense of an event through the telling of a coherent story about what happened in order to reach a verdict (a *vere dictum*, literally, a "saying of the truth"). To do this, the story must be simplified by limiting the narrative to specific actors for specific crimes during a specific timeframe. For US policymakers, "justice" is served in transitional justice contexts when a high-profile perpetrator, like Pol Pot or Charles Taylor, is the focus of attention. By "getting the bad guy," transitional justice also reinforces a dualistic narrative about "good versus evil" that is a core element of American identity, making the field appealing to support. Such symbol-laden arguments can help engender public support for, interest in, and commitment to transitional justice.

The United States also promotes a retributive model of transitional justice. Transitional justice measures can be broadly grouped into two categories: those that focus on punishing a perpetrator, primarily through criminal prosecutions; and those that focus on more "victim-centric" mechanisms like truth commissions and reparation programs. The American tradition of punishment through law, coupled with a US foreign policy bureaucracy that has dedicated significant resources to supporting criminal prosecutions, means that the United States tends to provide greater support to trials than other measures of transitional justice.

The US approach is strategic because of the way that it uses transitional justice instrumentally to advance its interests, or blocks it when it fails to advance these interests. For example, a transitional justice measure may be supported as an alternative to a more costly response, to enhance the US reputation, or even as a way to encourage regime change. In contrast, if transitional justice is perceived as interfering with US objectives, the United States may lessen its support or actively block assistance.[6] Whenever a new mechanism is established or investigation is begun, the United States will invariably work to ensure that it does not claim jurisdiction or authority over US nationals.

These three themes are explored in an examination of the development of US foreign policy over time and through three illustrative case studies. From World War I to the present, we see the features of the US approach begin to take shape. Four influential war crimes tribunals—Nuremberg, the International Criminal Tribunals for the Former Yugoslavia and Rwanda, and the International Criminal Court—provide a particularly helpful foundation for analyzing US involvement in the field. A more in-depth examination of three case studies allows for a closer look at US involvement in specific transitional justice measures.

Before describing these cases, it is helpful to note the wider universe of cases from which this study's cases were chosen.

Table 0.1 US Involvement in Transitional Justice, 1993–2007

Country	Measure type	Transition type	US involvement
Africa			
The Democratic Republic of Congo	Prosecutions	Ongoing conflict	Political support
Liberia	Prosecutions/ truth commission	Post-conflict	Technical, financial, and political support
Rwanda	Prosecutions/ truth commission/ reparations	Post-conflict	Technical, financial, and political support
Sierra Leone	Prosecutions/ truth commission/ reparations	Post-conflict	Technical, financial, and political support
South Africa	Truth commission/ reparations	Post-apartheid	No statement found
Americas			
Argentina	Reparations	Past conflict	No statement found
Brazil	Truth commission/ reparations	Past dictatorship	No statement found
Colombia	Prosecutions/ truth commission/ reparations	Ongoing conflict	Technical, financial, and political support
Guatemala	Prosecutions/ truth commission/ reparations	Post-conflict	Technical support

(continued)

Table 0.1 *(Continued)*

Country	Measure type	Transition type	US involvement
Peru	Prosecutions/ truth commission/ reparations	Post-conflict	Technical, financial, and political support
Asia			
Cambodia	Prosecutions	Past conflict	Technical, financial, and political support
Timor-Leste	Prosecutions/ truth commission/ reparations	Post-conflict	Political support
Europe			
Former Yugoslavia	Prosecutions	Post-conflict	Technical, financial, and political support
Middle East and North Africa			
Morocco	Truth commission/ reparations	Past repression	Political support

Table 0.1 highlights countries where a transitional justice measure was established between 1993 and 2007 and is accompanied by a short description of US involvement.[7]

From this list, three cases were selected. The first examines US involvement in and support for the Khmer Rouge Tribunal, a hybrid court established in 2004 by the UN and Cambodia to prosecute the crimes of senior Khmer Rouge leaders committed from 1975 to 1979. The second case focuses on US involvement in two measures involving Liberia: the trial of former Liberian president Charles Taylor, who was indicted by the Special Court for Sierra Leone in 2003, and the Liberian Truth and Reconciliation Commission (TRC), established in 2005. The third case examines US involvement in the Colombian Justice and Peace Law, passed in 2005, to investigate paramilitary crimes and support victims' rights and reparation.

These cases represent different transitional justice mechanisms (criminal prosecutions, truth-seeking, and reparation programs), different "transition" types (past abuse, post-conflict, and ongoing conflict), and different geographic regions (Asia, Africa, and Latin America).[8] They also each involve a case where the United States provided technical, financial, and political support. This variation permitted the identification of different US government participants involved in transitional justice, different types of involvement, as well as different motives and interests for their involvement. In addition, since the measures were all established in the early 2000s, they remain under-examined in the transitional justice literature, offering an opportunity to present new empirical data and analytical insights.

The wealth and richness of original material generated through nearly 200 interviews on five continents with officials in government, transitional justice measures, international organizations, nongovernmental organizations (NGOs), academia, and the media underpins much of the analysis and conclusions reached in this research.[9] Data collection also involved a longitudinal analysis of US diplomatic initiatives, strategic messaging, and programming, drawing on US government documents, UN and NGO reports, media reporting, and scholarly literature from different disciplines.

Aimed at a better understanding of the US approach to transitional justice, this book may serve as a basis for further analysis and improved policymaking in a field that is critical to addressing 21st-century problems. It is structured as follows: Chapter 1 establishes a framework for analyzing US foreign policy and introduces the three themes that characterize the US approach to transitional justice. Chapter 2 provides a historical overview of US foreign policy on transitional justice from World War I through the early 2010s. Chapters 3–5 explore three case studies (Cambodia, Liberia, and Colombia) to look at how US foreign policy on transitional justice has been implemented. The book concludes with a summary of key findings, implications of the study, and avenues for further research.

Notes

1 For more information about these trials, see the Nuremberg Trials Project at Harvard Law School.

2 A 2004 UN report of the secretary-general outlined the purpose of transitional justice and the measures most commonly associated with the field: "The notion of 'transitional justice' . . . comprises the full range of processes and mechanisms associated with a society's attempts to come to terms with a legacy of large-scale past abuses, in order to ensure accountability, serve justice and achieve reconciliation. These may include both judicial and non-judicial mechanisms, with differing levels of international involvement (or none at all) and individual prosecutions, reparations, truth-seeking, institutional reform, vetting and dismissals, or a combination thereof." UN Report of the Secretary-General to the UN Security Council, "The Rule of Law and Transitional Justice in Conflict and Post-conflict Societies," S/2004/616, 23 August 2004.

3 See William Muck and Eric Wiebelhaus-Brahm, "Patterns of Transitional Justice Assistance Among the International Community," Paper presented at the Sixth European Consortium for Political Research General Conference, Reykjavik, 25 August 2011, 31–34. They found that five donors provide most assistance to transitional justice: Canada, the United Kingdom, Japan, the Netherlands, and the United States.

4 For example, see Rosemary Nagy, "Transitional Justice as Global Project: Critical Reflections," *Third World Quarterly* 29, no. 2 (2008): 287; Chandra Lekha Sriram, "Justice as Peace? Liberal Peacebuilding and Strategies of Transitional Justice," *Global Society* 21, no. 4 (2007): 579–91; and Patricia Lundy and Mark McGovern, "Whose Justice? Rethinking Transitional Justice from the Bottom Up," *Journal of Law and Society* 35, no. 2 (2008): 276–77.

5 Much of the discussion of the US role has centered around its position on the ICC. For example, see William A. Schabas, "United States Hostility to the International Criminal Court: It's All about the Security Council," *European Journal of International Law* 14, no. 4 (2004): 701–20; Ruth Wedgwood, "Fiddling in Rome: America and the International Criminal Court," *Foreign Affairs* 77, no. 6 (1998): 20–24; Ruth Wedgwood, "The International Criminal Court: An American View," *European Journal of International Law* 10, no. 93 (1999); Diane Marie Amann and M. N. S. Sellers, "United States of America and the International Criminal Court," *American Journal of Comparative Law* 50 (supplement) (2002): 381–404; Bartram Brown, "U.S. Objections to the Statute of the International Criminal Court: A Brief Response," *New York University Journal of International Law and Politics* 31 (1999): 855; Bartram Brown, "Unilateralism, Multilateralism,

and the International Criminal Court," in *Multilateralism and US Foreign Policy: Ambivalent Engagement*, ed. Stewart Patrick and Shepard Forman (Boulder, CO: Lynne Rienner, 2002); Bruce Broomhall, *International Justice and the International Criminal Court: Between Sovereignty and the Rule of Law* (New York: Oxford University Press, 2003); Jack Goldsmith, "The Self-Defeating International Criminal Court," *University of Chicago Law Review* 70, no. 1 (2003): 89–104; Gerhard Hafner, Kristen Boon, Anne Rübesame, and Jonathan Huston, "A Response to the American View as Presented by Ruth Wedgwood," *European Journal of International Law* 10, no. 1 (1999): 108–23; Henry T. King and Theodore C. Theofrastous, "From Nuremberg to Rome: A Step Backward for US Foreign Policy," *Case Western Reserve Journal of International Law* 31, no. 1 (1999): 47–106; Daryl Mundis, "United States of America and International Justice—Has Lady Liberty Lost Her Way? The Editorial Comments on the USA and the ICC," *Journal of International Criminal Justice* 2, no. 1 (2004): 2–10; Monroe Leigh, "The United States and the Statute of Rome," *American Journal of International Law* 95, no. 1 (2001): 124–31; William K. Lietzau, "The United States and the International Criminal Court: Concerns from a US Military Perspective," *Law and Contemporary Problems* 64, no. 119 (2001): 119–40; Diane F. Orentilicher, "Unilateral Multilateralism: United States Policy toward the International Criminal Court," *Cornell International Law Journal* 36 (2003–4):415–33; Leila Nadya Sadat and S. Richard Carden, "The New International Criminal Court: An Uneasy Revolution," *Georgetown Law Journal* 88 (2000): 381–474; Michael P. Scharf, "The United States and the International Criminal Court: A Recommendation for the Bush Administration," *ILSA Journal of International and Comparative Law* 7 (2001): 385–89; Sarah B. Sewall and Carl Kaysen, *The United States and the International Criminal Court: National Security and International Law* (London: Rowman & Littlefield, 2000); Francisco Orrego Vicuna, "International Criminal Court and the In and Out Club," *Journal of International Criminal Justice* 2, no. 1 (2004): 35–37; Patricia M. Wald, "Is the United States' Opposition to the ICC Intractable?" *Journal of International Criminal Justice* 2, no. 1 (2004): 19–25.

6   By "costly," I am referring both to the financial expense of an alternative response, as well as to a response that may damage other interests.

7   The International Center for Transitional Justice (ICTJ) is a prominent international NGO working in countries where transitional justice measures have been established. Countries where the ICTJ has worked offer one way to list a broader universe of transitional justice cases. ICTJ's list of countries can be found at http://ictj.org/our-work/regions-and-countries. Research for this book began in 2007, which is why any measure established after this year was not selected. US involvement was determined by conducting an advanced

Google search of all US government documents where the measure was mentioned. For the DRC, see, e.g., US State Department, "U.S. Denounces 'Climate of Impunity' in Democratic Republic of Congo," 7 July 2003. For Sierra Leone, see Chapter 4 references. For Guatemala, see "DCI Statement on Declassification," 15 July 1998. For Peru, see US White House, "Support for Democracy" at http://georgewbush-whitehouse.archives.gov/infocus/perutrip/01.html, and The Bureau of Democracy, Human Rights and Labor, "Supporting Human Rights and Democracy: The U.S. Record 2003–2004." For Timor-Leste, see the US Senate Report 108-106, "Foreign Operations, Export Financing, and Related Programs Appropriations Bill," 2004, and the US House Report 108-105, "Foreign Relations Authorization Act, Fiscal years 2004 and 2005." For the former Yugoslavia, see US State Department, "Domestic and International Law," in History of the Department of State During the Clinton Presidency (1993–2001). For Morocco, see US State Department press statement on Morocco, 13 January 2006.

8   By "past abuse," I am referring to transitional justice measures that are aimed at addressing abuses several years after they were committed. For example, the Khmer Rouge stopped abuses in the 1970s, but the Khmer Rouge Tribunal was not established until the 2000s.

9   Appendix 1 provides a list of those interviewed.

1 :: The US Approach to Transitional Justice

Despite significant US involvement in transitional justice, no study thus far has attempted to provide a systematic explanation of the US approach to the field. The US government itself has not articulated a transitional justice policy, even though it has provided extensive political, technical, and financial support to measures. It is important to unpack the US approach since it can play a particularly influential role in transitional justice when it becomes involved.

A useful starting point when trying to understand why states behave as they do is the foreign policy literature. This scholarship helps illustrate how multiple sources of foreign policy collectively shape state behavior abroad. Key sources include the external environment, the societal environment of the nation, the bureaucratic setting in which policymaking occurs, and the individual characteristics of policymakers. Together, these sources help "open the black box" of US foreign policy by identifying the range of factors and actors that explain why the United States behaves as it does in the world.

Analysis of these sources helps reveal a distinctive US approach to transitional justice that is symbolic, retributive, and strategic. It is symbolic because of the powerful symbolic role that "justice" plays in American society. It is retributive because of the US preference for criminal prosecutions over other measures. It is strategic because of the way that the United States uses transitional justice instrumentally to advance its interests. This chapter first discusses the sources of foreign policy that underpin the US approach to transitional justice, and then turns to a discussion of each characteristic of the US approach. It concludes with a discussion of the implications of the US approach for the field of transitional justice and for US foreign policy.

The Sources of US Foreign Policy

Key sources of US foreign policy include the external environment, societal influences, the bureaucratic setting, and the individual characteristics of policymakers.[1] Together, these four sources give shape and direction to the actions the United States pursues abroad and provide a framework for understanding US foreign policy on transitional justice. These sources are described here, along with an explanation of their theoretical basis in the international relations and foreign policy scholarship.

The *external* source category refers to the ways in which attributes of the international system (i.e., changing distributions of power, rising interdependence, globalization, world political economy) and the characteristics and behaviors of the state and non-state actors comprising it shape US foreign policy.[2] Two mainstream international relations theories—realism and liberalism—along with constructivism broadly help explain the external source of US foreign policy.

Structural realists equate a state's national interest with power.[3] Power is viewed as the proper object of a state's foreign policy as well as a measure of its capacity. Calculation of the national interest can be arrived at rationally through careful analysis of the material conditions of states, as well as the particulars of a given foreign policy dilemma. The pursuit of security and the efforts to enhance material wealth place states in competition with each other, limiting the scope for cooperation to a series of selective, self-interested strategies.[4]

Liberals, in contrast, highlight how individuals and the ideas and ideals they espouse (such as human rights, liberty, and democracy), social forces (capitalism and markets), and political institutions (democracy and representation) can have direct effects on foreign relations. They disagree with the assumptions of structural realists regarding the determinative role of system structure (unipolar, bipolar, or multipolar) and the consequent assumption of state homogeneity (rational, material, and unitary actors). By opening the box of state action and allowing for the effects of varying ideas, interests, and institutions, liberals claim to produce better predictions of foreign policy behavior and incorporate modern conceptions of ethical foreign policy.[5]

Constructivists focus on the role of norms and ideational factors in foreign policy.[6] They believe the "national interest" is not objectively given or based solely on material interests, but also must be interpreted through the prism of ideas, which are seen to construct both identities and interests. Constructivists argue that agents will consider which action is most appropriate for their identity, even if such action may have costly consequences.[7] Some hold the view that the moral force of commonly held values and norms and increasing exposure to a globalized social environment exerts pressure on policymakers to act in a certain way.[8]

The *societal* source category comprises those characteristics of the domestic social and political system that shape a state's orientation toward the world. This category looks at how US political culture—Americans' beliefs about their political system and the way it operates—and their foreign policy attitudes and preferences— public opinion—affect American foreign policy. It also considers the roles that interest groups, the mass media, and presidential elections play in transmitting beliefs, attitudes, and preferences into the policymaking process.[9]

The *bureaucratic* source category refers to the way the US government is organized for making foreign policy decisions. The US foreign policy bureaucracy consists of those involved in making and implementing foreign policy, specifically the president, Congress, the State Department, and other federal agencies where relevant.

The bureaucratic politics literature describes the importance of understanding the diverse interests of each participant in the foreign policy bureaucracy. In any foreign policy decision widely believed at the time to be important, the president will almost always be the principal figure determining the general direction of actions.[10] Furthermore, the president's perception and judgment of what is in the national interest are dominant in the system. Congress serves as an important forum for the discussion of national interests. It also enjoys certain rights to control the operations and budgets of the executive branch, and the exercise of those rights can have a very direct effect on either the outcome of a particular foreign policy decision or the decision-making process itself.[11] The State Department is the lead institution for the conduct of American diplomacy, and the secretary of state is the president's principal foreign policy advisor.[12] Depending on the issue, other agencies are also involved in developing and implementing foreign policy decisions.

The bureaucratic politics literature highlights the fragmented and often institutionally driven nature of foreign policy. Different institutional settings mean officials and politicians view foreign policy issues through different prisms resulting in distinctly different views. These tensions result in competing imperatives that can be an impediment to formulating a coherent foreign policy. For example, when considering a particular issue, the Treasury tends to focus on the budgetary implications, the Department of Defense on the repercussions for national security, while the State Department focuses on the diplomatic and international political ramifications. Foreign policy is thus depicted as the unintended result of a bargaining process involving the principal participants.[13]

The *individual* source category refers to the individual characteristics of decision-makers that define the kind of people they are and the types of behavior they exhibit.[14] Behavioral accounts investigate the role of the individual decision-maker—focusing on psychological and cognitive factors, beliefs, biases and stereotypes, personality and emotions, leadership style and role—as an explanatory source of foreign policy choice.[15]

These source categories are interrelated and collectively determine foreign policy decisions. First, they generate the necessity for foreign policy decisions that result in foreign policy action. Second, they influence the decision-making process that converts inputs

Figure 1.1 The sources of US foreign policy as a funnel of causality

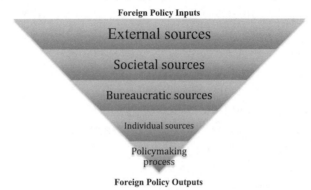

into outputs.[16] Figure 1.1 adapts Wittkopf, Kegley, and Scott's theoretical "funnel of causality" to describe this process.[17]

According to Eugene Wittkopf, Charles Kegley, and James Scott, the policymaking process is what converts inputs into outputs, and is where US foreign policy decisions are made. The process is complex because of its many participants and because policymaking procedures cannot be divorced from the multiple sources that shape decision-makers' responses to situations demanding action. Still, we can think of the foreign policymaking process as the intervening variable that links foreign policy inputs into outputs. Although it is sometimes difficult to separate the process from the resulting product, once that conversion has occurred, we can begin to examine the recurring behaviors that describe and explain how the United States responds to the world around it.[18]

Figure 1.1 also illustrates how each source of US foreign policy is nested within an ever-larger set of variables. Individual decision-makers are constrained by their positions within the foreign policy bureaucracy. Those bureaucratic variables in turn are cast within their more encompassing societal setting, which is nested within an even larger international environment consisting of other states, non-state actors, and global trends and issues to which the United States, as a global actor, believes it must respond.[19]

The framework's attention to the multiple sources of US foreign policy implicitly rejects the widespread impulse to search for its single cause. Since foreign policy actions almost invariably result from multiple sources, it is better to think in multicausal terms in order to move toward an understanding of the complex reality underlying US foreign policy.[20]

Symbolic, Retributive, and Strategic Justice

The foreign policy literature helps us better understand the multiple sources that shape US foreign policy on transitional justice. US foreign policy reflects the tensions and competing imperatives between and within the external, societal, bureaucratic, and individual sources of foreign policy, which can be a real impediment to formulating a coherent approach to transitional justice.

Despite this complexity, careful analysis of these sources helps reveal a distinctive US approach to transitional justice that is symbolic, retributive, and strategic. Figure 1.2 provides examples of how these sources of foreign policy help explain the US approach to transitional justice.

Each feature of the US approach, as well as the sources of US foreign policy that support these themes, is explored here.

Figure 1.2 The US approach to transitional justice

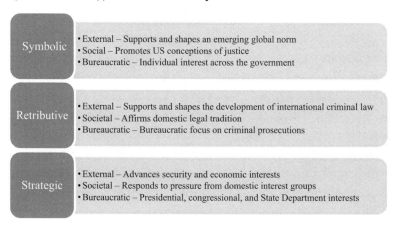

Symbolic
• External – Supports and shapes an emerging global norm
• Social – Promotes US conceptions of justice
• Bureaucratic – Individual interest across the government

Retributive
• External – Supports and shapes the development of international criminal law
• Societal – Affirms domestic legal tradition
• Bureaucratic – Bureaucratic focus on criminal prosecutions

Strategic
• External – Advances security and economic interests
• Societal – Responds to pressure from domestic interest groups
• Bureaucratic – Presidential, congressional, and State Department interests

Symbolic Justice

The United States supports transitional justice first and fore-most because of the powerful symbolic role that "justice" plays in American society.[21] Trials, in particular, are seen as an enactment of justice by making sense of an event through the telling of a coherent story about what happened in order to reach a verdict (a *vere dictum*, literally, a "saying of the truth").[22] To do this, however, the story must be radically simplified by limiting the narrative to specific actors for specific crimes during a specific timeframe.[23] For US policymakers, "justice" is served in transitional justice contexts when a high-profile perpetrator, like Pol Pot or Charles Taylor, is the focus of attention.

By "getting the bad guy," transitional justice also reinforces a dualistic narrative about "good versus evil" that is a core element of American identity, making the field appealing to support. Professor John Ciorciari explains:

> The backdrop of US foreign policy is that America is promoting values. Trials are a good institutional mechanism for this—not only for advancing the cause of justice, but also because they are useful political processes. A foreign power can come in and support them. There are substantive merits, like reducing impunity, but trials also feel right. US foreign policymakers usually view themselves as the good guys. In criminal trials, there are winners and losers. Fighting to be on the right side gives policymakers a sense of mission and connects to US founding myths and principles.[24]

The Holocaust is connected to this narrative. As Helmut Dubiel argues, the term "Holocaust" identifies not only the historical event, but has developed into a symbolic repertoire, which has been adopted by political groups all over the world who are subjected to extreme pain and distress. "It has come to denote political evil itself," he writes.[25] In the US imagination, the Nuremberg trials represented a supremely successful example of how the ceremonial process of the trial transformed the normative values of a deeply conflicted society. In addition, US support of the Nuremberg trials, as a response to the Holocaust, continues to play into American self-perceptions as the global "good guy."

Symbolic arguments can assist US policymakers with a genuine interest in and commitment to transitional justice to obtain public acceptance for US engagement in such activities overseas. For example, when marshaling support for the international criminal tribunals in 1995, President Clinton said:

> With our purpose and with our position comes the responsibility to help shine the light of justice on those who would deny to others their most basic human rights. We have an obligation to carry forward the lessons of Nuremberg. That is why we strongly support the United Nations War Crimes Tribunals for the former Yugoslavia and for Rwanda.[26]

Global and societal acceptance of transitional justice has also allowed US officials to rely on the symbolic power of the field to explain or advocate for US involvement. The emergence of transitional justice as a body of customary international law and normative standards, as well as the role of "transnational advocacy networks" that encourage the establishment of transitional justice measures, and an "epistemic community" that provides specialized, technical expertise to such mechanisms when established all contribute to US support for transitional justice.[27] Within the United States, interest groups dedicated to advocating for these issues, the variety of diaspora communities, and the diverse views expressed by the media sources that report on transitional justice also play a role.[28]

US officials also get involved based on their personal interest in transitional justice or the country in question, and their belief that transitional justice is the "right" thing to do after atrocities have been committed. For example, Secretary of State Madeleine Albright's personal history of being forced into exile as a child is cited as partly related to her support of war crimes tribunals.[29] Former US ambassador to the UN and NSC advisor Susan Rice cited her guilt about the US failure to respond to the Rwandan genocide as justification for a more interventionist foreign policy.[30] Samantha Power's experiences as a journalist covering the Bosnian war in the 1990s and her subsequent best-seller on the failure of the United States to stop genocide was a key reason for her appointment as President Obama's director for global affairs during his first administration and US ambassador to the UN during his second administration.

Retributive Justice

The retributive approach is closely connected to the symbolic approach of transitional justice. Transitional justice measures can be broadly grouped into two categories: those that are retributive and focused on punishing a perpetrator of abuse mainly through criminal prosecutions; and those that are restorative, more "victim-centric," and mainly refer to measures like truth commissions and reparation programs. The American tradition of punishment through law leads to the privileging of trials over other measures of transitional justice.[31] Trials are familiar to Americans and thus more likely to receive public support than other transitional justice measures like truth commissions and reparations, which are less common in the United States.[32] There is also a sense of pride about the US justice system, the legal institutions it has created, and the standards it abides by, which leads to the desire to "export" this system abroad. Beth van Schaack, professor of law and former deputy in the State Department Office of Global Criminal Justice, explains:

> We're so proud of our legal system. It's one of our biggest exports: legal ideas and laws and lawyers. . . . It really is our contribution to the world. We see ourselves as being a place where justice happens.[33]

The retributive model is reinforced by the structure of the US government and the roles that people occupy within it. There are a number of offices across the foreign policy bureaucracy that are focused on supporting criminal prosecutions abroad. These offices are staffed with people who provide policy guidance, as well as technical and financial assistance to trials. Other measures of transitional justice do not receive the same level of focus within the bureaucracy. The creation of the War Crimes Office (now called the Office of Global Criminal Justice) in the State Department in the 1990s is an obvious example, established specifically to formulate and guide US war crimes policy. In addition to the war crimes office, other bureaus support a retributive approach. For example, the Office of the Legal Adviser promotes the development of international law and furnishes advice on legal issues. The Bureau of Democracy, Human Rights, and Labor supports human rights investigations and criminal accountability. The Bureau of International Narcotics and Law Enforcement Affairs works to develop host nations' criminal justice systems and the establishment of the rule of law in transitional countries. Several bureaus and offices at USAID support criminal prosecutions in transitional contexts, including its Bureau for Democracy, Conflict, and Humanitarian Assistance.

In addition to the State Department and USAID, the Department of Justice has an International Criminal Investigative Training Assistance Program and an Office of Overseas Prosecutorial Development, Assistance and Training, which are dedicated to developing foreign justice sector institutions, and a Human Rights and Special Prosecutions Section, which investigates and prosecutes cases against human rights violators and other international criminals. Since 9/11, the formation of the Department of Homeland Security has added another agency focused on retribution into the mix. The fact that this range of agencies, and bureaus and offices within agencies, are focused on criminal prosecutions means there is a bureaucratic driver for this policy area that does not exist for other measures of transitional justice.

Decision-makers are also influenced by the socially prescribed behaviors and legally sanctioned norms attached to the positions they occupy. Because the positions they occupy shape their behavior, policy outcomes are inevitably influenced by the roles extant in the policymaking arena. Role theory helps explain why, for example, American presidents act, once in office, like their predecessors, as well as why certain policy decisions are habitually made within large bureaucratic organizations.[34]

The individual characteristics of policymakers also contribute to the retributive approach. The first war crimes ambassador, David

Scheffer, was a forceful advocate for the establishment of war crimes tribunals. The profiles of the three subsequent war crimes ambassadors further illustrate the retributive focus of this office. They each came to the position with specialized, prosecutorial experience in international criminal tribunals, including the International Criminal Tribunals for the Former Yugoslavia and Rwanda, and the Special Court for Sierra Leone.[35] This individual expertise on criminal prosecutions influences a US policy emphasis on retributive justice.

The global growth of the field of international criminal law—or what Kathryn Sikkink calls the "justice cascade," which she defines as the rapid increase in international, foreign, and domestic human rights prosecutions around the world—also contributes to the retributive approach of the United States.[36] The United States has been a key "norm entrepreneur" for the growth of the field.[37] US support for criminal prosecutions has arguably influenced the dramatic shift in the legitimacy of the norms of individual criminal accountability for human rights violations, and the increase in actions, like trials, on behalf of those norms.[38]

Strategic Justice

The US approach to transitional justice is strategic in the way that it uses measures instrumentally to advance its interests or blocks transitional justice when it fails to advance these interests. In contrast to the other two features of the US approach, the strategic nature of the US approach explains the variability in when the United States gets involved and, once it gets involved, any fluctuations in US support. This characteristic of the US approach helps explain the ambivalence and inconsistency that some scholars have asserted is present in the US response to atrocities.[39]

The United States may get involved in transitional justice in order to exclude discussion of any US role in the violence examined by a measure.[40] In the Nuremberg, Yugoslavia, and Rwanda tribunals, the possibility of prosecution of US nationals was either expressly precluded or otherwise remote.[41] The US may also support transitional justice as an alternative to a more costly response (i.e., a military or humanitarian response), or as a way to express support for or opposition to a transitional government's behavior. It might offer, block, or condition economic assistance for a measure as a way to express approval or disapproval of a government. The United States may also use transitional justice as a way to encourage regime change in a country where the United States opposes its leadership.

Transitional justice also offers a way to expand American "soft power" in the world.[42] Anne-Marie Slaughter, former State Department director of policy planning, pointed out that "standing for accountability for genocide, crimes, against humanity, war crimes, and ethnic cleansing . . . is a huge source of US power in the world."[43] The United States may therefore use transitional justice as a diplomatic tool, or as a way to promote its cultural influence, its role in international institutions, to obtain recognition, and so on. Other scholars, such as Anne Orford, criticize the international community's absence "from the scene of violence and suffering until it intervenes as the heroic savior."[44] In this way, the United States may strategically use transitional justice to promote an image as a global "hero."

Societal sources of US foreign policy also explain its strategic approach. Policymakers may support transitional justice as a response to domestic public outrage, as Gary Bass point out in his explanation of Western governments' support for international war crimes tribunals.[45] They may respond to effective lobbying from domestic interest groups, including human rights groups, faith-based groups, or diaspora communities in the United States that advocate for transitional justice.[46]

Within the US government, the diverse interests of the foreign policy bureaucracy and individuals within it also contribute to the strategic approach. Presidential interests in transitional justice might be based on a measure's effect on the president's overall agenda and his ability to accomplish other goals.[47] Members of Congress are likely to be affected by the interests of their domestic constituencies.[48] Federal agencies may support or oppose transitional justice based on the extent to which measures further their organizational objectives or individual interests.[49]

Implications of the US Approach

US involvement in transitional justice is thus characterized by an approach that is symbolic, retributive, and strategic. In general, these three characteristics are present when analyzing a case of US involvement in transitional justice and intersect with one another in various ways. The symbolic and retributive characteristics of the US approach tend to go hand in hand: US officials believe something has to be done after atrocities have been committed, and trials of a limited number of high-profile perpetrators are viewed as an appropriate response. However, strategic interests may stop the United States from getting involved, or may lead to fluctuations in US support. This tension often results in a battle among US foreign policy participants, or with actors outside the US government, until a compromise is reached.

The US approach has implications for the field, and for the transitional justice objectives of communities where atrocities have been committed. The fact that trials for a narrow set of high-profile perpetrators receive more US support than other forms of transitional justice, and that US interests play such an important role, has influenced decisions to establish transitional justice measures, their design, and their implementation. For example, the call for transitional justice within a community may align with US strategic interests, but it is possible that US foreign policy objectives are vastly different. Similarly, some communities may prefer trials over other transitional justice measures, yet others may call for a model that does not involve a retributive approach. In addition, some communities may call for the examination of a wider set of actors involved in past abuses, or of the social or institutional causes of violations rather than the symbolic approach of the United States which prioritizes a simplified version of what happened that is imbued with US conceptions of justice. The challenge lies in ensuring that the US approach avoids becoming, as Rosemary Nagy writes, "detrimentally abstracted from [the] lived realities" of communities attempting to deal with the aftermath of atrocities.[50]

The US approach also has implications for US foreign policy. It shows how external and societal influences, as well as how bureaucracy and individual decision-makers, are key to understanding the US approach to this relatively new area in US foreign policy. The study also contributes an empirical account of how the interest-versus-values debate in American foreign policy plays out in practice. In addition, the retributive characteristic of US foreign policy may offer insight into US foreign policy in other areas.

It is important to note that other actors approach transitional justice in different ways. Switzerland, for example, has laid out a framework for transitional justice that is broader than the US approach. The Swiss emphasize "combating impunity in the context of human security strategies . . . because real and significant difficulties persist for which neither the creation of the ICC nor international tribunals have provided a full and final solution." The Swiss Department of Foreign Affairs designate this work as "Dealing with the Past," which is based on the UN principles for the protection and promotion of human rights through action to combat impunity.[51] They developed a "holistic approach to Dealing with the Past" that involves the "right to know," the "right to reparation," the "right to justice," and a "guarantee of non-recurrence."[52] It would be useful to study cases that the Swiss have supported to see how they compare with the conceptual framework that they have laid out.

Other foreign state governments will likely share the strategic characteristic of the US approach, supporting transitional justice in ways that align with their national interests, but additional research would need to be undertaken to understand whether they also adopt the symbolic or retributive features of the US approach. International human rights organizations may tilt toward a retributive model of transitional justice, whereas peacebuilding organizations may lean more toward restorative approaches. Civil society groups in states where atrocities have taken place may lean toward a community or victim-centric approach and prioritize reparative and truth-telling measures of transitional justice. Unfortunately, it was outside the scope of this research to compare different approaches since the focus is on understanding the US approach. The next chapter begins this examination by exploring the development of US foreign policy on transitional justice over time.

Notes

1   These sources of foreign policy were drawn from Charles W. Kegley, Eugene R. Wittkopf, and James M. Scott, *American Foreign Policy: Patterns and Process*, 6th ed. (Belmont: Wadsworth/Thomson Learning, 2003).

2   Ibid., 17.

3   See William C. Wohlforth, "Realism and Foreign Policy," in *Foreign Policy: Theories, Actors, Cases*, ed. Steve Smith, Amelia Hadfield, and Tim Dunne (New York: Oxford University Press, 2012), 52.

4   Realist scholars include, e.g., John J. Mearsheimer, *The Tragedy of Great Power Politics* (New York: Norton, 2001); Jack Donnelly, *Realism and International Relations* (New York: Cambridge University Press, 2000). For rational accounts, see, e.g., Glen Herald Snyder and Paul Diesing, *Conflict among Nations: Bargaining, Decision Making, and System Structure in International Crises* (Princeton, NJ: Princeton University Press, 1977); Thomas C. Schelling, *The Strategy of Conflict* (Cambridge: Harvard University Press, 1960); R. Putnam, "Diplomacy and Domestic Politics: The Logic of Two Level Games," *International Organization* 42, no. 3 (1988): 427–60; Gilat Levy and Ronny Razin, "It Takes Two: An Explanation for the Democratic Peace," *Journal of the European Economic Association* 2, no. 2 (2004): 1–29.

5   See Michael Doyle, "Liberalism and Foreign Policy," in Smith, Hadfield, and Dunne, *Foreign Policy*; and Michael W. Doyle, *Ways of War and Peace: Realism, Liberalism, and Socialism* (New York: Norton, 1997).

6   For more on constructivism, see, e.g., David Patrick Houghton, "Reinvigorating the Study of Foreign Policy Decision Making: Toward a Constructivist Approach," *Foreign Policy Analysis* 3, no. 1 (2007): 24–45; Martha Finnemore and Kathryn Sikkink, "Taking Stock: The Constructivist Research Program in International Relations and Comparative Politics," *Annual Review of Political Science* 4 (2001): 391–416; E. Adler, "Constructivism and International Relations," in *Handbook of International Relations*, ed. W. Carlnaes, T. Risse, and B. Simmons (London: Sage, 2002); Michael Barnett and Raymond Duvall, "Power in International Politics," *International Organization* 59 (2005): 39–75; Trine Flockhart, "Constructivism and Foreign Policy," in Smith, Hadfield, and Dunne, *Foreign Policy*; Alexandra Gheciu, "Security Institutions as Agents of Socialization? NATO and the 'New Europe,'" *International Organization* 59 (2005): 973–1012; Audie Klotz

and Cecelia Lynch, *Strategies for Research in Constructivist International Relations*, International Relations in a Constructed World (Armonk, NY: M.E. Sharpe, 2007); Stefano Guzzini and Anna Leander, *Constructivism and International Relations: Alexander Wendt and His Critics* (London: Routledge, 2006).

7   See Trine Flockhart, "Constructivism and Foreign Policy," in Smith, Dunne, and Hadfield, *Foreign Policy*, 93.

8   Checkel, "Constructivism and Foreign Policy," 74–75.

9   See Kegley, Wittkopf, and Scott, *American Foreign Policy*, 242. For additional discussion of domestic influences on foreign policy, particularly the role of public opinion and the media, see W. Lance Bennett and David L. Paletz, *Taken by Storm: The Media, Public Opinion, and U.S. Foreign Policy in the Gulf War* (Chicago: University of Chicago Press, 1994); Ole Holsti, "Public Opinion and Foreign Policy, *International Studies Quarterly* 36 (1992): 439–66. For more on interest groups, see, e.g., Barry Hughes, *The Domestic Context of American Foreign Policy* (San Francisco: W. H. Freeman, 1978); Richard J. Payne and Eddie Ganaway, "The Influence of Black Americans on US Policy towards Southern Africa," *African Affairs* 79 (1980): 567–85; Putnam, "Diplomacy and Domestic Politics"; Charles Kegley, ed., *The Domestic Sources of American Foreign Policy: Insights and Evidence* (New York: St. Martins Press, 1987). Some scholars have focused on the structure and nature of state political institutions, the features of society and the institutional arrangements linking state and society and channelling societal demands into the political system, e.g., Peter Katzenstein, "International Relations and Domestic Structures: Foreign Economic Policies of Advanced Industrial States," *International Organization* 30, no. 1 (1976): 1–45; Thomas Risse-Kappen, "Public Opinion, Domestic Structure and Foreign Policy in Liberal Democracies," *World Politics* 43 (1991): 491–517; James N. Rosenau, *Domestic Sources of Foreign Policy* (New York: Free Press; London: Collier-Macmillan, 1967). Others view foreign policy-making as driven by the nature of the economic system within states and, concurrently, in the interests of a narrow elite that traditionally has acted in what it perceives to be the national interest, e.g., Bruce Moon, "The State in Foreign and Domestic Policy," in *Foreign Policy Analysis: Continuity and Change in Its Second Generation*, ed. Laura Neack, Jeanne Hey, and Patrick Haney (Edgewood Cliffs, NJ: Prentice Hall, 1995); C. Wright Mills, *The Power Elite* (London: Oxford University Press, 1956).

10   Morton H. Halperin, Priscilla Clapp, and Arnold Kanter, *Bureaucratic Politics and Foreign Policy* (Washington, DC: Brookings Institution Press, 2006), 16.

11   Ibid., 18–19.

12   Ibid., 17.

13   See Graham T. Allison, *Essence of Decision: Explaining the Cuban Missile Crisis* (Boston: Little, Brown, 1971); Halperin, Clapp, and Kanter, *Bureaucratic Politics and Foreign Policy.*

14   Kegley, Wittkopf, and Scott, *American Foreign Policy,* 19.

15   For behavioral accounts, see, e.g., Harold Sprout and Margaret Sprout, *Man-Milieu Relationship Hypotheses in the Context of International Politics* (Princeton, NJ: Princeton University Press, 1956); Robert Jervis, *Perception and Misperception in International Politics* (Princeton, NJ: Princeton University Press, 1976); Leon Festinger, *A Theory of Cognitive Dissonance* (Stanford, CA: Stanford University Press, 1957); Kenneth Boulding, "National Images and International Systems," *Journal of Conflict Resolution* 3, no. 2 (1959): 120–31; Irving Lester Janis, *Personality and Persuasibility* (Westport, CT: Greenwood Press, 1982); Irving Lester Janis and Leon Mann, *Decision Making: A Psychological Analysis of Conflict, Choice, and Commitment* (New York: Free Press; London: Collier Macmillan, 1977); Cynthia Orbovich and Richard Molnar, "Modeling Foreign Policy Advisory Processes," in *Political Psychology and Foreign Policy,* ed. Eric Singer and Valerie Hudson (Boulder, CO: Westview, 1992); Irving Janis, *Groupthink: Psychological Studies of Policy Decisions and Fiascos* (Boston: Houghton Mifflin, 1982); Martin Hollis and Steve Smith, "Roles and Reasons in Foreign Policy Decision Making," *British Journal of Political Science* 16 (1986): 269–86.

16   Kegley, Wittkopf, and Scott, *American Foreign Policy,* 15–16.

17   Ibid.

18   Ibid.

19   Ibid.

20   Ibid.

21   See Thurman Arnold, The Symbols of Government (New Haven: Yale University Press, 1935). In this book, Arnold examines the symbolic role that the trial plays in the United States. See He suggests at the end of the book that a more "rational" approach to the law might someday be achieved by society, but later in his life, after he had experience in government and as a judge on the federal court of appeals, he explicitly abandoned that view, and recognized that the symbolic function was as essential to the operation of the law as any rational cost-benefit analysis was. Arnold explicitly discusses his changed views on the matter in a collection of letters dating from the 1950s that was published by his law firm, Arnold and Porter, after he died. See Peter Winn, email communication, 25–26 April 2014. For more on legal ritual, see Peter A. Winn, "Legal Ritual," *Law and Critique* 2, no. 2 (1991): 207–32.

22   Mark Osiel writes that this need for public reckoning with the question of how such horrific events could have happened is particularly salient in the aftermath of atrocities. He argues that trials, when effective as public

spectacle, stimulate public discussion and shape collective memory in a way that is difficult to accomplish through other means. See Mark Osiel, *Mass Atrocity, Collective Memory, and the Law* (New Brunswick, NJ: Transaction Publishers, 1997), 1–2.

23 Nagy, "Transitional Justice as Global Project," 279.

24 John Ciorciari, interview, 10 March 2010.

25 See Helmut Dubiel, "The Remembrance of the Holocaust as a Catalyst for a Transnational Ethic?" *New German Critique* 90 (Autumn 2003): 59. Also see Jeffrey C. Alexander, *Remembering the Holocaust: A Debate* (New York: Oxford University Press, 2009).

26 William J. Clinton, "Remarks at the University of Connecticut," 31 *Weekly Compilation of Presidential Documents* 1840, 1842 (23 October 1995).

27 On the emergence of transitional justice as a global norm, see Nagy, "Transitional Justice as Global Project." For more on transnational advocacy networks, see Margaret E. Keck and Kathryn Sikkink, *Activists beyond Borders: Advocacy Networks in International Politics* (Ithaca, NY: Cornell University Press, 1998); For more on epistemic communities, see P. Haas, "Introduction: Epistemic Communities and International Policy Coordination," *International Organization* 46, no. 1 (1992): 1–35.

28 See, e.g., Daniel Drezner, "The Future of U.S. Foreign Policy," *Internationale Politik und Gesellschaft* 15 (January 2008): 20–21. Drezner discusses the kinds of interest groups that hold particular sway over narrow aspects of American foreign policy, including NGOs fueled by religious or secular motives. Both conservative Christians and human rights groups, for example, campaigned for the United States to be more proactive in the crisis in Darfur. There is a wealth of literature on the impact of human rights groups on the domestic politics of countries where atrocities have occurred, and, to a lesser extent, their impact on foreign state governments. See, e.g., Steve C. Ropp, Thomas Risse-Kappen, and Kathryn Sikkink, *The Power of Human Rights: International Norms and Domestic Change* (Cambridge: Cambridge University Press, 1999).

29 David Scheffer, *All the Missing Souls: A Personal History of the War Crimes Tribunals* (Princeton, NJ: Princeton University Press, 2011).

30 Samantha Power, "Bystanders to Genocide," *The Atlantic*, September 2001.

31 E.g., see Alexis Tocqueville, *Democracy in America*, trans. Henry Reeve, 2nd ed., 2 vols. (London: Saunders and Otley, 1836); James Bryce, *The American Commonwealth* (London: Macmillan, 1888); D. W. Brogan, *America in the Modern World* (New Brunswick, NJ: Rutgers University Press, 1960); D. W. Brogan, *Politics in America* (Garden City, NY: Doubleday, 1960); Samuel P. Huntington, *American Politics: The Promise of Disharmony* (Cambridge: Harvard University Press, 1981); Anne-Marie Slaughter, *The Idea That Is America: Keeping Faith with Our Values in a Dangerous World*

(New York: Basic Books, 2007); Judith Shklar, *Legalism: Law, Morals and Political Trials* (Cambridge: Harvard University Press, 1986); Robert Hogan and Nicholas P. Emler, "Retributive Justice," in *The Justice Motive in Social Behavior: Adapting to Times of Scarcity and Change*, ed. Melvin J. Lerner and Sally C. Lerner (New York: Plenum Press, 1981).

32 Sriram, "Justice as Peace?" 589.

33 Beth van Schaack, interview, 31 October 2009.

34 Kegley, Wittkopf, and Scott, *American Foreign Policy*, 18. Path-dependent explanations are also useful here. See, e.g., Jack A. Goldstone, "Initial Conditions, General Laws, Path Dependence, and Explanation in Historical Sociology," *American Journal of Sociology* 104 (1998): 829–45; James Mahoney, "Path Dependence in Historical Sociology," *Theory and Society* 29, no. 4 (2000): 507–48; Jens Meierhenrich, *The Legacies of Law: Long-Run Consequences of Legal Development in South Africa, 1652–2000* (Cambridge: Cambridge University Press, 2010); Paul A. David, "Clio and the Economics of QWERTY," *American Economic Review* 75 (1985): 332–37; W. Brian Arthur, *Increasing Returns and Path Dependence in the Economy* (Ann Arbor: University of Michigan Press, 1994).

35 Annie Bird, "The Development of US Foreign Policy on Transitional Justice: The Role of the US War Crimes Ambassadors," International Studies Association Annual Convention, San Diego, CA, 2012.

36 Sikkink, *The Justice Cascade*.

37 Acharya, A. (2004). How ideas spread? Whose ideas matter - norm localisation and institutional change in Asian regionalism. International Organization, 58, 239-275.

38 Cass Sunstein, *Free Markets and Social Justice* (New York: Oxford University Press, 1997).

39 See, e.g., Wedgwood, "Fiddling in Rome"; Power, *A Problem from Hell*.

40 Nagy, "Transitional Justice as Global Project," 276.

41 John P. Cerone, "Dynamic Equilibrium: The Evolution of US Attitudes toward International Criminal Courts and Tribunals," *European Journal of International Law* 18, no. 2 (2007): 315.

42 Joseph Nye coined this term to refer to the ability to pursue one's foreign policy through co-opting and attracting other states toward your position. See Joseph Nye, *Soft Power: The Means to Success in the World* (New York: Public Affairs, 2004).

43 Anne-Marie Slaughter, interview, 23 May 2012.

44 A. Orford, "Commissioning the Truth," *Columbia Journal of Gender and Law* 15 (2006): 862.

45 Gary Jonathan Bass, *Stay the Hand of Vengeance* (Princeton, NJ: Princeton Princeton University Press, 2002).

46 Elyda Mey, "Cambodian Diaspora Communities in Transitional Justice," International Center for Transitional Justice, March 2008.

47 Halperin, Clapp, and Kanter, *Bureaucratic Politics and Foreign Policy*, 67–80.

48 Ibid., 38.

49 Ibid., 26.

50 Nagy, "Transitional Justice as Global Project," 276.

51 Directorate of Political Affairs, "Introduction," in *Politorbis* (Bern: Federal Department of Foreign Affairs, 2010), 9.

52 Swiss Peace/FDFA, "Dealing with the Past: Conceptual Framework," 2006.

2 :: The Development of US Foreign Policy on Transitional Justice

This chapter provides a historical overview of the development of US foreign policy on transitional justice from World War I to the 2010s. It focuses on four influential war crimes tribunals—Nuremberg, the International Criminal Tribunals for the Former Yugoslavia and Rwanda, and the International Criminal Court—because, although they are all courts, they are the institutions where we see the US approach to transitional justice begin to take shape. This review highlights the leadership role taken by the United States, the reliance on American legal rights and tradition as a guide for US support, the importance of American lobby groups, and the significance of individuals who took on these issues.

The Nuremberg Precedent

Before examining the Nuremberg trials—which are commonly viewed as the modern origin of the field of transitional justice—it is interesting to note US opposition to a proposal for an international criminal tribunal during World War I. The British wanted a tribunal to prosecute German combatants and officials for "violations of the laws and customs of war and the laws of humanity." Despite some American support for the idea of individual criminal liability, the United States was against the idea of a tribunal.[1] American representatives at the Paris Peace Conference believed that the nations should

> use the machinery at hand, which had been tried and found competent, with a law and a procedure framed and therefore known in advance, rather than to create an international tribunal with a criminal jurisdiction for which there is no precedent, precept, practice, or procedure.[2]

British prime minister Lloyd George was determined to hold trials, however, and eventually reached a compromise with President Woodrow Wilson for the former German emperor Kaiser Wilhelm II to stand trial "for a supreme offence against international morality and the sanctity of treaties."[3] The United States went along with the proposal, but only after negotiating language that would reduce the prospects of it being implemented.[4] Shortly after, the Dutch gave asylum to the German emperor and refused to extradite him.[5]

President Wilson was more concerned with a viable democratic government for Germany and a League of Nations to secure future peace than with accountability for war crimes.[6] Early in its existence, the Council of the League of Nations had before it a proposal to create a "High Court of International Justice," which would be competent to criminally prosecute individuals for violations of the "universal law of nations."[7] However, the proposal was rejected for reasons similar to those given by the US delegation at the Paris Peace Conference.[8] During the interwar years, there was little activity within international organizations concerning the establishment of international criminal tribunals. European academics and policymakers kept the idea alive, but American international lawyers watched the process from the sidelines.[9]

In contrast to the aftermath of World War I, the period after World War II witnessed an explosion of war crimes trials in Europe and Asia. Telford Taylor, who served as chief prosecutor of the

Nuremberg trials, explains the differences in part by the changing outlook in the late 1920s, reflected in international agreements like the Kellogg-Briand Pact. More importantly, the "perceived evil of Nazism" was viewed as "far deeper and more pervasive than was that of Imperial Germany."[10] The Hague and Geneva conventions became applicable after the German invasion of Poland in 1939, where German violation of its obligation to the Polish civilian population clearly constituted war crimes. By 1942, most of Europe had fallen under the occupation and administration by Germany or its satellites.

In October 1941, President Franklin Roosevelt and Prime Minister Winston Churchill simultaneously issued statements condemning the Germans' execution of "scores of innocent hostages" and other atrocities in the occupied territories. Retribution for these crimes was envisaged, but the statements did not address any of the problems that this prospect presented. In January 1942, nine governments-in-exile in London, which had been collecting information about events in their respective countries, organized themselves as the Inter-Allied Commission on the Punishment of War Crimes and issued the war's first principled utterance about war crimes. The "Declaration of St. James" repudiated retribution "by acts of vengeance" and declared that "the sense of justice of the civilized world" required that the signatory powers

> place among their principal war aims the punishment, through the channel of organized justice, of those guilty of or responsible for these crimes, whether they have ordered them, perpetrated them, or participated in them.[11]

According to Taylor, their declaration was accurately predictive. These leaders did not "merely want to see the heads of their oppressors roll; they wanted vindication and retribution by *law*, applied through judicial process."[12] In 1942, the signatory powers sought public support from the United States, the United Kingdom, and the Soviet Union. In reply, Roosevelt, Churchill, and Stalin approved the proposal that those accused of war crimes should stand trial.

However, the British failure to hold trials after World War I for German leaders resulted in a complete reversal of British war crimes policy after World War II. Churchill's first attempt to block the tribunal idea was illustrated in the "Moscow Declaration" of June 1943, which stated that "the major criminals whose offenses have no particular location" will be "punished by a joint decision of the Governments of the Allies." This statement made no reference to a trial and made clear that punishment would be decided by the United Kingdom, United States, and the Soviet Union, and perhaps France. Churchill opposed the creation of an international war crimes tribunal and pushed for summary execution of the major criminals instead.[13]

In Washington, no significant attention was given to war crimes policies until the late summer of 1944, when an Allied victory appeared imminent. That year, however, the United States, like Britain, "made a 180-degree turn from its 1919 war crime policies, but in the opposite direction."[14] In 1945, it was the United States that took the lead in planning and establishing an international tribunal and in expanding international penal law beyond the traditional limits of the laws of war. In addition to the White House, at least six different federal agencies had concern with war crimes questions—the Departments of State, War, Treasury, Navy, and Justice, and the Office of Strategic Services.

Initially, the War and Treasury departments were the most vigorous participants, and early discussions led to a sharp confrontation between their two chiefs: Secretary of War Henry Stimson and Secretary of the Treasury Henry Morgenthau Jr.[15] Morgenthau supported the summary execution proposal, which President Roosevelt initially entertained. Stimson was repelled at the prospect of executions, and felt it was beneath America's standards—even for Nazi war criminals. He was a lawyer and had long been a believer in punishing war crimes; in 1916, he had signed a letter to President Woodrow Wilson protesting Germany's deportation of Belgians, "in violation of laws and humanity." His standards grew out of his respect for basic American legal rights, with explicit reference to the Bill of Rights. He clung to the idea of individual responsibility for war crimes, which would focus Allied vengeance against the guilty rather than all Germans. His respect for law also encompassed a fondness for trials. For Stimson, Morgenthau's summary executions simply stood against American domestic legal tradition.

Stimson's views may not have taken hold, however, if parts of Morgenthau's proposal had not been leaked and resulted in a negative public reaction.[16] The US government's preference for a "judicial" solution to the problem of war criminals was made clear in the Yalta Memorandum, which had been prepared to guide President Roosevelt when he attended the Yalta conference:

> We think that the just and effective solution lies in the use of the judicial method. Condemnation of these criminals after a trial, moreover, would command maximum public support in our own times and receive the respect of history. The use of the judicial method will, in addition, make available for all mankind to study in future years an authentic record of Nazi crimes and criminality.[17]

This same memorandum envisioned the creation of an International Military Tribunal (IMT) to be established by executive agreement, and formed the groundwork of the later drafts submitted by the United States for international agreement. Upon taking office, President Harry Truman made it clear that he opposed summary execution and supported the establishment of a tribunal, and, in May 1945, he appointed Robert Jackson to prepare and prosecute "charges of atrocities and war crimes against such of the leaders of the European Axis powers."[18] The inclusion of atrocities and war crimes had not been the focus of Stimson's efforts. He and others were mostly interested in prosecuting the Nazis for the crime of aggressive war.[19] It was Jewish American lobby groups and other domestic interest groups that empathized with the plight of European Jews that successfully influenced the inclusion of these crimes.[20]

The IMT at Nuremberg was established on the basis of the London Agreement, a treaty concluded among the four allies, and the IMT for the Far East (Tokyo) was created by a special proclamation of General Douglas MacArthur, acting as supreme commander of the allied forces. Both tribunals were given jurisdiction to prosecute crimes against peace, war crimes, and crimes against humanity. Their jurisdiction was limited to prosecuting those fighting on behalf of enemy states, with no possibility of prosecuting those who fought on behalf of the Allies. Although France, Britain, and the Soviet Union were equal players in theory, from the start, the initiative lay with the Americans.[21]

Reflecting on the motivation of the Americans, Taylor concluded that the "members of the Stimson group shared the prevailing wish for retribution" for the Nazi leaders. He also noted the significance of the simultaneous establishment of the UN Charter and the first international consensus on war crimes:

> Essentially, in the minds of Stimson and his colleagues, their prime purpose was to bring the weight of law and criminal sanctions to bear in support of the peaceful and humanitarian principles that the UN was to promote by consultation and collective action.[22]

Nazi leaders Hermann Göring, Rudolf Hess, Albert Speer, and others were convicted on September 30 and October 1, 1946. The plan at the London Conference had been to hold at least one additional trial, but there was declining enthusiasm for the idea except for in the United States.[23] Instead, the United States organized a series of additional trials before their own military tribunals. Built around groups of defendants who were identified thematically—the Nazi judges, the SS, the military leaders, and so on—these were held in the same Nuremberg courtroom as the trial of the International Military Tribunal. Judges were drawn from US courts.[24]

US interest in drafting a code of "international criminal law" continued in 1946. Attorney General Francis Biddle, who served as a judge at the Nuremberg tribunal, urged President Truman to support the development of permanent procedures and institutions in order to enforce international law and utilize the experience of Nuremberg. President Truman was strongly supportive:

> That tendency will be fostered if the nations can establish a code of international criminal law to deal with all who wage aggressive war. The setting up of such a code as that which you recommend is indeed an enormous undertaking but deserves to be studied and weighed by

the best legal minds the world over. It is a fitting task to be undertaken by the governments of the United Nations. I hope that the United Nations, in line with your proposal, will reaffirm the principles of the Nürnberg Charter in the context of a general codification of offences against the peace and security of mankind.[25]

Some days later, the United States submitted a proposal to the UN General Assembly directing the International Law Commission (ILC) to begin work on "a general codification of offences against the peace and security of mankind or in an International Criminal Code."[26]

The following year saw the negotiation of the Genocide Convention. An early draft prepared by the Secretariat included alternative proposals for a permanent, ad hoc international criminal court to try to punish acts of genocide. However, the United States proposed that this issue be considered separately. This proposal was formalized in article VI of the Genocide Convention, which established that genocide would be punished by the territorial state or by the international criminal court, yet to be created.[27]

Exacerbated by the nascent Cold War, enthusiasm in the United States for the Genocide Convention and for multilateral commitments in the field of international justice and human rights soon met with fierce opposition in the Senate.[28] At the UN, work on the code of offenses was halted in 1954 and did not revive until the early 1980s. Some argue that the incomplete internationalization of justice represented by the Nuremberg tribunal was foreclosed by the emergence of the Cold War. Despite the development of human rights law after World War II, the incorporation of human rights criteria into national foreign aid and the selective linkage between human rights promotion and military sales and trade policies by Western governments in the 1970s profoundly politicized human rights, and violations often went unaddressed during this period.[29]

The International Criminal Tribunals for the Former Yugoslavia and Rwanda

The end of the Cold War and the rise of the United States as a global superpower, along with the eruption of mass violence during and after the breakup of Yugoslavia, led to an increase in US attention to human rights. Just a few months into the Bosnian war, evidence of systematic executions, expulsions, and indiscriminate shelling attacks committed by Serbia were evident. By the time the war ended in 1995, some 200,000 Bosnians had been killed.[30]

The United States was not prepared to intervene, but recommended that a UN Commission of Experts be deployed to examine and analyze information about violations being committed in the former Yugoslavia.[31] Although the UK, France, and China disagreed, the United States pushed for a body similar to the 1943 war crimes commission that prepared the ground for the Nuremberg trials.[32] In December 1992, Secretary of State Lawrence Eagleburger "named names" of persons suspected of crimes against humanity, and said that the United States had provided details to the Commission of Experts "whose decision it will be to prosecute or not." At a conference on the Balkan conflict, Eagleburger said:

> We know that crimes against humanity have occurred, and we know when and where they occurred. We know, moreover, which forces committed those crimes, and under whose command they operated. And we know, finally, who the political leaders are and to whom those military commanders were—and still are—responsible.[33]

The names included the Bosnian Serb leaders Radovan Karadžić and Ratko Mladić, who figured in early ICTY indictments, and Serbian president Slobodan Milošević.[34] Eagleburger warned that "a second Nuremberg awaits the practitioners of ethnic cleansing."[35]

When President Clinton entered office, Secretary of State Warren Christopher investigated how best to organize an international war crimes tribunal, and submitted a report to the UN on human rights violations during the Balkan conflict based on material collected by US intelligence agencies.[36] UN Security Council Resolution 808 established the International Criminal Tribunal for the Former Yugoslavia (ICTY) in February 1993, and drew substantially from the US report.[37] US ambassador to the UN Madeline Albright was a strong advocate for the tribunal. "We oppose amnesty for the architects of ethnic cleansing," she said in a 1994 speech. "We believe that establishing the truth about what happened in Bosnia is *essential* to—not an *obstacle* to—national reconciliation. And we know the tribunal is no substitute for other actions to discourage further aggression and encourage peace." The tribunal, Albright said, would deter war criminals now and in the future, help bring reconciliation, and strengthen international law. But she knew the difficulties too. "This is not Nuremberg," she said. "The accused will not be the surrendered leaders of a broken power." She emphasized money, investigations, staff, and political will.[38] Albright confronted the Pentagon on the issue of arresting war criminals, and eventually got the secretary of defense to agree to have the international forces be more active in making arrests, and applied significant pressure on European governments to take a more active stance as well.[39]

A year after the ICTY was established, the Rwanda genocide claimed 800,000 lives during the summer of 1994.[40] The United States, which failed to intervene to stop the violence, focused on efforts to establish a tribunal similar to the one created for the former Yugoslavia. Albright initiated discussions about prosecution of those responsible for atrocity crimes, which received the support of Secretary of State Christopher.[41] In early August, senior State Department human rights official John Shattuck visited Kigali and convinced Rwanda's new regime to go along with the idea.[42] David Rawson, who was the US ambassador to Rwanda at the time, said that the Rwandan request was prepared in the US Embassy in Kigali and taken for signature to the Rwandan minister of justice by Shattuck.[43] In November 1994, the UNSC established the International Criminal Tribunal for Rwanda (ICTR).[44]

When Albright became secretary of state, she created a new ambassadorship for war crimes issues, which made support for the investigation and prosecution of atrocity crimes an official diplomatic function of the United States. Albright's creation of this post demonstrated to some that the United States "recognized the gravity of the situation and rose to the challenge. No other nation had seen fit to designate anyone as an ambassador to cover atrocity crimes."[45] Albright considered this work as part of her legacy in office, and construed herself as the "mother of the war crimes tribunals."[46] To Albright, herself twice a refugee from Nazi and Soviet

totalitarianism in Czechoslovakia, the wars in Bosnia were remi-
niscent of Nazism. She was not afraid of using force or putting pressure on the Pentagon when it was reluctant to do battle. While most
Americans had grown up in the shadow of Vietnam, she said, her
views had been formed by another searing experience. "My mindset
is Munich," she liked to say.[47]

The Office of War Crimes was responsible for "formulat[ing] US
policy responses to atrocities committed in areas of conflict and elsewhere throughout the world" and "coordinat[ing] US government
support for war crimes accountability in regions where crimes have
been committed against civilian populations on a massive scale."[48]
David Scheffer, who served as USUN senior advisor and counsel to
Albright from 1993 to 1996 and the first ambassador-at-large for war
crimes issues from 1997 to 2001, took a special interest in supporting accountability for war crimes, which he documents in *All the
Missing Souls*, a personal account of his involvement building the
ICTY, ICTR, and other tribunals.[49]

US support to the ICTY and ICTR took several forms, including
technical assistance. Scheffer claims that much of the American-
generated evidence ultimately made its way, directly or indirectly,
into trials, despite challenges in coordinating intelligence-sharing.[50]
In addition, investigators and attorneys from the Department of
Justice (DOJ) were deployed to the tribunals, and many stayed on
for many years, eventually joining the tribunal payroll.[51] ICTY
prosecutor Richard Goldstone said the American deployment
enabled the tribunal to launch its work and was instrumental in
preparing early indictments and trials.[52] An ICTY special advisor
to the prosecutor said that DOJ personnel were "some of the most
senior trial attorneys at the court" and were key to the tribunal's
success.[53]

US financial assistance was also significant. The United States
was the largest donor, contributing at least a quarter of the budgets
for the ICTY and ICTR, plus additional voluntary contributions.[54]
The tribunals enjoyed bipartisan support in Congress, who se members supported policies like conditioning economic infrastructure
aid on the arrest and transfer of indicted suspects to the tribunals.[55]
Scheffer writes, "although other governments pitched in, the United

States often became the one-stop shopping ally of the war crimes tribunals."[56] In comparison to the cost of intervening to stop the atrocities committed in both places, observers have pointed out that supporting the ad hoc tribunals was a less costly response.[57]

The International Criminal Court

The increase in attention to war crimes, crimes against humanity, and genocide, and the establishment of the two ad hoc tribunals renewed international interest in an international criminal court that would serve as a permanent institution to prosecute those crimes. In the United States, after the Genocide Convention was finally ratified in 1988, Congress passed legislation urging the president to investigate establishing an international criminal court. The legislation also stated: "Such discussions shall not include any commitment that such court shall have jurisdiction over the extradition of United States citizens."[58]

President Clinton supported the establishment of an international criminal court. In 1995, he stated: "nations all around the world who value freedom and tolerance [should] establish a permanent international criminal court to prosecute, with the support of the United Nations Security Council, serious violations of humanitarian law."[59] He reiterated this support in a 1997 address before the UN General Assembly: "we must maintain our strong support for the United Nations war crime tribunals and truth commissions. And before the century ends, we should establish a permanent international court to prosecute the most serious violations of humanitarian law."[60]

In 1998, the statute for the International Criminal Court was negotiated in Rome. Led by David Scheffer, the US delegation to the Rome Conference was the largest of any government. A number of US agencies, including the Departments of Justice, State, Defense, Treasury, the Joint Chiefs of Staff, and the intelligence community, were all involved in developing the US position.[61]

However, the United States failed to attract support for its views and the Rome Statute passed by a large majority without US support.[62] The United States voted against the statute primarily because it objected to the breadth of the court's jurisdiction and, in particular, its jurisdiction over nationals of non-states parties absent a Security Council referral.[63] Scheffer said that he "could not break the logjam" between Security Council control, which satisfied the Justice Department, and the precondition requiring consent of the state of nationality, which Justice rejected and the Pentagon strongly preferred.[64]

On the last day that the Rome Statute was open for signature, President Clinton signed the treaty despite internal disagreement.[65] Upon signature, Clinton made clear that the United States was not prepared to ratify the treaty unless "significant flaws" in the statute—language that was heavily negotiated in order to satisfy DOD—were addressed.[66] According to Scheffer, signing the treaty would allow the United States to maintain influence in ongoing negotiations, influence national judges and prosecutors to take a positive view of the Court, and enhance US leadership on international justice issues.[67]

The Bush administration was more hostile toward the Court, however, and "unsigned" the statute in May 2002.[68] Under Secretary of State for Political Affairs Marc Grossman said that the ICC undermined the role of the UN Security Council in maintaining international peace and security and asserted jurisdiction over citizens of states that had not ratified the treaty, which threatened US sovereignty. He also said that the ICC created a prosecutorial system that was an unchecked power that left it open for exploitation and politically motivated prosecutions.[69] The second war crimes ambassador, Pierre Prosper, explained how the prosecutor might unfairly target Americans:

> We are in a unique position internationally. We have the unique responsibility to preserve international peace and security. Whenever there is a conflict, whenever there is a hot spot, the first nation that people look to is the United States. Currently we have service members deployed in over 100 countries at a given time. We feel that this is a process that exposes us to politicization. We believe that a prosecutor with this unbridled authority to pursue any case that he or she feels is appropriate is a dangerous one and will expose us.[70]

Despite these concerns, Grossman and Prosper stated that the United States "respects the decision of those nations who have chosen to join the ICC" and did not intend to "take aggressive action or wage war" against the ICC or its supporters.[71]

Shortly after, however, the United States did in fact pursue an aggressive strategy to limit the exposure of US citizens to the jurisdiction of the ICC. By June 2005, the United States, at times applying tremendous political and financial pressure, had persuaded 100 states to sign "Article 98 agreements." These agreements ensured that those states would not surrender US citizens to the court.[72] The United States also worked through the Security Council to obtain an exemption for peacekeepers from states that had not ratified the Rome Statute. In addition, Bush signed into law the American Service-Members' Protection Act (ASPA), which was dubbed the "Hague Invasion Act" by critics because it granted the president permission to use "all means necessary and appropriate" to free US citizens and allies from ICC-ordered detention or imprisonment. The legislation also contained provisions that restricted US cooperation with the ICC, made US support of peacekeeping missions largely contingent on achieving an ICC exemption for all US personnel, and cut off military assistance to states that refused to sign Article 98 agreements.[73] Observers believed that US support of the Special Court for Sierra Leone (SCSL) was partially linked to its opposition to the ICC.[74]

During this period, Prosper emphasized the importance of domestic prosecutions within states where atrocities were committed. He stated: "international tribunals are not and should not be the courts of first redress, but of last resort," and "international practice should be to support sovereign states seeking justice domestically when it is feasible and would be credible."[75]

Although not intentional, the situation in Sudan began to soften US policy on the ICC. In September 2004, Secretary of State Colin Powell told members of Congress that genocide had been committed in Darfur. Use of the word "genocide" led to a US request for UN investigations into Darfur violations "with a view to ensuring accountability."[76] In January 2005, a UN Commission of Inquiry (COI) concluded that abuses in Sudan constituted war crimes and crimes against humanity, but not genocide, and recommended the immediate UNSC referral of the matter to the ICC. The United States needed to support these recommendations after its earlier statements, but also had to deal with its opposition to the court.[77] US faith-based groups added pressure on the United States to stop the violence.[78] Ultimately, the United States decided to abstain on the UNSC vote to refer the Darfur situation to the ICC.[79] Acting US ambassador to the UN Anne Patterson stated:

> We decided not to oppose the resolution because of the need for the international community to work together in order to end the climate of impunity in Sudan, and because the resolution provides protection from investigation or prosecution for US nationals and members of the armed forces of non-state parties.[80]

A few months later, Deputy Secretary of State Robert Zoellick suggested that the United States might cooperate and offer assistance to the ICC.[81] Although observers viewed the US abstention as tacit acceptance of the ICC, Prosper said that the abstention did not signal a radical departure from earlier US policy. "We've always envisioned that the Security Council has the authority to grant jurisdiction over particular matters," Prosper said, alluding to the US position that the Security Council should have the sole authority to trigger ICC jurisdiction.[82]

Nevertheless, the communication lines between the United States and the ICC were opened because of the Darfur referral, and opposition to the ICC continued to decrease. The following year, Congress approved legislation eliminating some of the aid restrictions on states parties to the ICC statute. President Bush also waived the penalties imposed upon countries that refused to reach Article 98 agreements, in part because they were interfering with other US foreign policy objectives, such as counterterrorism and counter-drug policy.[83] In June 2006, the *Wall Street Journal* reported on an interview with State Department legal advisor John Bellinger:

> US officials concede they can't delegitimize a court that now counts 100 member countries, including such allies as Australia, Britain and

Canada. While insisting the Bush administration will never allow Americans to be tried by the court, "we do acknowledge that it has a role to play in the overall system of international justice," John Bellinger, the State Department's chief lawyer, said in an interview. . . . In a May speech, Mr. Bellinger said "divisiveness over the ICC distracts from our ability to pursue these common goals" of fighting genocide and crimes against humanity.[84]

Clint Williamson, appointed by President Bush in his second term as the third war crimes ambassador, explained that the Bush administration had acknowledged the need to walk back from its more extreme positions and return to the status quo on these issues.[85] At a conference, Williamson said that the United States first looked to support "local courts and non-judicial mechanisms, when these institutions are robust enough and may simply need a small amount of training and additional resources. If this is not a possible solution to the problem of accountability," he said that the United States examines "options for a hybrid-type of accountability mechanism." Finally, if domestic or hybrid courts are not a viable option, he said, the United States looks "at a purely international process, which now, with the new Administration, presumably would be through the International Criminal Court."[86]

Indeed with the election of President Barack Obama, State Department legal advisor Harold Koh outlined the new US policy on the ICC:

Significantly, although during the last decade the US was largely absent from the ICC, our historic commitment to the cause of international justice has remained strong. As you all know, we have not been silent in the face of war crimes and crimes against humanity. As one of the vigorous supporters of the work of the ad hoc tribunals regarding the former Yugoslavia, Rwanda, Cambodia, Sierra Leone, and Lebanon, the United States has worked for decades, and we will continue to work, with other States to ensure accountability on behalf of victims of such crimes. But as some of those ad hoc war crimes tribunals enter their final years, the eyes of the world are increasingly turned toward the ICC. . . . Even as a non-State party, the United States believes that it can be a valuable partner and ally in the cause of advancing international justice. The Obama Administration has been actively looking at ways that the US can, consistent with US law, assist the ICC in fulfilling its historic charge of providing justice to those who have endured crimes of epic savagery and scope. And as [Obama's War Crimes] Ambassador [Stephen] Rapp announced in New York, we would like to meet with the Prosecutor at the ICC to examine whether there are specific ways that the United States might be able to support particular prosecutions already underway in the Democratic Republic of Congo, Sudan, Central African Republic, and Uganda.[87]

The United States first attended the ICC's Assembly of States Parties in 2009, where the fourth war crimes ambassador, Stephen Rapp, confirmed that the United States was back where it had been a decade earlier in terms of a positive, if critical, approach to the court, and made clear that the United States was "content to see other countries join" the court.[88] Rapp also made clear that the United States believed that the ICC would be where international justice is delivered:

> We are now coming to the end of the era of the Yugoslavia and Rwanda Tribunals and Sierra Leone Special Court; institutions with narrow jurisdictions and ad hoc mandates. In the future, for crimes committed after 2002, there will not be the will to establish temporary international courts for single situations. If international justice is required, it will be delivered at the International Criminal Court. That is where these trials will be conducted. That is where the mass butchers and rapists will face justice, and that is where the United States needs to provide support to ensure success.[89]

According to Rapp, the United States would help the ICC succeed in the cases that it has undertaken, serving as a "non-party partner." The United States has supported a number of ICC cases thus far. For example, Congress passed legislation to support the arrest and trial of LRA leader Joseph Kony.[90] President Obama issued a statement expressing support for the ICC's arrest of Sudanese president Omar al-Bashir.[91] In February 2011, the United States and other members of the Security Council unanimously referred the Libya case to the ICC.[92]

However, the United States will not be ratifying the ICC statute anytime soon. When asked about US ratification of the ICC statute, Rapp relied on arguments based on American exceptionalism: the United States takes a "very long time" to decide whether to ratify international treaties and conventions. The United States has "a tradition of self-reliance, an aspiration to do what is right in our own way, and a pride in the protections provided by our constitution and laws." In addition, he noted the "well-developed system of military justice" that already fulfills military obligations.[93] Rapp has also said that it will take the development of case standards in actual practice by a succession of prosecutors and judges to relieve US concerns about the court.[94]

Legal scholar William Schabas finds that US concerns will continue to lessen "as long as the politics of the institution are compatible with its own national interests."[95] He argues that the gradual warming of the United States to the ICC, which began early in the second term of the Bush administration, is the result of "a growing level of comfort with the policy choices and the political orientations of the prosecutor."[96] The prosecutor has pursued cases in Uganda, Sudan, and Kenya, but not against British forces in Iraq. Investigations in Afghanistan will probably target the Taliban, not North Atlantic Treaty Organization (NATO) forces. Schabas writes:

> All of this is reassuring to the US, which feared a radical prosecutor who would complicate American foreign policy. Instead, it has a tame institution that focuses its energies where the US would prefer, helping pursue perceived American interests in the same way as the Nuremberg, Yugoslavia, and Rwanda tribunals. . . . While the US would be happier with an ICC whose subservience to the Security Council was clearly established, its anxiety level with the institution has declined to the extent that the prosecutor seems to respect American interests and spheres of influence.[97]

Similarly, an ICC legal advisor said: "So far, all cases have converged with US interests (i.e., in Libya, Darfur, Uganda), but it is unclear what will happen if a case comes up that is more sensitive for the US."[98]

Conclusions

This chapter provided a historical overview of US foreign policy on transitional justice from World War I through the 2010s. What is most glaring in this review is the focus on courts. Albright's statement that a court could achieve truth, reconciliation, and justice highlights the US position. For the United States, transitional justice has been equated with criminal prosecutions.

Although the United States initially resisted the idea of international prosecutions proposed by Britain after World War I, this view changed after World War II, "and the US became a keen supporter, indeed the keenest supporter, of individual criminal accountability for perpetrators of war crimes and other atrocities."[99] Gary Bass writes: "Nuremberg was the American thing to do."[100] The trials were a result of Henry Stimson's narrow triumph, establishing trials over summary execution, which was based on his belief in American legal rights and tradition. Stimson and others were primarily interested in prosecuting the crime of aggression, not the Holocaust. If it were not for the successful lobbying of American Jewish groups, the trials would not have prosecuted Nazi leaders for crimes against humanity.

US interest declined during the Cold War, but re-emerged in the early 1990s when "no other nation showed such enthusiasm" for the ad hoc tribunals for the former Yugoslavia and Rwanda. The ICTY and ICTR would not have been created without the United States, but did not have the same level of political will as the Nuremberg trials. They offered a response to the atrocities that had been committed, and were continuing to be committed, which was less costly than intervening to stop the violence. Nevertheless, agencies across the government, some more grudgingly than others, supported these courts by helping to identify indictees, arrest them, gather intelligence, investigate suspects, and pay for the tribunals. Albright stands out as a particularly forceful advocate for US war crimes policy, based on her personal experience growing up as a refugee from

Nazi and Soviet totalitarianism in Czechoslovakia. She institution-alized this support through the establishment of the war crimes office in the State Department.

US leadership on international criminal justice declined when the Bush administration "unsigned" the Rome Statute of the ICC and through its various attempts to undermine the court. These extreme positions were reversed, however, by Bush's second term, in part because they contrasted so sharply with earlier US support and in part because the United States came to see the court's util-ity for specific policy goals, as was the case with the Darfur refer-ral. The US approach on the ICC during the Obama administration as a "non-party partner" is likely to be maintained in subsequent administrations.

This chapter's historical overview should serve as a useful basis for understanding the development of US foreign policy on tran-sitional justice. The Cambodia, Liberia, and Colombia cases offer an opportunity for a more in-depth look at US involvement in spe-cific transitional justice measures. The Cambodia case is explored first, with an examination of US involvement in the Khmer Rouge Tribunal.

Notes

1   At the 1915 annual meeting of the American Society of International Law, a former Yale University law professor, Theodore S. Woolsey, proposed that war criminals be tried before "an international court . . . previously agreed to in treaty form." See Theodore S. Woolsey, "Retaliation and Punishment," *Proceedings of the American Society of International Law* 62 (1915): 62–69.

2   Commission on the Responsibilities of the Authors of the War and on the Enforcement of Penalties, "Report Presented to the Preliminary Peace Conference, March 29, 1919, Annex II: Memorandum of Reservations Presented by the Representatives of the United States to the Report of the Commission on Responsibilities," *American Journal of International Law* 14 (1920): 142.

3   James F. Willis, *Prologue to Nuremberg: The Politics and Diplomacy of Punishing War Criminals of the First World War* (Westport, CT: Greenwood Press, 1982), 80.

4   John P. Cerone, "U.S. Attitudes toward International Criminal Courts and Tribunals," in *The Sword and the Scales: The United States and International*

Courts and Tribunals, ed. Cesare P. R. Romano (New York: Cambridge University Press, 2009), 136.

5   Willis, *Prologue to Nuremberg*, 80.

6   Telford Taylor, *The Anatomy of the Nuremberg Trials: A Personal Memoir* (New York: Alfred A. Knopf, 1992), 15.

7   Richard J. Alfaro, Special Rapporteur, "Report on the Question of International Criminal Jurisdiction," A/CN.4/15, *Yearbook of the International Law Commission* 2 (1950).

8   Cerone, "Dynamic Equilibrium," 282.

9   Schabas, "International War Crimes Tribunals and the United States," 771.

10 Taylor, *The Anatomy of the Nuremberg Trials*, 21.

11 The full text of the declaration is in Woolsey, "Retaliation and Punishment," 68.

12 Taylor, *The Anatomy of the Nuremberg Trials*, 25–26.

13 Ibid., 29–32.

14 Ibid., 33.

15 Ibid.

16 Bass, *Stay the Hand of Vengeance*, 64, 155–57.

17 Yalta Memorandum, "Memorandum to President Roosevelt from the Secretaries of State and War and the Attorney General," 22 January 1945.

18 Taylor, *The Anatomy of the Nuremberg Trials*, 39.

19 Bass, *Stay the Hand of Vengeance*, 174–75.

20 Ibid., 179–80.

21 Schabas, "International War Crimes Tribunals and the United States," 772.

22 Taylor, *The Anatomy of the Nuremberg Trials*, 42.

23 Hilary Earl, *The Nuremberg SS-Einsatzgruppen Trial, 1945–1958: Atrocity, Law, and History* (New York: Cambridge University Press, 2009).

24 Schabas, "International War Crimes Tribunals and the United States," 772.

25 J. Spiropoulos, "Draft Code of Offences against the Peace and Security of Mankind, Report by Special Rapporteur," A/CN.4/25, *Extract from the Yearbook of the International Law Commission* 2 (1950): para. 10.

26 UN General Assembly Resolution 177 (II), 21 November 1947.

27 UN Convention on the Prevention and Punishment of the Crime of Genocide, 1948.

28 Lawrence J. LeBlanc, *The United States and the Genocide Convention* (Durham, NC: Duke University Press, 1991).

29 Ruti G. Teitel, *Transitional Justice* (New York: Oxford University Press, 2000), 21.

30 Bass, *Stay the Hand of Vengeance*, 210.

31 See UN Security Council Resolution 780, "Requesting the Establishment of a Commission of Experts in the Former Yugoslavia," 6 October 1992. Read Power's discussion of the internal US debates about intervention in her chapter on Bosnia. See Power, *A Problem from Hell*.

32   UN Commission on Human Rights, "The Situation of Human Rights in the Territory of the Former Yugoslavia," CHR Res. 1992/S-2/1, 1992. See Mark Tran and Hella Pick, "UN to Set Up Commission to Investigate Atrocities in Former Yugoslavia; Europeans Dilute US Call for War Crimes Tribunal," *Guardian*, 7 October 1992; Virginia Morris and Michael Scharf, *An Insider's Guide to the International Criminal Tribunal for the Former Yugoslavia*, vol. 1 (Irvington-on-Hudson: Transnational Publishers, 1995), 26.

33   Elaine Sciolino, "U.S. Names Figures It Wants Charged with War Crimes," *New York Times*, 17 December 1992, 1.

34   See the Karadžić Indictment, "Prosecutor v. Karadžić et al. (IT-95-5-I), Indictment," 14 July 1995; and Milošević Indictment, "Prosecutor v. Milošević (IT-01-51–I), Indictment," 22 November 2001. Milošević was not indicted for alleged crimes committed in Bosnia and Herzegovina until November 2001.

35   B. G. Ramcharan, *The International Conference on the Former Yugoslavia: Official Papers* (Boston: Kluwer, 1997).

36   Schabas, "International War Crimes Tribunals and the United States," 776.

37   See "Letter Dated 5 April 1993 from the Permanent Representative of the United States of America to the United Nations Addressed to the Secretary-General," UN Document S/25575, 1993; and Morris and Scharf, *An Insider's Guide*, 451–57.

38   Bass, *Stay the Hand of Vengeance*, 262–63.

39   Ibid., 263–64.

40   See Alison Des Forges, *"Leave None to Tell the Story": Genocide in Rwanda* (New York: Human Rights Watch, 1999).

41   See USUN, "Rwanda: Bringing the Guilty to Justice," Cable 02491, 15 June 1994; Scheffer, *All the Missing Souls*, 71.

42   See also Paul Lewis, "Rwanda Agrees to a U.N. War-Crimes Tribunal," *New York Times*, 9 August 1994, 6; Jerry Gray, "At Rwanda Border, Mass Graves and the Start of a Journey Home," *New York Times*, 26 July 1994, 1. After losing power in mid-July, the remnants of the Rwandan regime that presided over the genocide issued a call for the creation of an international tribunal, adding that its jurisdiction should cover human rights violations in Rwanda since October 1990, when the civil war had begun.

43   D. Rawson, "Coping with Chaos While Acting Justly: Lessons from Rwanda," in *Effective Strategies for Protecting Human Rights*, ed. David Barnhizer (Burlington, VT: Dartmouth, 2001), 125–34.

44   See UN Security Council Resolution 955, 8 November 1994. Also see "Letter Dated 28 September 1994 from the Permanent Representative of Rwanda to the United Nations Addressed to the President of the Security Council," UN Document S/1994/1115, 1994. During the negotiations, however, Rwanda objected to a number of provisions, such as the time period

(wanting it to end in July 1994, not December), the death penalty, the seat of the tribunal in Rwanda, and the participation of Rwandans. Because of its dissatisfaction with the final design of the tribunal, Rwanda was the only country at the UNSC to vote against the resolution establishing the ICTR in November 1994. See Thierry Cruvellier, email communication, 3 June 2014. Some of these original points of tension remain as issues that may tend to limit or at least to call into question the efficacy of the ICTR. Also see Madeline H. Morris, "Trials of Concurrent Jurisdiction: The Case of Rwanda," *Duke Journal of Comparative and International Law* 7 (1996): 349.

45 Scheffer, *All the Missing Souls*, 3.

46 Ibid., 8.

47 Bass, *Stay the Hand of Vengeance*, 262.

48 This description was formerly posted on the State Department's website before a change in the office's description. See http://www.state.gov/j/gcj/.

49 Scheffer, *All the Missing Souls*, 3.

50 Ibid., 44.

51 Mark Harmon, Alan Tieger, Peter McCloskey, and Dermot Groome are some of the US attorneys who stayed on at the ICTY. ICTY Special Advisor to the Prosecutor, interview, 13 January 2012.

52 Richard J. Goldstone, *For Humanity: Reflections of a War Crimes Investigator* (New Haven, CT: Yale University Press, 2000), 82.

53 ICTY Special Advisor to the Prosecutor, interview, 13 January 2012.

54 Wierda and Triolo, "Resources," 116–17.

55 The US launched a Rewards for Justice program, which offered up to $5 million for information leading to the arrest or conviction of ICTY and ICTR indictees. Also see Cerone, "Dynamic Equilibrium," 289.

56 Scheffer, *All the Missing Souls*, 29.

57 See, e.g., Peter Ronayne, *Never Again? The United States and the Prevention and Punishment of Genocide since the Holocaust* (Lanham, MD: Rowman & Littlefield, 2001).

58 US PL 100–690, 102 Stat. 4267, 1988.

59 Clinton, "Remarks at the University of Connecticut."

60 William J. Clinton, "Remarks to the 52d Session of the United Nations General Assembly in New York City," 33 *Wkly. Comp. Pres. Docs.* 1386, 1389 (29 September 1997).

61 Senior Subcommission on International Operations of the Commission on Foreign Relations, "Is a U.N. International Criminal Court in the U.S. National Interest?" (1998).

62 In the drafting of the Rome Statute, a coalition of middle and small powers, including allies of the United States like Germany and Canada, coalesced into a group known as the "like-minded," which agreed on the following

issues: inherent jurisdiction of the court over the "core crimes" of geno-cide, crimes against humanity, and war crimes (and, perhaps, aggression); the elimination of a Security Council veto on prosecutions; an indepen-dent prosecutor with the power to initiate proceedings on his or her own initiative (*proprio motu*); and the prohibition of reservations to the stat-ute. See Philip Kirsch and Darryl Robinson, "Reaching Agreement at the Rome Conference," in *The Rome Statute for an International Criminal Court: A Commentary*, ed. Antonio Cassese (New York: Oxford University Press, 2002), 70–71. The United States found itself at odds with all of these propositions. But it was outmaneuvered at the Rome Conference by the "like-minded," which managed to dominate much of the debate and the organization. Their program was incorporated into the final draft. In the final sessions of the Rome Conference, the United States tried des-perately to block the groundswell of support for a court that was largely independent of the Security Council, unsuccessfully proposing some last-minute amendments and then calling for an unrecorded vote on the final version of the statute, thereby preventing adoption of the draft statute by consensus. The result was 120 in favor to 7 against with 21 abstentions, a comfortable majority. See UN Diplomatic Conference of Plenipotentiaries on the Establishment of an International Criminal Court, UN Document A/CONF.183/C.1/L.70; A/CONF.183/C.1/L.90; A/CONF.183/SR.9, 1998.

63 Senior Subcommission on International Operations of the Commission on Foreign Relations, "Is a U.N. International Criminal Court in the U.S. National Interest?"

64 Scheffer, *All the Missing Souls*, 181.

65 See Cerone, "Dynamic Equilibrium," 293. The Department of Defense and the Joint Chiefs of Staff did not want to sign; however, there was division even within DOD.

66 Ibid.

67 David J. Scheffer, "Staying the Course with the International Criminal Court," *Cornell International Law Journal* 35 (2002): 47.

68 See US State Department, "International Criminal Court: Letter to United Nations Secretary General Kofi Annan." A wariness about international law and institutions was evident on the part of Bush, Vice President Dick Cheney, and a number of the administration's appointees, including Donald Rumsfeld, secretary of defense, and John Bolton, under secretary of state for arms control and international security. Bolton, whose anti-ICC position was clearly set forth in a 1998 Senate hearing, had an influence greater than his title would ordinarily imply because he was perceived to have helped Bush win the 2000 presidential election. Very few Democratic legislators went on record to support US adherence to the ICC statute. Even Chris Dodd, who was the chief opponent of the anti-ICC provisions of the

ASPA, stated that he would not support US ratification of the ICC statute. See Cerone, "Dynamic Equilibrium," 293 and footnote 110.

69 US State Department, "American Foreign Policy and the International Criminal Court," Press Release, Marc Grossman, Under Sec'y for Political Affairs, 6 May 2002.

70 PBS, "Ambassador Pierre-Richard Prosper of the Office of War Crimes Issues discusses war tribunals with host Daljit Dhaliwal," *Wide Angle*, 25 August 2002.

71 US State Department, "American Foreign Policy and the International Criminal Court"; US State Department, "Issues Update," Press Release, Pierre-Richard Prosper, US Ambassador for War Crimes Issues, 6 May 2002.

72 US Fact Sheet, "The International Criminal Court," Bureau of Political-Military Affairs, 2 August 2002.

73 American Service-Members' Protection Act (ASPA), 22 USCA §§ 7423–27 (2002).

74 SCSL, ICTR, Special Tribunal for Lebanon (STL) officials, interviews, 12–13 January 2012. See also Cerone, "Dynamic Equilibrium," 293; and Tom Perriello and Marieke Wierda, "The Special Court for Sierra Leone under Scrutiny," International Center for Transitional Justice, March 2006, 12. The SCSL, for example, exempted peacekeepers from its jurisdiction.

75 Pierre-Richard Prosper, "Address at the Peace Palace in the Hague," Press Release, US Ambassador for War Crimes Issues, 19 December 2001. See also Pierre-Richard Prosper, "War Crimes in the 21st Century," Press Release, US Ambassador for War Crimes Issues, 26 October 2004. "Tribunal fatigue," a term Scheffer claims to have coined, had also begun to set in, with the international community concerned about the high costs and lengthy time frame of the ad hoc tribunals. See Scheffer, *All the Missing Souls*, 118.

76 Adele Waugaman, "The United States in Darfur: Trapped by 'Genocide,'" *International Justice Tribune*, 21 November 2005.

77 Ibid.

78 Ibid.

79 UN Security Council Resolution 1593, 2005.

80 Waugaman, "The United States in Darfur."

81 Ibid. Also, Assistant Secretary of State for African Affairs Jendayi Frazer told the House International Relations Committee, "if the ICC requires assistance, the United States stands ready to assist . . . we don't want to see impunity for any of these actors."

82 Waugaman, "The United States in Darfur."

83 Schabas, "International War Crimes Tribunals and the United States," 783.

84 Jess Bravin, "U.S. Warms to Hague Tribunal: New Stance Reflects Desire to Use Court to Prosecute Darfur Crimes," *Wall Street Journal*, 14 June 2006.

85   Clint Williamson, interview, 21 April 2010.

86   American Society of International Law, Transitional Justice, Rule of Law and the Creation of the Civilian Response Corps, 22 January 2009, http://www.crs.state.gov/index.cfm?fuseaction=public.display&shortcut=C4MB.

87   Harold Hongju Koh, "The Obama Administration and International Law," address by Harold Hongju Koh to the American Society of International Law, 15 March 2010.

88   Schabas, "International War Crimes Tribunals and the United States," 784. See also Stephen J. Rapp, "Remarks by Ambassador-at-Large for War Crimes Issues at Question and Answer Session at the Forum Hosted by the Women of Ateneo," Makati, Philippines, 10 May 2011.

89   Stephen J. Rapp, "Remarks by the Ambassador-at-Large for War Crimes Issues on International Justice and the Use of Force," International Humanitarian Law Dialogs, Chautauqua, NY, 30 August 2010.

90   Ibid.

91   Ibid.

92   UNSCR 1970, "Peace and Security in Africa," 2011.

93   Rapp, "Remarks by Ambassador-at-Large for War Crimes Issues at Question and Answer Session at the Forum Hosted by the Women of Ateneo"; Rapp, "Remarks by the Ambassador-at-Large for War Crimes Issues on International Justice and the Use of Force."

94   Ibid.

95   Schabas, "International War Crimes Tribunals and the United States," 785.

96   Ibid.

97   Ibid., 786.

98   Rod Rastan, ICC visit, 13 January 2012.

99   Schabas, "International War Crimes Tribunals and the United States," 785.

100 Bass, *Stay the Hand of Vengeance*, 181.

3 :: US Involvement in the Khmer Rouge Tribunal

Nearly 20 years after the Cambodian genocide, and after years of domestic pressure, Congress made it US policy to investigate and help establish a tribunal for the crimes committed by the Khmer Rouge in the 1970s. The decision was made long before the Cambodian government and UN had come to such a conclusion, however, and it took another decade to bring both on board. The first war crimes ambassador, David Scheffer was determined to see the court established, and encouraged a number of compromises to get the court up and running. When the court was finally established, Congress refused to fund it, primarily because one well-placed staffer on the Hill did not trust Hun Sen— Cambodia's prime minister. Eventually, this position shifted and the US provided some funds to support the court. Before examining the tribunal, this chapter briefly reviews US involvement in Cambodia starting with the period of Khmer Rouge rule.

From 1975 to 1979, an estimated 1.7 million of Cambodia's seven million people died through disease, overwork, starvation, or execution under the Khmer Rouge regime of Democratic Kampuchea, led by Pol Pot, Nuon Chea, Ta Mok, Ieng Sary, Son Sen, and Khieu

Samphan, among others.[1] In an attempt to revolutionize Cambodia into a purely agrarian-based Communist society without class or ethnic differences, those living in cities were deported to the countryside and subjected to forced labor.

Just before Pol Pot seized power, the Nixon administration had heavily bombed border towns in Cambodia between 1969 and 1973 in the fight against Vietnam.[2] When the Khmer Rouge regime took control, the United States withdrew its embassy staff and did not re-establish a diplomatic mission until 1991. Although there was limited information about Khmer Rouge crimes while they were committed, Rep. Stephen Solarz held hearings on the human rights abuses taking place and Senator George McGovern tried to get support for an international force to stop the violations.[3] However, the Carter administration's position was clear. A State Department spokesman said: "While the US takes great exception to the human rights record of the government of Kampuchea, we, as a matter of principle, do not feel that unilateral intervention against the regime of any third power is justified."[4]

Vietnamese troops invaded Cambodia in late 1978 and installed the People's Republic of Kampuchea (PRK), a Communist government made up mostly of former Khmer Rouge cadres who had defected to Vietnam, including current prime minister Hun Sen. The Khmer Rouge retreated to camps on the Thai border, allied with two smaller noncommunist parties, and called themselves the Coalition Government of Democratic Kampuchea (CGDK). Fighting continued between the government and Khmer Rouge between 1979 and 1998, while millions of Cambodians remained in refugee camps.

Since the United States did not want to recognize a Cambodian government controlled by Vietnam, it recognized the CGDK as the legitimate government.[5] The primary objective of the United States at this time was to enhance US-China strategic relations in the common anti-Soviet effort.[6] President Carter's national security advisor, Zbigniew Brzezinski, recalls: "I encouraged the Chinese to support Pol Pot. I encouraged the Thai to help Democratic Kampuchea. . . . ol Pot was an abomination. We could never support him, but China could."[7] According to Brzezinski, the United States "winked, semi-publicly" at Chinese and Thai aid to the Khmer Rouge forces, while the United States pushed through additional UN and other international aid to their camps on the Thai border.[8] Although official US policy was that all covert aid was nonlethal and that none of it went to the Khmer Rouge, there was evidence of unreported American assistance to the Khmer Rouge.[9]

Without the support of the Soviet Union after it collapsed, Vietnamese troops withdrew from Cambodia in 1989, and a political settlement, as opposed to a military settlement, became possible. The United States helped negotiate a Security Council agreement for a UN-managed peace process. Because the United States wanted to find a settlement that China would approve, this meant including the Khmer Rouge in the settlement.[10] The 1991 Paris Accords established the UN Transitional Authority in Cambodia (UNTAC), which led to the elections in 1993, where a power-sharing arrangement was made for a two-headed administration led by Hun Sen and Prince Norodom Ranariddh.

This new moment in Cambodian history allowed for long-standing calls for accountability for violations committed by the Khmer Rouge to gain traction, including in the United States. These calls eventually led to a request by the Cambodian government in July 1997 for international assistance in setting up a court. This request resulted in years of negotiations for the eventual establishment of the Extraordinary Chambers in the Courts of Cambodia (ECCC), also known as the Khmer Rouge Tribunal, in 2004. The aim of this tribunal was to bring to justice surviving senior leaders of Democratic Kampuchea and those most responsible for genocide, crimes against humanity, serious war crimes, and certain other Cambodian crimes during the Pol Pot era.[11] This chapter documents US involvement in this process, from its decision to make support for accountability a policy goal, to its role in court negotiations and operations. This chapter draws on 38 Cambodia-specific interviews undertaken in Phnom Penh and Washington, DC, with officials from the US government, the ECCC, international organizations, NGOs, academia, and the media.[12]

The Policy Shift in Favor of Accountability

It took many years before the US position shifted to support accountability for human rights violations committed by the Khmer Rouge. Interest in Cambodian trials initially came from a small group of advocates in the 1980s.[13] After visiting the exhumations of the Choeung Ek "killing fields" site with Australian historian Ben Kiernan, Yale law student Gregory Stanton founded the Cambodian Genocide Project in order to gather evidence for the charge of genocide. This project gathered documentary evidence and testimony of a multitude of eyewitnesses in Cambodia, including scores of hours of videotaped testimony funded by the US Institute of Peace.[14] Stanton took the case to Australia in 1986, and Bill Hayden, minister of foreign affairs, announced his support for a trial of the Khmer Rouge. The Australian prime minister, under State Department pressure, however, stopped that initiative. Stanton states:

> We learned a crucial lesson: human rights are not lost because of the absence of law, but because of the lack of political will to enforce it. We needed to change the political will of crucial nations, notably the United States, which opposed pursuing the case because it might legitimize the Vietnamese-backed government in Phnom Penh.[15]

Stanton and others believed that before they could advocate for accountability, they first needed to convince the United States to stop supporting a role for the Khmer Rouge in Cambodia. Stanton, along with Ben Kiernan, Craig Etcheson, Sally Benson, and a number of others, formed a coalition called the Campaign to Oppose the Return of the Khmer Rouge (CORKR) in 1989.[16] This group felt that power-sharing was impossible and there was no choice but to back Hun Sen and help the Thais disengage from the forces of Pol Pot.[17] Congressional Democrats became increasingly concerned about the return of the Khmer Rouge, and 203 members signed a petition requesting that Secretary of State James Baker identify a policy that would deny a role for Pol Pot and the Khmer Rouge in Cambodia.[18]

In July 1991, the US policy of support for the Khmer Rouge was reversed when Baker announced that the United States would no longer recognize the CGDK.[19] The primary goal became to keep the Khmer Rouge from taking power, a goal that, Baker acknowledged, the United States had not been able to achieve with its former policy. The United States "would no longer defer" to ASEAN countries and China on Cambodian matters.[20] It agreed to pay 30 percent of UN operations and, at least on the surface, warmed to Hun Sen's government.[21]

Baker also publicly acknowledged the Khmer Rouge crimes and offered support for justice if the Cambodian government chose to pursue this path:

> What makes the case of Cambodia so extraordinary—and its claim for international support so compelling—is the magnitude of the suffering its people have endured. The Khmer Rouge were no ordinary oppressors. In the name of revolution, they used violence against their own people in a way that has few parallels in history. We condemn these policies and practices of the Khmer Rouge as an abomination to humanity that must never be allowed to recur. To prevent such a recurrence, we have encouraged the incorporation of strong human rights guarantees into this settlement agreement. And I can assure . . . that we will steadfastly sustain our efforts to ensure that the human rights of the Cambodian people are supported by the international community. Cambodia and the US are both signatories to the Genocide Convention, and we will support efforts to bring to justice those responsible for the mass murders of the 1970s if the new Cambodian government chooses to pursue this path.[22]

Although this statement signaled a shift, the United States was still not prepared to support a tribunal. Australia and Japan suggested a court, but China and the United States were opposed and it was not included in the peace accords.[23] Part of the reason that the United States was unwilling to support a tribunal was because, as one reporter noted, it would

> dredge up no little amount of embarrassment about the American role in recent Cambodian history. . . . We were indeed there at the creation of Cambodia's troubles. For purely prudential reasons, then, a

US initiative aimed at exhuming our own policy ancestor, so to speak, seems very ill-advised.[24]

For others, this history was a reason to support accountability. War crimes ambassador David Scheffer said:

> The Cambodian tribunal is a reminder that a titanic explosion occurred in Indochina after we left there. That's one of the lessons of the Vietnam War, that the aftermath was just as important as the event itself. . . . For Americans in particular, the secret bombing of Cambodia during the Nixon presidency, which helped to destabilize that country as the Khmer Rouge were gaining power, leaves us no moral choice but to make every possible effort to achieve some measure of credible accountability for the slaughter that ensued.[25]

Lobbying continued and was focused on legislation that would make it US policy to prosecute the leaders of the Khmer Rouge. Senator Charles Robb took the issue on and drafted the Cambodian Genocide Justice Act, with the assistance of Craig Etcheson.[26] Although the bill was opposed by the State Department, it was passed in 1994 and signed by President Clinton.[27] The act declared that it was US policy "to support efforts to bring to justice members of the Khmer Rouge for their crimes against humanity committed in Cambodia between April 17, 1975, and January 7, 1979." It also directed the creation of an "Office of Cambodian Genocide Investigations" within the State Department, and earmarked $500,000 for the investigation of Khmer Rouge crimes.

The Office of Cambodian Genocide Investigations was created inside the Bureau of East Asia Affairs, headed by Alfonse La Porta. The job was not sought after at the State Department since officials "didn't want to rock the boat" with Thailand and China.[28] Nevertheless, work began, starting with an initial grant that supported the establishment of the Cambodian Genocide Program (CGP) at Yale University, led by Professor Ben Kiernan, and its Cambodian counterpart, the Documentation Center of Cambodia (DC-Cam), led by Youk Chhang. Stanton, who had joined the State Department, helped convince Assistant Secretary of State John

Shattuck to give the Cambodian Genocide Program another $1 million, during which time DC-Cam become an independent NGO.

With these grants, CGP and DC-Cam produced hundreds of thousands of pages of evidence of the atrocities committed by the Khmer Rouge that could be used by a prosecutor. This work contributed to recommendations proposed in a legal study commissioned by the State Department, which found culpability for charges of war crimes, crimes against humanity, and genocide, and weighed various avenues for prosecution.[29]

Negotiating the Court's Design

Meanwhile, with the urging of the UN special representative for human rights in Cambodia, Thomas Hammarberg,[30] Cambodian co-prime ministers Hun Sen and Prince Ranariddh requested assistance from the UN and the international community in establishing a tribunal. The request stated that a tribunal should prosecute

> those persons responsible for the genocide and crimes against humanity during the rule of the Khmer Rouge from 1975 to 1979. . . . Cambodia does not have the resources or expertise to conduct this very important procedure. Thus, we believe it is necessary to ask for the assistance of the United Nations. We are aware of similar efforts to respond to the genocide and crimes against humanity in Rwanda and the former Yugoslavia, and ask that similar assistance be given to Cambodia. . . . We believe that crimes of this magnitude are of concern to all persons in the world, as they greatly diminish respect for the most basic human right—the right to life. We hope that the United Nations and the international community can assist the Cambodian people in establishing the truth about this period and bringing those responsible to justice. Only in this way can this tragedy be brought to a full and final conclusion.[31]

Shortly after this request, however, tensions between the two coalition parties escalated and Hun Sen ousted Prince Ranariddh in a coup in July 1997. At the same time, the disintegration of the Khmer

Rouge sped up with the defection of important leaders, the amnesty of Ieng Sary, the return to Cambodia of close to 40,000 refugees, and Pol Pot's trial by a "people's court" close to the Thai border where he was sentenced to lifelong detention.

The plausible arrest of Pol Pot drew the attention of US officials who worked on a scheme to capture him. The United States approached Canada, Denmark, Sweden, and Israel, among others, about hosting a trial of Pol Pot, yet failed to inform the UN, which believed that no country was prepared to host this type of trial.[32] One of the reasons motivating US interest in Pol Pot's capture was the view that this effort would boost President Clinton's credibility as he embarked on his long-awaited trip to Rwanda to confront the memory of genocide there.[33]

Although the US effort was unsuccessful, the death of Pol Pot in April 1998 reaffirmed US resolve to bring senior Khmer Rouge leaders to justice. President Clinton stated:

> Although the opportunity to hold Pol Pot accountable for his monstrous crimes appears to have passed, senior Khmer Rouge, who exercised leadership from 1975 to 1979, are still at large and share responsibility for the monstrous human rights abuses committed during this period. We must not permit the death of the most notorious of the Khmer Rouge leaders to deter us from the equally important task of bringing these others to justice.[34]

Scheffer noted: "No other government was so determined to launch a tribunal-building initiative, and no other government became so deeply involved for four years (1997–2000) in negotiations leading to the constitutional documents of the Cambodia Tribunal."[35] The process began with Scheffer's drafting of a UNSC Chapter VII resolution to establish an International Criminal Tribunal for Cambodia. The US draft envisioned sharing much of the infrastructure and resources of the ICTY, and prosecuting "senior members of the Khmer Rouge leadership who planned or directed serious violations of international and humanitarian law" committed in Cambodia between April 1975 and January 1979.[36]

The United States was therefore partly responsible for limiting the temporal jurisdiction of the court to violations committed between 1975 and 1979. Scheffer acknowledged that limiting the court's focus in this way was in part due to the desire "to avoid giving any individuals an excuse for using the [US] bombing to justify their own action in Cambodia."[37] DC-Cam legal advisor Beth van Schaack said: "There was no way [the United States] would have supported the trial if those dates had not been very clear from the start."[38]

Nonetheless, the US proposal failed to attract support. China was opposed to the idea and it was reported that Russia and France also had problems with the initiative. Instead, the UN recommended that a group of experts evaluate evidence of responsibility for the Khmer Rouge human rights violations. The group (which included Steven Ratner, who had undertaken the earlier State Department study on this issue in 1995)[39] found that serious crimes had been committed under both international and Cambodian law and that sufficient evidence existed to justify legal proceedings against Khmer Rouge leaders.[40] The group also recommended that the UN establish an ad hoc international tribunal because they found that the Cambodian judiciary would not be fair or effective.[41] Upon submitting the report, UN secretary-general Kofi Annan said that the tribunal should be international in character, but that other models could be explored as well.[42]

By the time the experts' report was released, further defections from senior Khmer Rouge leaders had decreased Hun Sen's support for a court. He rejected the recommendations for an international criminal tribunal, asserting a potential conflict between a trial and peace and his preference for trials in Cambodian courts or a South African–style truth commission, which could investigate crimes committed from 1970 to 1998. Secretary of State Madeleine Albright rejected the truth commission proposal, and made US support for an international criminal tribunal clear.[43] There was a concern about Hun Sen's proposal for a longer time frame, which would have implicated US involvement in Cambodia in the early 1970s. Scheffer said the United States continued to press for an international criminal tribunal in part because it "had to keep the matter out of the control of the General Assembly, which could, by major-ity vote, create a tribunal with wide-ranging jurisdiction."[44]

In response to the lack of support by the Cambodian govern-ment and some UNSC members for an international criminal tri-bunal, Scheffer began to explore other options. He wrote: "As is often the case in negotiations, my task in this situation was to push the envelope to find an acceptable means to a desired end."[45] One idea being discussed was a "mixed" tribunal that would guarantee international standards and be based in Cambodia. Senator John Kerry, a Vietnam veteran and chairman of the East Asian Foreign Relations Subcommittee, supported the idea and proposed it to Hun Sen in April 1999. Hun Sen expressed interest and requested techni-cal assistance from the UN in creating the Cambodian draft law. The United States officially shifted its position to support a mixed tribunal.

Although the UN was not convinced about this model, the UN Office of Legal Affairs (OLA) began discussions with the Cambodian government on the task of its establishment. When UN assistant secretary-general for legal affairs Ralph Zacklin and Cambodian senior minister Sok An met in August 1999 to discuss their respective drafts of the enabling law, there were major dif-ferences between the two. They differed on several issues, includ-ing the issue of personal jurisdiction, the method of appointing judges and prosecutors, and the numbers of foreigners and Cambodians among them.[46] Zacklin came to these discussions with negative impressions about tribunals, depicted in an article he wrote about his experience establishing the ICTY—a court he viewed as plagued with "major" legal, political, and institutional problems.[47]

In late 1999, Scheffer prepared a draft law that addressed some of the differences between the UN and Cambodia drafts. He pro-posed the establishment of "Extraordinary Chambers"—a special trial chamber and special appeals chamber in the Cambodian courts with participation by an international prosecutor and judges. He suggested that the Cambodians be in the majority but that a "supermajority" vote would require at least one international judge behind decisions. He wrote:

I introduced the supermajority vote rule because I was convinced that some formula had to be developed to ensure the participation of Cambodian judges in the court, but in a way that preserved international influence and oversight. . . . There was no magical historical reflection or precedent that brought it to mind. I simply tried to figure out how to manage a Cambodian majority on the bench (if that proved to be the endgame) and determined that requiring the vote of at least one international judge could establish the minimum threshold of international oversight in the decision-making process of the judges. . . . The supermajority would be a lower threshold than required in the US and yet an appropriately higher bar to surmount than that found in civil-law jurisdictions.[48]

Hammarberg disagreed: the supermajority notion "was clearly a compromise" and not without problems. "It carries an implicit notion of there being two categories of judges—which would be an unfortunate perception even in more normal circumstances," he added.[49]

Regarding the issue of personal jurisdiction, there was a need to find a legal formulation that would limit the number of prosecutions without giving an implicit amnesty to those outside that limited group.[50] The UN Group of Experts had used the notion that only "the most responsible for the most serious crimes" be tried, an approach that had been echoed in General Assembly and Human Rights Commission resolutions. Scheffer foresaw two groups of suspects: Khmer Rouge senior leaders and all persons responsible for the most serious violations of Cambodian law.[51] This issue was (and continued to be) contentious. In order to assuage Cambodian government fears that the court might indict a large number of persons, US ambassador to Cambodia Kent Wiedemann suggested limiting the personal jurisdiction to six or seven persons, "that is, the senior most leaders of the Khmer Rouge most responsible for crimes against humanity, war crimes, genocide, etc."[52] The UN had cautioned against limiting prosecution only to senior leaders since it might not correspond to those most responsible for human rights violations; certain top leaders may have been removed from knowledge and decision-making power, while others not in the chart of senior leaders may have played a significant role in the atrocities.[53] An informal UN paper noted that Kofi Annan gave in to US and Cambodian demands to limit prosecution only to senior leaders of the Khmer Rouge.[54] Former ECCC official and Cambodia expert Steve Heder was more critical of US pressure on the UN to accept personal jurisdiction clauses that were intended to limit prosecutions of those responsible exclusively to senior leaders and one other official. He said:

> This was part of a larger pattern of pressure on the UN by the US and other governments with diplomatic interests to pursue vis-à-vis the Royal Government of Cambodia (RGC). Most importantly, after obtaining UN acquiescence to a severely limited personal jurisdiction, they also forced it to agree to involve itself in assisting with what the UN was certain would be much less than fair trials, as the CPP's control over the Cambodian court system via its domination of the RGC was sufficient to ensure that the extraordinary chambers would not adhere to international standards of judicial independence and impartiality. They have further limited the court's prosecutorial reach by insisting that the budget for investigations, trials and defense be kept low.[55]

Shortly after Wiedemann formally delivered Scheffer's proposal to the Cambodian government, Hun Sen said: "At this hour, we and the UN, especially considering the US position towards us, can reach a deal. I have agreed to this proposal, there is no more doubt left."[56] Hammarberg said that the United States had not coordinated with the UN and that "Hun Sen, and others, obviously believed that with US support any trial would not be much criticized abroad."[57] He said that the feasibility of a mixed tribunal would require guarantees for the integrity of the process, including watertight protection against the risk of direct or indirect political pressure. The fact that Hun Sen "dominated every bit" of the process "and most often made no secret of that fact" was a problem.[58] Although the UN did not approve the draft law, the Cambodian government adopted the draft ECCC Law in January 2000.

While the UN continued to apply pressure on the Cambodian government on various elements of the law, the French condemned the United States and the UN for pushing too hard for an international element to the trials.[59] The French expressed support for Hun Sen's desire not to be "dispossessed" by any trial process and sympathy for the position that political stability and economic development should be Cambodia's overriding priorities.[60] China encouraged Hun Sen to resist, and threatened to withdraw aid to the government if it allowed UN participation in a tribunal.[61] China was providing the government with low-interest loans worth about $200 million and some military assistance, and encouraged Chinese state-owned enterprises to invest there.[62]

Despite French and Chinese support to resist US and UN pressure, in order to preserve the economic assistance linked to the trials, Hun Sen wanted to at least appear serious about trying some former Khmer Rouge leaders.[63] When Japan pledged new aid if Hun Sen would "go just one step further in efforts with the UN," Hun Sen announced that he would allow a second foreign judge.[64] Hun Sen used this announcement to garner diplomatic support for pressuring the UN to send a delegation to Phnom Penh on his terms.[65] In this, he had the support of the United States, whose diplomats criticized the UN for lacking enthusiasm for making a deal, and for "bungling" negotiations so far by being reluctant to engage Hun Sen.[66]

US officials suggested that the UN team going to Cambodia include legal experts, but be guided by "someone with a good feel for political realities," because, according to the United States, the main stakes in the negotiations were "political, not legal."[67] The UN conceded to this request, sending a personal representative of Annan, who, as one UN official put it, "was there to ensure that political considerations overrode legal considerations," and that the "tremendous ... pressure" from the United States and other governments to make a deal was translated into concessions.[68] Before the UN visit, a senior State Department official

was despatched to persuade Hun Sen to be more accommodating, enough at least to give the deal an appearance of a mutual compromise arising from a willingness on the part of Hun Sen and the UN "to work flexibly together." The sweetener, as it had been with the Japanese, was aid, although the payoff had to be put in the future. The official made it clear to Hun Sen that if he would move sufficiently to find common ground with a UN already forced into a climb down by the US, Japan, France, Russia and India, any resulting agreement with Corell [UN legal counsel] would be a "hugely positive thing" that would "encourage the climate in Washington and elsewhere," and could bring about a lifting of US congressional restrictions on aid to Cambodia.[69]

Despite these efforts, little progress was made at the meeting between Hun Sen and UN legal counsel Hans Corell. A sticking point in the negotiations during this period centered on how disagreements between the Cambodian and international prosecutors and judges would be resolved.[70] This led to another US-crafted proposal delivered by Senator John Kerry that a separate panel of judges (three Cambodians and two international) would resolve disputes, requiring a supermajority vote of at least four judges to block a proposal from one of the two prosecutors for an indictment.[71]

The UN again took issue with the US proposal: "Though this approach seemed unconventional and even unprincipled, it was described in some media as a major compromise on the side of the Cambodian government."[72] Others familiar with international judicial standards decried the fact that it would create a "problem of multiple judges performing a task that should not be theirs," ruling on prosecution decisions and then being involved in further adjudicating the same case.[73] Together with the supermajority formula for decisions on verdicts, it set up a "horrendously complicated" and "unworkable system" that was insufficient to ensure that "evidence—and not politics— . . . determines who is indicted, arrested and convicted."[74]

Non-US diplomats and the UN remained skeptical about whether Hun Sen would agree to a credible tribunal or travel the route prescribed by the United States. Hans Corell was sent back to Phnom Penh in June. Upon his departure, he warned that Kofi Annan had established a time limit beyond which the UN would no longer wish to proceed in the negotiations, and although he did not

name a date, he said that the UN would not tolerate further procras-
tination. Disregarding this threat, the Cambodian Assembly and
Senate approved a proposal for a special court within the existing
Cambodian judicial system, with a majority of Cambodian judges
and Cambodian government approval required for the appointment
of foreign judges. Decisions would be settled by a supermajority
voting requirement. The Cambodia proposal did not meet the UN
requirement that the majority of judges be foreign and appointed by
the secretary-general.

After more disagreement throughout 2001, Kofi Annan withdrew from the negotiations in February 2002. Corell stated:

> The United Nations has come to the conclusion that the Extraordinary
> Chambers, as currently envisaged, would not guarantee the indepen-
> dence, impartiality and objectivity that a court established with the
> support of the United Nations must have. . . . Therefore . . . the United
> Nations has concluded . . . to end its participation in this process.[75]

Key governments were not informed in advance about the UN decision to withdraw from negotiations and were surprised by it.[76] In
response, Japan and France sponsored an UNGA resolution calling
for the resumption of negotiations, which forced the UN to recom-
mence negotiations with Cambodia despite its misgivings about the
process.[77]

In June 2003, the text was finalized and the "Agreement between
the UN and the Royal Government of Cambodia Concerning the
Prosecution Under Cambodian Law of Crimes Committed during
the Period of Democratic Kampuchea" was signed by both parties.[78]
It took another year for the agreement to be ratified by Cambodia's
National Assembly and it was officially promulgated on 19 October
2004 following amendment of the ECCC law to ensure that the two
documents were consistent.

Court Operations

Despite significant US involvement in establishing the court, this
involvement did not initially extend to funding it. Congress had cut

off all bilateral assistance to Cambodia after Hun Sen's 1997 coup. Although Congress could have supported the UN side of the tribunal, it blocked all funding to the court for the first few years of its operations. Because the United States was a top donor for other tribunals and because it had been so involved in the establishment of the Cambodian court, this funding block was noticeable.

The United States justified the block by citing the court's failure to meet international standards of justice. The United States also noted its contributions to the Cambodian Genocide Program and the Documentation Center of Cambodia, which totaled approximately $9 million by 2006.[79] A key reason for the funding restriction, however, was Republican senator Mitch McConnell's chief of staff Paul Grove's distrust of Hun Sen. Before his work in Congress, Grove worked for the International Republican Institute in Cambodia where his colleague, Ron Abney, had been injured in a grenade attack during a rally of an opposition party in 1997, at which 13 Cambodians were killed. Because a number of sources had found that Hun Sen was responsible for the attack, Grove was convinced of the need for regime change in Cambodia.[80] He persuaded McConnell, then chair of the Appropriations Subcommittee on Foreign Operations, to block funding to the court.[81]

McConnell had the support of key Democratic senators for this position, including Senator Patrick Leahy. In 2003, the two senators wrote a letter to Kofi Annan, arguing that the mixed tribunal was "doomed to failure."[82] They co-sponsored the Cambodia Democracy and Accountability Act, which, although it never became law, would have provided additional foreign assistance to Cambodia if Hun Sen was no longer in power and directed the FBI to resume its investigation into the 1997 grenade attack.[83]

Although this legislation was not passed, appropriations legislation still precluded the United States from providing financial assistance to Cambodia and, specifically, "to any tribunal established by the Government of Cambodia":

> The Committee directs that no funds be made available for a contribution to the tribunal unless the Secretary of State reports to the

Committee that the tribunal is capable of delivering justice that meets internationally recognized standards of justice for crimes against humanity and genocide in an impartial and credible manner.[84]

The only way to provide funding would be if the secretary of state determined that Cambodia's judiciary was "competent, independent, free from widespread corruption, and its decisions [were] free from interference by the executive branch"—a stipulation most recognized was impossible to meet.[85] The tribunal-specific provision, however, was removed in the 2006 Appropriations Act, signaling a moderation of the US position.

To help address a number of challenges faced by the court, the UN appointed David Tolbert as special expert to the court. One of Tolbert's goals was to lift the US funding block. Table 3.1 shows the amount pledged to the court by international donors in 2005, with the notable exception of the United States.[86]

"I lobbied the Hill really hard," Tolbert said. "I think I convinced them that we were undertaking serious reforms."[87] He added:

I argued that the Duch [Kaing Guek Eav] case was going to be historic and important. I said we were addressing the issues and it was becoming a serious court. We removed the head of administration and put in someone that was more serious. We brought in someone for witness protection, someone for court management and court structure. I went through everything I did with [US officials]. I said,

Table 3.1 International Assistance to the ECCC

Donor	Amount (in USD)	Percentage
Japan	21,600,000	52
France	4,800,000	12
United Kingdom	2,873,563	7
Australia	2,351,097	5.5
Netherlands	1,981,506	4.5
Canada	1,612,903	4
Others	6,239,121	15
Total	41,458,190	100

"I understand and I agree with you. . . . But this is our one chance. If we don't address it now, we're going to lose this opportunity." We had support from the democratic side. Senator Kerry was very supportive. . . So it was just a matter of convincing the Republicans.[88]

Tolbert thought that US support for the ECCC was important because "the US was the only major country with interest in the country that wasn't paying."[89] He also felt that the US would help on the corruption issue: "I had the UK in my corner, but some of the other countries were not strong on corruption, so I thought the US would be tough on that issue." Tolbert also felt that the United States should be engaged because of its past responsibility for events, though he did not rely on this argument in his discussions.[90]

War crimes ambassador Clint Williamson was supportive of Tolbert's efforts and conducted a review of the ECCC, which fueled rumors that the United States was considering funding the court. An embassy official stated: "If we were to consider funding the ECCC, we must be convinced that it is capable of meeting international standards of justice."[91] Shortly after, Senator Kerry called for direct US funding: "The court faces a looming financial crisis . . . there is a real danger that the ECCC will collapse before it even gets off the ground." Though Kerry admitted that there were legitimate concerns about the court's independence and alleged financial improprieties, he proposed the United States contribute $2 million to support victims' rights and witness protection programs.[92]

In August 2008, the United States announced that it would fund the tribunal upon resolution of a corruption investigation. The following month, at the end of his visit to Cambodia, Deputy Secretary of State John Negroponte announced that the United States would give $1.8 million to the tribunal.[93] In total, Japan provided 50 percent of all contributions made to the international component of the court and 40 percent of all contributions to the national component. Donations from the United States, Australia, France, and Germany constitute 31 percent of contributions to the international component of the tribunal.[94]

Despite the funding block, the United States remained involved in court operations. For example, the United States was concerned about French and Japanese leadership of the "Friends of the ECCC"—the donor coordinating body for the court. A cable titled "Friends of the ECCC or RGC (Royal Government of Cambodia)?" illustrated US concerns:

> We are concerned that the two countries are focusing exclusively on the preservation of their bilateral relationship with the RGC in their discussions about the ECCC, and are not taking a more nuanced approach as co-chairs of the Friends. The Japanese position is particularly sensitive due to the balancing act the Japan government plays with China in Cambodia. The Chinese, [one Cambodian official] believes, are placing pressure on the government with respect to moving forward with the Tribunal. The Japanese want the Tribunal to succeed at virtually any cost, and therefore will be loath to put any pressure on the government that might make the RGC accord more sympathy to Chinese views. . . . As co-chair of the Friends, we believe Japan and France have some measure of responsibility to engage with the government or the ECCC if exceptional circumstances warrant the waving of a red flag. Absent a push from their respective capitals, the French or Japanese embassies in Phnom Penh will not be receptive to changing their views on the Friends mechanism and their roles as co-chairs. We would welcome Washington views on the possibility of demarching both capitals, and would be willing to send suggested talking points to that end.[95]

Another example of US engagement was its support of the Open Society Justice Initiative (OSJI), one of the few international NGOs following the ECCC, after the organization called for an investigation into the corruption allegations by Cambodian judges and staff.[96] In response to an OSJI press release on this topic, the Cambodian government considered evicting OSJI from Cambodia and ending its monitoring role of the court. Scheffer was informed of this by a Cambodian government official, who requested that Scheffer alert the US Embassy "so that a pre-emptive intervention with Deputy Prime Minister Sok An might be made to turn off the RGC's plan."[97] Scheffer did so and expressed his concern that OSJI's departure would be interpreted by the UN legal office as a breach of the UN/

RGC agreement. He also made clear that he personally believed that OSJI had made a mistake by going public with the corruption allegations so quickly. The US Embassy met with representatives of several embassies about the possibility of a joint demarche with the RGC. However, this step was not needed since Scheffer was able to resolve the issue by seeking assurance from OSJI director James Goldston that future disclosures of information potentially damaging to the ECCC would be provided to the court with adequate notice and advance consultation before going to press.[98]

An embassy cable reporting on the OSJI issue stated that kickbacks were common in the Cambodian public sector and that the corruption allegations at the court "surprised no one. . . . No whistleblower culture exists, and people have legitimate fears when it comes to making public information that could be embarrassing to senior officials." The cable said the Cambodian government's reaction to the OSJI press release revealed RGC unease with a high-profile judicial process designed to limit political influence. While OSJI "could have handled this matter better"—especially by anticipating that Hun Sen would take the OSJI letter very personally—"RGC sensitivities cannot be allowed to derail what must be a non-political tribunal."[99]

The court's first case began in 2009 and resulted in the conviction of Kaing Guek Eav, alias Duch, in 2010 for crimes against humanity and war crimes committed while he ran Tuol Sleng (S-21) prison camp. In July 2010, the fourth war crimes ambassador, Stephen Rapp, attended the verdict of the Duch trial, and his staff participated in meetings discussing the court's legacy. The United States agreed to fund a second UN special expert to assist the ECCC as long as the position was given to former war crimes ambassador Clint Williamson.[100] Scheffer was appointed as the third UN special expert to the court in January 2012, and said the United States has been more aggressive than other governments in seeing the additional cases go forward.[101] Scheffer also created the Cambodia Tribunal Monitor website, a key source for accessing information about the ECCC.

The court's second case began in November 2011, which accused Khieu Samphan, Nuon Chea, Ieng Thirith, and Ieng Sary of crimes against humanity, war crimes, and genocide, as well as homicide, torture, and religious persecution within Cambodian law. However, the case ultimately only prosecuted Samphan and Chea because Sary died during the trial and Thirith was declared unfit to stand trial. The prospect of two additional cases involving five suspects caused significant debate for several years. The Cambodian government publicly opposed extending prosecutions, and the resulting controversy contributed to the resignation of two international co-investigating judges.[102] It remains unclear whether or not these trials will proceed, although the court has published information about crime sites for the two cases.

Conclusions

This chapter examined how the United States eventually came to support accountability for the crimes committed by the Khmer Rouge, its close involvement in court negotiations, and its role in the operations of the court once established. DC-Cam director Youk Chhang said: "The ECCC was [established] because of the Cambodian Genocide Justice Act. . . . The US government was the only government that believed in the court and consistently supported the whole effort."[103] This support did not come easy. The CGJA was passed nearly 20 years after the violations had been committed, and was in large part due to sustained lobbying efforts in the United States that started in the 1980s and found a receptive group of key members on the Hill. This group was successful in shifting a long-standing lack of support for accountability and passed legislation specifically dedicated to collecting data on crimes of genocide and supporting the establishment of a tribunal.

This group set the parameters for Cambodian transitional justice early on by focusing on the documentation of crimes that could be used in legal proceedings. Through congressional funding of CGP and DC-Cam, the United States supported the gathering of much of the evidence that eventually made trials possible.

US efforts did not initially include the involvement of Cambodians. "The idea for the ECCC came from the West," said the director of the Cambodian Human Rights Action Committee.[104]

DC-Cam board member Jaya Ramji-Nogales similarly concluded: "The ECCC was a very American response."[105]

Despite a decade of negotiations between the Cambodian government and the UN, the court was established, with many compromises encouraged by war crimes ambassador David Scheffer.
Scheffer was motivated by "a supreme responsibility to those who
perished in Cambodia to bring the leading perpetrators to justice,"
especially given that the United States had been a part of destabilizing the country.[106] But he also ensured that the court's jurisdiction
was limited to crimes committed between 1975 and 1979 so that it
would not be able to turn up incriminating evidence concerning
the US bombings of Cambodia in the early 1970s or other acts of
warfare. Scheffer stewarded through compromises on the structure
of the court, a supermajority requirement, issues of personal jurisdiction, and a dispute resolution mechanism. For him, these ideas
represented solutions; for the UN they were compromises that pri-
oritized politics over principles to appease the Cambodian government.[107] In response to this criticism, Scheffer said:

> I was advised many times to walk away from this project. Just walk
> away. And I refused to do so. If that opens me up to criticism that
> we built an imperfect tribunal that does not deliver perfect jus-
> tice to as many people as possible, then so be it. I will live with that
> imperfection.[108]

Scheffer, like Albright, was a true believer. He believed establishing
a court was the right thing to do, and that the United States had a
responsibility to do it. Whether or not the compromises he negotiated ultimately helped or hindered the overall justice effort is for
ongoing debate among experts.

Because the United States was so involved in building this tribunal, it was surprising that Congress refused to fund it. A single congressional staffer was principally responsible for this block because
of his distrust of the Cambodian government. This position shifted
eventually with a targeted effort to convince the Hill about the "historic nature" of the court. Ultimately, more study of Cambodian
perceptions of the court is needed to determine whether US efforts

were effective in meeting the transitional justice objectives of Cambodians.

The next chapter examines a second case study about US involvement in the trial of Liberian president Charles Taylor and the Liberian Truth and Reconciliation Commission.

Notes

1   Ben Kiernan estimates 1.7 million deaths; Craig Etcheson estimates between 2.2 and 2.5 million deaths. See Ben Kiernan, "The Demography of Genocide in Southeast Asia," *Critical Asian Studies* 35, no. 4 (2003): 193; and Craig Etcheson, "'The Number': Quantifying Crimes against Humanity in Cambodia," Documentation Center of Cambodia, 2000, 171.

2   See Richard Bernstein, "As Notorious Khmer Figure Is Tried, Few in U.S. Take Notice," *New York Times*, 3 December 2009. During 1966–69, South Vietnamese and American forces mounted frequent small raids across the Cambodian border, despite protests by the Cambodian government. In 1970, Sihanouk was overthrown by a coup and Lon Nol seized power. US attacks against Communist bases continued with Nixon's support. See William Shawcross, *Sideshow: Kissinger, Nixon and the Destruction of Cambodia* (New York: Simon and Schuster, 1979). The January 1973 Paris Agreement, which ended the Vietnam War, included a provision on the withdrawal of foreign troops from Cambodia. However, massive B-52 and F-111 bombings of Cambodia resumed after the ceasefire. Congress opposed the bombing but agreed that the attacks could continue until 15 August 1973. On 7 August, an off-target B-52 plane bombed the government-held town of Neak Luong, killing over 125 people and injuring more than 250. From 1969 to 1973, the US bombing resulted in 50,000 to 150,000 deaths. See Ben Kiernan, "The US Bombardment of Cambodia, 1969–1973," *Vietnam Generation* 1, no. 1 (1989): 4–41.

3   See US House of Representatives, Human Rights in Cambodia, 26 July 1977; *New York Times*, "Senator George McGovern calls for international force to overthrow Khmer Rouge government," 22 August 1978.

4   *Washington Post*, 4 January 1979, 22.

5   Ben Kiernan, "Cambodia's Twisted Path to Justice," *The History Place* (1999); and Margo Picken, "The Beleaguered Cambodians," *New York Review of Books*, 13 January 2011.

6   Fred Z. Brown, *Second Chance: The United States and Indochina in the 1990s* (New York: Council on Foreign Relations Press, 1989), 43.

7   Elizabeth Becker, *When the War Was Over: The Voices of Cambodia's Revolution and Its People* (New York: Simon and Schuster, 1986), 440.

8 Ibid.

9 See Ben Kiernan, *Genocide and Democracy in Cambodia: The Khmer Rouge, the United Nations, and the International Community* (New Haven: Yale University Southeast Asia Studies, 1993), note 48. Cambodian historian Kenton Clymer finds that the most persuasive indication was US Public Law 99-83, which made it illegal to spend any funds to bolster Khmer Rouge military capacity. This was part of the legislation that ultimately allowed lethal assistance to the non-Communist resistance, introduced in the House by Representative Solarz. See US Public Law 99-83, US International Security and Development Cooperation Act (1985), 141. Clymer questions why a law was needed if aid had not been getting to the Khmer Rouge. Legislation from the House of Representatives, HR 5114, deleted language that prohibited any assistance for the Khmer Rouge and non-Communist resistance forces in Cambodia. It substituted language that provided $7 million for the non-Communist resistance forces and non-Communist civilians in Cambodia. It included a prohibition on direct or indirect assistance for the Khmer Rouge. In a widely seen documentary in 1990 that is thought to be a major factor in changing American policy toward Cambodia in the 1990s, *From the Killing Fields*, Peter Jennings argued that the United States was covertly supporting the return to power in Cambodia of the Khmer Rouge. See Kenton Clymer, *The United States and Cambodia, 1969–2000: A Troubled Relationship* (New York: Routledge, 2004), 142; and Peter Jennings, "From the Killing Fields," *Peter Jennings Reporting* (1990).

10 Ben Kiernan, personal communication, 14 April 2011.

11 These chambers are considered a "hybrid" court because of its mixed Cambodia-UN structure. It has two components, one national and one international. Each side has its own staffing, management, and budget.

12 See Appendix 1 for interview list.

13 Shortly after, to document abuses and advocate for a war crimes tribunal, the Cambodia Documentation Commission was started by David Hawk, former executive director of Amnesty International USA. Around this same time, the film *The Killing Fields* helped increase public attention to human rights violations committed by the Khmer Rouge.

14 Gregory Stanton, "Seeking Justice in Cambodia," in *Genocide Watch* (no date).

15 Ibid.

16 According to Ben Kiernan, CORKR was founded in January 1990 at a meeting in Washington, DC, that was convened by a group of former antiwar activists, including Anne Gallivan, Paul Shannon, Kathy Knight, Sally Benson, Walter Teague, Chan Bun Han, and others. CORKR then asked Kiernan to join their board. Kiernan involved Gregory Stanton in the project. Chan Bun Han and Kiernan invited a number of key Cambodians to join the CORKR board, including former Cambodian prime minister In

Tam, former information minister Chhang Song, and Kim Eng Chantarit. Executive directors Ruth Cadwallader (1990–92) and Craig Etcheson (1992–94), Anne Gallivan, and Kathy Knight undertook CORKR's lobbying and other Washington work with the support of Jeremy Stone and others. Ben Kiernan, personal communication, 14 April 2011. Stone identified the main actors he felt were responsible for pushing US policy on the Khmer Rouge, including the Indochina Project, a group run by William Herod that spread information about Indochina problems to Washington policy analysts; Chhang Song, a former minister of the Lon Nol government and a Cambodian who was respected on Capitol Hill; William E. Colby, former director of central intelligence from 1973 to 1976; Edmund Muskie, former secretary of state; Michael Horowitz, a Reagan administration official; and those involved with CORKR. See Jeremy Stone, *Every Man Should Try: Adventures of a Public Interest Activist* (New York: Public Affairs, 1999), 270.

17 William Colby and Jeremy Stone, "Thailand Can Become the Key to Restraining the Khmer Rouge," *Los Angeles Times*, 23 October 1989.

18 Melanie C. Greenberg, John H. Barton, and Margaret E. McGuinness, *Words over War: Mediation and Arbitration to Prevent Deadly Conflict* (Lanham, MD: Rowman & Littlefield, 2000), 151.

19 Clymer, *United States and Cambodia*, 155.

20 Ibid.

21 Ibid., 162.

22 Steve Heder, "A Review of the Negotiations Leading to the Establishment of the Personal Jurisdiction of the Extraordinary Chambers in the Courts of Cambodia," 1 August 2011, 6–7; See also, Agreement on a Comprehensive Political Settlement of the Cambodia Conflict, 23 October 1991, Preamble and Article 15. *Bangkok Post*, "Column Reports Interview with Hun Sen," 3 May 1991, 4; *Le Monde*, "Hun Sen Interviewed on Cease-Fire, Peace Talks," 22 May 1991; FBIS EAS-91-174, "Demand on Genocide Reference Reiterated," 9 September 1991.

23 Kiernan, *Genocide and Democracy in Cambodia*, 207, 31, 46.

24 Adam Garfinkle, "Be Careful Which Graves We Exhume," *Los Angeles Times*, 24 January 1999.

25 Bernstein, "As Notorious Khmer Figure Is Tried, Few in U.S. Take Notice."

26 Peter Cleveland, congressional aide to Senator Chuck Robb (Democrat from Virginia), proposed the idea of a Cambodia tribunal to the senator, after attending several conferences run by the Aspen Institute's Indochina Program, where he had met Ben Kiernan and others. See Ben Kiernan, personal communication, 14 April 2011. Cleveland drafted a bill initially entitled The Khmer Rouge Prosecution and Exclusion Act, which was introduced by Senator Robb to Congress in May 1992, but was not adopted.

27 See US Cambodian Genocide Justice Act, 22 U.S.C. 2656, (1994): Part D, §§ 571–74. The law urged the president to (1) to collect, or assist appropriate

organizations and individuals to collect, relevant data on crimes of genocide committed in Cambodia; (2) in circumstances that the president
deems appropriate, to encourage the establishment of a national or international criminal tribunal for the prosecution of those accused of genocide
in Cambodia; and (3) as necessary, to provide such national or international tribunal with information collected pursuant to item (1). The legislation also directed the creation of an Office of Cambodian Genocide
Investigations within the State Department. The office was meant to support, through organizations and individuals, efforts to bring to justice
members of the Khmer Rouge, including the following: (1) to investigate
crimes against humanity; (2) to provide Cambodians with access to documents and records as a result of investigation; (3) to submit relevant data to
a national or international penal tribunal that may be convened to formally
hear and judge the genocidal acts committed by the Khmer Rouge; and (4)
to develop the US proposal for the establishment of an international criminal tribunal for the prosecution of those accused of genocide in Cambodia.
The president was to report to the Senate and House Committees on
Foreign Relations/Affairs every six months on the activities of the new
State Department office; new facts learned about past Khmer Rouge practices; and the steps the president had taken "to promote human rights, *to
support efforts to bring to justice the national political and military leadership of the Khmer Rouge*, and to prevent the recurrence of human rights
abuses in Cambodia through actions which are not related to UN activities
in Cambodia" (emphasis added).

28   Fred Z. Brown, interview, 6 November 2009.
29   Steven Ratner and J. S. Abrams, "Striving for Justice: Accountability and the
     Crimes of the Khmer Rouge," A Study for the United States Department of
     State under the Cambodian Genocide Justice Act (1995).
30   In June 1996, Thomas Hammarberg was appointed as the special represen-
     tative of the UN secretary-general for human rights in Cambodia. During
     the UN Commission on Human Rights session in April 1997, Hammarberg
     suggested that a resolution on Cambodia mention the possibility of inter-
     national assistance to enable Cambodia to address past serious violations of
     human rights. On initiative of the United States, the commission said that
     any request by Cambodia for international assistance in responding to past
     serious violations should be examined. See UN Commission on Human
     Rights, "Situation of Human Rights in Cambodia: Report of the Special
     Representative of the Secretary-General for Human Rights in Cambodia,"
     Thomas Hammarberg, Submitted in Accordance with Commission
     Resolution 1997/49, 20 February 1998; and Tom Fawthrop and Helen Jarvis,
     Getting Away with Genocide? Elusive Justice and the Khmer Rouge Tribunal
     (London: Pluto Press, 2004), 117.

31 Thomas Hammarberg, "How the Khmer Rouge Tribunal Was Agreed: Discussions between the Cambodian Government and the UN," Searching for the Truth, Documentation Center of Cambodia, 2001.

32 Ibid.

33 Scheffer, *All the Missing Souls*, 352.

34 Associated Press, "Clinton to Pursue Khmer Leaders," 17 April 1998.

35 Scheffer, *All the Missing Souls*, 343–44.

36 See USUN, "Resolution to Establish an International Tribunal for the Prosecution of Certain Persons Responsible for Serious Violations of International Humanitarian Law in the Territory of Cambodia during the Period 15 April 1975–7 January 1979," 28 April 1998; Scheffer, *All the Missing Souls*, 364–66.

37 Scheffer, *All the Missing Souls*, 378.

38 Beth van Schaack, interview, 31 October 2009.

39 See Ratner and Abrams, "Striving for Justice."

40 UN Report of the Group of Experts for Cambodia established pursuant to General Assembly resolution 52/135, 18 February 1999.

41 Ibid. Para. 126 of the report stated: "It is the opinion of the Group that the Cambodian judiciary presently lacks three key criteria for a fair and effective judiciary: a trained cadre of judges, lawyers, and investigators; adequate infrastructure; and a culture of respect for due process." Para. 133 stated: "First, in the light of what we heard during our mission to Cambodia, even from some high official sources, the level of corruption in the court system and the routine subjection of judicial decisions to political influence would make it nearly impossible for prosecutors, investigators, and judges to be immune from such pressure in the course of what would undoubtedly be very politically charged trials. The decisions on whom to investigate and indict, and to convict or acquit, must be based on the evidence and not serve to advance the political agenda of one or another political group. This is necessary in order to respect the integrity of the proceedings and to accord fundamental fairness to defendants."

42 Hammarberg, "How the Khmer Rouge Tribunal Was Agreed."

43 Scheffer, *All the Missing Souls*, 382.

44 Ibid.

45 Ibid., 381.

46 Hammarberg, "How the Khmer Rouge tribunal Was Agreed."

47 Ralph Zacklin, "Some Major Problems in the Drafting of the ICTY Statute," *Journal of International Criminal Justice* 2, no. 2 (2004): 361–67.

48 Scheffer, *All the Missing Souls*, 387.

49 Hammarberg, "How the Khmer Rouge Tribunal Was Agreed."

50 Ibid.

51 David Scheffer, "The Negotiating History of the ECCC's Personal Juris-diction," *Cambodia Tribunal Monitor*, 22 May 2011.

52 Heder, "Review of the Negotiations," 30.

53 Brad Adams, "Snatching Defeat from the Jaws of Victory?" *Phnom Penh Post*, 25 January 1999.

54 The UN Non-paper on the Khmer Rouge Trial on 5 January 2000 is refer-enced in Heder, "Review of the Negotiations," 31.

55 Steve Heder, "Politics, Diplomacy, and Accountability in Cambodia: Severely Limiting Personal Jurisdiction in Prosecution of Perpetrators of Crimes against Humanity," in *Historical Justice in International Perspective: How Societies Are Trying to Right the Wrongs of the Past*, ed. Manfred Berg and Bernd Schaefer (Washington, DC: German Historical Institute; New York: Cambridge University Press, 2009), 191.

56 Hammarberg, "How the Khmer Rouge Tribunal Was Agreed."

57 Ibid.

58 Ibid.

59 In February 2000, Kofi Annan raised four concerns: (1) that there be guar-antees that those indicted be arrested; (2) that there would be no amnesties or pardons; (3) that the prosecutor be foreign in order that independence be guaranteed; and (4) that the majority of the judges be foreign and appointed by the secretary-general. See Hammarberg, "How the Khmer Rouge Tribunal Was Agreed"; and UN Secretary-General Briefing, "The Secretary-General Briefing to the Security Council on Visit to Southeast Asia," 29 February 2000.

60 See AFP, "Khmers Rouges—Védrine favorable à un procès au Cambodge," 14 January 2000; Ministry of Foreign Affairs, "Point de Press," 14 January 2000.

61 UN Non-paper, 30.

62 *Asian Wall Street Journal*, "The Growing Cambodia-China Alliance," 28 July 2000.

63 *Far Eastern Economic Review*, "Cambodia: The Price of Justice," 17 February 2000.

64 Reuters, "Japan Announces 2.5 Billion Yen in Fresh Cambodian Aid," 11 January 2000; Associated Press, "Progress for Khmer Rouge Trial Seen," 10 January 2000.

65 *South China Morning Post*, "Compromise Offered on Trial Judges," 12 January 2000.

66 *South China Morning Post*, "Hun Sen's Trial Offer Puts UN on the Spot," 13 January 2000.

67 *Phnom Penh Post*, "PM-UNSG Talks Agree: More Talks," 18 February–2 March 2000.

68 See UN Non-paper, 17; Associated Press, "UN Pressured over Cambodia Tribunal," 14 March 2000.

69 UN Non-paper, 18. See also Associated Press, "U.S. Envoy Backs Cambodia Tribunal," 9 March 2000; Reuters, "US Official Optimistic about Cambodia Trial Talks," 9 March 2000.

70 See David Scheffer, "The Value of Steve Heder's Research on the ECCC's Personal Jurisdiction, and an Afterword on the Purpose of the Dispute Settlement Mechanisms," Cambodia Tribunal Monitor, 8 August 2011. He states: "The prospect of disputes was driven primarily by the concern of key negotiators that the Cambodian Co-Prosecutor or the Cambodian Co-Investigating Judge, or both, might balk at investigating and indicting certain individuals who objectively fall within the personal jurisdiction of the court. Their international counterparts presumably would be less susceptible to political influence in the identification of two groups of individuals, 1) senior Khmer Rouge leaders and 2) those individuals most responsible for the crimes falling within the subject matter jurisdiction of the ECCC. If everyone thought that the only likely suspects would be a small number of long and prominently identified individuals (limited now to the surviving Khieu Samphan, Nuon Chea, Ieng Sary, Ieng Thirith, and Kaing Guek Eav ["Duch"]), the likelihood of disputes would have been seen as so minimal as to discourage such pro-tracted negotiations over a dispute mechanism. It was precisely because nego-tiators foresaw a possible rift between the Co-Prosecutors, in particular, over additional individuals to bring to trial that the dispute mechanism was devel-oped. We did not anticipate that the International Co-Investigating Judge might take a radically different view of the evidence from that held by the International Co-Prosecutor, but that is technically possible under the ECCC Law and may yet occur with respect to Case 003 and/or Case 004. We did not build into the constitutional framework how to resolve a dispute between one of the Co-Prosecutors and any joint determination of both Co-Investigating Judges to dismiss a case. Also see Scheffer, "Negotiating History of the ECCC's Personal Jurisdiction," Cambodia Tribunal Monitor, 22 May 2011.

71 Agence France-Presse, "Cambodia Lauds Fresh US Proposal to Break Khmer Rouge Trial Deadlock," 17 April 2000.

72 Hammarberg, "How the Khmer Rouge Tribunal Was Agreed."

73 UN Non-paper, 28.

74 Bangkok Post, "Politicians Still at Play in 'Killing Fields,'" 29 April 2000; Brad Adams, "No Pass for the Khmer Rouge," Washington Post, 18 April 2000.

75 UN Press Statement by Legal Counsel Hans Corell, "Negotiations between the UN and Cambodia regarding the Establishment of the Court to Try Khmer Rouge Leaders," 8 February 2002.

76 Margo Picken, interview, 18 June 2011.

77 See UN General Assembly Resolution 57/228, "Khmer Rouge trials," 22 May 2003; and UN Report of the Secretary General on the Khmer Rouge Trials, UN Doc. A/57/761. The Cambodian Genocide Program offered

to assist in breaking the legal logjam, and with funding from the Open Society Institute, provided legal advice to the Cambodian government. The Coalition for International Justice convened a group of legal advisors to key missions to the UN, who drafted a General Assembly Resolution that ordered the UN's Office of Legal Affairs back into negotiations based on the Cambodian law. See Stanton, "Seeking Justice in Cambodia."

78 See Agreement between the United Nations and the Royal Government of Cambodia on the ECCC, 2004. In the ensuing negotiations, the Cambodian government met three demands of the UN. It agreed to amend the Cambodian law to simplify the tribunal's appeals process. It agreed to amend the law so it refers specifically to the rights of the accused enshrined in Articles 14 and 15 of the International Covenant on Civil and Political Rights (ICCPR)—to which Cambodia is already a state-party. And it agreed to amend the law to explicitly affirm that the Vienna Convention on the Law of Treaties prohibits invocation of national law to escape international treaty obligations. See also Stanton, "Seeking Justice in Cambodia."

79 See US State Department, "Daily Press Briefing," 1 February 2005. This briefing cited the US contribution of an additional $2 million for DC-Cam's endowment fund in August 2006. See also *Phnom Penh Post*, "The American Role in Putting Together a KR Trial Deal," 28 April–11 May 2000. In this article, US Ambassador to Cambodia Kent Wiedemann said: "it's not at all unusual that we establish new customized models to fit certain national situations." See also Niko Kyriakou, "Cambodia Steps Closer to Justice," *Asia Times Online*, 31 March 2005.

80 Andrew Wells-Dang, "Republican Group Meddles in Cambodia," *Asia Times Online*, 16 April 2004.

81 Ibid. In one series of op-ed articles published in 2002 and early 2003, McConnell and Grove wrote, "It is in America's interests that the opposition win . . . it is time for the State Department to take sides." This was followed by calls for "regime change" and attempts to link the "paranoid evil dictator" Hun Sen to the "war on terrorism."

82 Craig Etcheson, *After the Killing Fields: Lessons from the Cambodian Genocide* (Westport, CT: Praeger, 2005), 157.

83 US Cambodia Democracy and Accountability Act, 2003.

84 US P.L. 109-102, Foreign Operations, Export Financing, and Related Programs Appropriations Act, 2006, 14 November 2005.

85 Cerone, "Dynamic Equilibrium," note 228.

86 Data obtained from Muck and Wiebelhaus-Brahm, "Patterns of Transitional Justice Assistance."

87 David Tolbert, interview, 10 May 2010.

88 Ibid.

89 Ibid.

90 Ibid.

91   *Phnom Penh Post*, "U.S. Special Adviser Assessing Khmer Rouge Court," 27 May 2008.

92   *Phnom Penh Post*, "Sen. John Kerry Urges U.S. to Help Fund ECCC," 27 May 2008.

93   US Embassy Phnom Penh, "Press Statement: Visit of Deputy Secretary of State John D. Negroponte to Cambodia," 16 September 2008.

94   Wierda and Triolo, "Resources," 148.

95   US Embassy in Cambodia, "Friends Of The ECCC Or RGC?" 16 March 2007.

96   See Cambodia Tribunal Monitor, "Composite Chronology of the Evolution and Operation of the Extraordinary Chambers in the Courts of Cambodia" (no date), 33. In February 2007, OSJI issued a press release alleging that Cambodian judges and other Cambodian personnel of the ECCC were compelled to kick back part of their wages to Cambodian government officials in exchange for their position. OSJI called for donors and the international community to investigate thoroughly the corruption allegations. In October, a UN Development Program (UNDP) commissioned report exposed widespread malpractice in hiring local staff members for the ECCC and handing out lucrative salaries to unqualified people. Cambodian officials objected to the recommendations that all staffing contracts on the Cambodian side of the ECCC be nullified and salaries cut and that the UNDP take a more direct oversight role. In March 2007 Scheffer visited Sok An and other ECCC officials to discuss proposals for resolving these disputes.

97   US Embassy in Cambodia, "The ECCC And OSJI," 15 March 2007.

98   Ibid.

99   Ibid.

100 UN official, interview, 17 June 2010. Williamson served in this position from August 2010 until September 2011.

101 David Scheffer, interview, 12 March 2012.

102 OSJI, "Recent Developments at the Extraordinary Chambers in the Courts of Cambodia," June 2011, 3.

103 Youk Chhang, interview, 15 July 2010.

104 President, Cambodian Human Rights and Development Association, interview, 19 July 2010.

105 Jaya Ramji-Nogales, interview, 2 November 2009.

106 David Scheffer, "Why the Cambodia Tribunal Matters to the International Community." http://www.cambodiatribunal.org/commentary/40.html.

107 Hammarberg, "How the Khmer Rouge Tribunal Was Agreed."

108 David Scheffer, interview, 12 March 2012.

4 :: US Involvement in the Taylor Trial and the Liberian Truth and Reconciliation Commission

The United States chose not to intervene in Liberia's two civil wars, which claimed the lives of 250,000 Liberians and displaced a million others. This view changed in the early 2000s when Congress decided that Liberian president Charles Taylor had to go, and found support for this position in the Bush administration. Discussions for a war crimes tribunal were already under way in neighboring Sierra Leone, which offered one way to remove Taylor from power since he had committed war crimes and crimes against humanity there. However, as time passed, another option appeared more viable, and the administration successfully brokered a deal to offer Taylor asylum in Nigeria instead. Congress disagreed with this decision and, for the next three years, increasingly pressured the administration to transfer Taylor to the Special Court for Sierra Leone (SCSL). The pressure for Taylor's prosecution eventually worked, and the administration crafted another deal to transfer Taylor to the court. Meanwhile, to meet the calls for transitional justice in Liberia, a Truth and Reconciliation Commission was established as an "acceptable alternative" to trials. Though the US Embassy supported the commission, when the final report recommended that Liberian president Ellen Johnson-Sirleaf be sanctioned from holding public office, the State Department withdrew support for the process because of US support for Sirleaf. Of the two transitional justice measures, prosecuting Taylor at the Special Court was clearly the priority. Before examining these measures, this chapter starts with a brief review of the historical relationship between the United States and Liberia.

US involvement in Liberia dates back to 1821, when African Americans established settlements in Liberia with the assistance of the American Colonization Society. In 1847, following a settler referendum, the colony's legislature declared the territory an independent, free republic, the first on the African continent. Liberia modeled its constitution after that of the United States, named its capital Monrovia, after the fifth US president, and chose a flag similar to that of the United States. American companies, like Firestone, received special rights to Liberian natural resources, particularly rubber.

US-Liberian relations deepened during World War II, and were further strengthened in the 1950s through the mid-1970s, as Liberia hosted major US security and communication facilities during the Cold War. A brief period of tensions characterized the mid to late 1970s during William Tolbert's administration, but relations warmed again after a coup led by Samuel Doe, which toppled and killed President Tolbert in April 1980. In August 1982, President Reagan met with Doe at the White House and paid tribute to 120 years of US-Liberian diplomatic relations, praising the two countries' "special friendship," "firm bond," and "long history of cooperation," which he said would be further strengthened in the years to come.[1] From 1980 to 1985, Liberia was the largest sub-Saharan Africa per capita recipient of US aid despite the regime's record of serious human rights violations and widespread corruption.[2] In 1985, Doe won a rigged election, but his victory was not viewed critically by the Reagan administration.[3] In response to a question about US friendship to "one dismal regime after another in Liberia," Assistant Secretary of State for African Affairs Chester Crocker said: "I would never in a million years tell you I was seeking what was in the best interests of Liberia. . . . I was protecting the interests of Washington."[4]

The end of the Cold War and US disillusionment with increasing corruption and dictatorial tendencies under Doe in the mid to late 1980s led to a gradual decline in US assistance, and in 1986, the United States suspended bilateral aid. As foreign embassies came under threat in 1990, the Bush administration evacuated them, cut direct financial and military aid to the government, withdrew Peace Corps operations, and imposed a travel ban on senior Liberian government officials.

In December 1989, Charles Taylor and a small group of Libyan-trained rebels called the National Patriotic Front of Liberia (NPFL) entered Liberia with the aim of overthrowing the Doe regime, initiating the first Liberian civil war from 1989 to 1996.[5] Before this, Taylor had attended college in the United States in the 1970s and was an official in the Doe administration in the 1980s before being dismissed for alleged embezzlement of government funds. Taylor fled to the United States, was arrested on Doe's request, and was put in US prison. Taylor escaped and returned to Liberia.[6] Following Doe's execution, Taylor gained increasing control in Liberia. From 1991 onward, Taylor also supported the rebel group, the Revolutionary United Front (RUF), in the civil war in Sierra Leone. Following a peace deal that ended the war, Taylor was elected president in 1997. New opposition groups emerged, renewing fighting throughout Liberia and resulting in the outbreak of the second Liberian civil war from 1999 to 2003.

From 1989 to 2003, the two civil wars claimed the lives of 250,000 Liberians and displaced a million others into refugee camps in neighboring countries. The conflicts were particularly vicious, with factions committing atrocities, including rape, torture, and civilian murders. Large numbers of children were forcibly enlisted as fighters. The country's unemployment rate hovered at 85 percent, and four out of five Liberians were living below the poverty line.

In the 1990s, State Department officials, including Assistant Secretary of State for Africa Hank Cohen, believed that the historically close relationship between the United States and Liberia obligated the United States to take special responsibility to respond to Liberia's humanitarian needs, to promote a democratic system, and to stop human rights abuses. Some in this camp believed it would not be inappropriate for the United States to send in troops to help restore order and protect noncombatants in Liberia, or at least to establish a zone of safety in Monrovia. They pointed to Haiti and Bosnia as recent examples of successful humanitarian intervention, and asked why the same was not done for a country with historic US ties.[7] However, the National Security Council, Central Intelligence Agency, and Defense Department saw little need for US involvement.[8] National security advisor Robert Gates described the historical relationship as "meaningless; it doesn't govern us anymore; we treat Liberia like any other country, we have no real interest there."[9] The latter perspective won, and US policy "quietly became one of letting the Liberians work out their conflicts themselves"—a position the United States maintained during the Bush and most of the Clinton administrations.[10] From 1991 to 2003, no military aid was provided to Liberia; US assistance consisted predominantly of food aid and support for the Economic Community of West African States Monitoring Group, and the UN Observer Mission in Liberia.

The US position drastically shifted in the early 2000s, and removing Taylor from power and Liberian reconstruction became top priorities. This chapter examines US efforts to remove Taylor from power, and eventually to transfer him to the Special Court for Sierra Leone to be prosecuted. It also explores the US role in the Truth and Reconciliation Commission (TRC). It draws on 55 Liberia-specific interviews with officials from the US government, SCSL, TRC, international organizations, international NGOs, and local civil society groups.[11]

Removing Taylor from Power

As political and economic conditions degenerated in Liberia, US views of the Taylor administration became increasingly negative.

The Clinton administration threatened to take punitive actions against the Taylor government in response to Liberian intervention in Sierra Leone's civil war, which also resulted in congressional calls for tough, activist US policy measures to counter such alleged actions.

Republican senator Judd Gregg of New Hampshire took it further by calling for Taylor's removal from office: "Taylor and his criminal gang must go; every feasible effort ought to be made to undermine his rule."[12] The position of Gregg and others emerged from the confluence of several factors: it provided an opportunity to make Congress seem pro-accountability; it allowed members of Congress to criticize the UN, by citing the failure of the UN Mission in Sierra Leone; it offered media attention; and it promoted anti-Clinton sentiment by publicizing the failure of the Lomé Accords, which had granted blanket amnesty to the RUF, appointed its leader Foday Sankoh as Sierra Leone's vice president, and gave him control of the country's diamond mines.[13]

Senator Gregg made the case to US ambassador to the UN Richard Holbrooke and the two discussed a shift in policy against Taylor, directed at the removal of his regime using a diversity of instruments. These included sponsoring an armed rebellion against Taylor's government, establishing a tribunal that would indict him, placing sanctions on his government that would weaken his ability to repel a rebel force, and providing support to local political opponents. Holbrooke and Gregg intended that one or a combination of these methods would force Taylor from power.[14]

Within a month of the meeting between Holbrooke and Gregg, developments on a tribunal moved forward, and an armed militia called LURD, which allegedly received US military training and ammunition for their offensive against Taylor, attacked Liberia from Guinea.[15] President Clinton denied entry into the United States to Taylor, senior members of the Liberian government, and their supporters and families for their failure to end trafficking in arms and illicit diamonds with the RUF.[16]

Because the idea for a tribunal for Sierra Leone had already gained support, especially from the United Kingdom, Holbrooke recommended that war crimes ambassador David Scheffer work on a proposal for a Security Council–backed international criminal tribunal.[17] Scheffer and his advisor Pierre Prosper shared the proposal with the Sierra Leonean president, who shortly after sent a letter to UN secretary-general Kofi Annan requesting a court similar to the American proposal. However, aside from the United States and United Kingdom, Security Council members were unwilling to establish another tribunal. In response, Scheffer suggested establishing an international criminal court with a treaty between the UN and the government.[18] This hybrid model would be less expensive than the ad hoc tribunals, funded by voluntary contributions instead of mandatory contributions from UN member states.

This proposal gained traction, and in August 2000, the Security Council passed Resolution 1315 to create the Special Court for Sierra Leone.[19] It was mandated to try those who bear the greatest responsibility for serious violations of international humanitarian law and Sierra Leonean law committed in the territory of Sierra Leone since November 1996. The White House asked Department of Defense (DOD) lawyer David Crane to "help set up an experiment in West Africa."[20] Crane agreed and began utilizing DOD intelligence to formulate who he believed was most responsible for crimes committed during the conflict.[21]

Several administration officials and members of Congress applied pressure on the UN to get Crane appointed as the Special Court's first chief prosecutor. DOD, which had been a source of opposition to international criminal courts, did not express opposition to the creation of the SCSL and at times seemed affirmatively supportive, largely because of Crane's DOD experience.[22] Crane's management experience at DOD, his experience as a former judge advocate, and his Africa background mirrored the Nuremberg model, and, for US officials, positioned him well for the role.[23]

As the court was set up, Crane visited the State Department approximately four times annually, where he sought the War Crimes Office's view as to who was to be prosecuted.[24] According to Scheffer, the decision to investigate Taylor was made in summer 2000, when the structure of the court was being negotiated. He said:

Taylor was front and center in our minds as negotiators. There was no ambiguity that this court would investigate Taylor. None. We couldn't actually say that in the statute, of course, but that was a clear mandate in the negotiating of this court.[25]

Scheffer said that his work on the court was not premised around an agenda about Taylor and was unaware of the earlier Gregg-Holbrooke meeting.[26] Whether or not Senator Gregg and others viewed the court as a way to remove Taylor or the structure of the court was negotiated in a way that would guarantee his prosecution, Taylor's transfer and trial to the Special Court were not inevitable, and it would be several years before this would come to pass.

At the State Department, meetings grew from the four people who had been tracking the country to a room full of interested people.[27] Michael Arietti, director of the Office of West African Affairs, said that he and US ambassador to Liberia John Blaney "felt it was worth giving Liberia another shot." In the Bush administration, they had the support of national security advisor Condoleezza Rice and NSC's senior director for African affairs, Jendayi Frazer.[28] "There was a sense that with a little bit of effort, we could make a difference. . . . It was hardest to sell to DOD."[29]

By June 2003, rebel forces had made significant inroads to the capital and threatened Taylor's stronghold on power. Taking advantage of Taylor's weakened position, the Economic Community of the West African States (ECOWAS) and the United States negotiated a new round of peace talks involving all the major parties to the conflict. They undertook a concerted campaign to convince Taylor to participate personally in the talks, which would be held in Accra, Ghana. Taylor yielded, and all parties to the conflict were guaranteed their security while attending the conference. Some diplomats considered the Accra talks the best chance in years to create a peaceful, durable solution for Liberia that would also remove Taylor by allowing him to exit the presidency as part of a negotiated settlement.[30]

While Taylor was in Ghana attending the opening day of the talks, the Special Court unsealed an indictment against him and appealed to Ghanaian authorities to arrest him for war crimes and transfer him to the court.[31] The timing of the indictment was not coincidental; Crane's strategy was to demonstrate "the power of the rule of law by stripping Taylor of his political power in front of his peers."[32] He gave 24 hours' notice to concerned parties, including the United States, of his intent to unseal the indictment.[33] The Ghanaians refused to enforce the warrant and gave Taylor a presidential plane to return quickly to Liberia. They said that arresting Taylor would be a violation of the commitment they had made to guarantee the security and freedom of participants in the talks.[34]

Although the United States had wanted the Special Court to indict Taylor in 2000, this view had changed by 2003 when the prospect of a negotiated settlement appeared imminent. The timing of the indictment infuriated State Department officials and members of the National Security Council, who tried unsuccessfully to persuade Crane to refrain from issuing it.[35] Ambassador Blaney said that "hundreds if not thousands of people would have died" in retribution if Taylor had been arrested in Ghana. "It would have ended the peace process and the war would have continued," he said.[36] US citizens and the embassy were reportedly directly threatened as a result of the indictment, given the belief widely held in Liberia that the United States was the real power behind the Special Court.[37] State Department official Michael Arietti said that this was the farthest from the truth since the United States was not heavily involved in the court at this time. After the indictment, he said that the State Department came up with a phrase used in official statements that indicated support for accountability, but did not expressly call for Taylor's prosecution.[38] For months after the indictment was unsealed, the State Department cut off all communication with Crane's office and the US ambassador to Sierra Leone refused access to court personnel.[39] Crane described the relationship between the court and the United States as "love-hate."[40]

The Bush administration was focused on Taylor's resignation— not his prosecution. During a speech on his Africa policy, President Bush called on Taylor to resign: "President Taylor needs to step down so that his country can be spared further bloodshed."[41] The Bush administration was working on a deal to provide Taylor with asylum in Nigeria, which Nigeria eventually agreed to in order to aid the Liberian peace process. Taylor accepted the offer with a promise from Nigeria that he would not later be prosecuted, provided he withdrew from political activity.[42]

Members of Congress were either unaware of or opposed to the Bush administration's efforts. They faulted Nigeria for its asylum offer, called for Taylor's immediate transfer to the Special Court, and authorized a $2 million reward for his capture.[43] US ambassador to Nigeria Howard Jeter "was stunned to learn that some members of the Senate were planning to sanction Nigeria for taking in Charles Taylor." He said, "I was incredulous. Instead of sanctioning Nigeria, I thought we should have been praising [Nigerian president Olusegun] Obasanjo for his political courage."[44] Ambassador Jeter added:

> Obasanjo did not take the decision on Charles Taylor lightly or alone. He consulted broadly and often with all key players in and outside the region. . . . President Obasanjo acted with our full knowledge and concurrence. . . . He said he would not move forward, however, if the American or British governments objected . . . what followed was a succession of phone calls from Washington telling the Embassy to urge President Obasanjo to move forward on getting Taylor out. "We wanted Taylor out of Liberia and we wanted him out quickly" was the refrain I heard many times. This message was echoed by State Department and National Security Council officials who accompanied President Bush to Abuja during his State Visit to Nigeria in mid-July. Even President Bush at that time publicly was saying that the US would not consider sending military forces to Liberia as long as Charles Taylor remained in the country. The President called for his immediate departure. . . . The decision to grant political asylum to Taylor prevented a humanitarian disaster and saved thousands, perhaps tens of thousands of lives. The 14-year civil war in Liberia was ended and the dreaded spill-over into neighboring countries was prevented. Liberia now has a chance and a future, and I am certain that the issue of justice for Charles Taylor will not go away.[45]

Despite congressional concerns, Taylor was granted asylum in Nigeria during the summer of 2003.

Taylor's Transfer to the Court and His Trial

The debate between Congress and the administration over Taylor's transfer to the Special Court continued for the following three years. Although a condition for asylum in Nigeria was that Taylor disengage from Liberian politics, he reportedly broke these conditions extensively.[46] Congress felt that the administration was not doing enough to press Nigeria to transfer Taylor to the Special Court.

Congressional interest in Taylor's prosecution was driven by the successful lobbying of human rights groups and faith-based groups. The Campaign Against Impunity, a coalition made up of some 300 African and international civil society groups, including members of the Liberian diaspora in the United States, was formed to ensure Nigeria's surrender of Taylor to the Special Court for Sierra Leone. The campaign was active, and included pressure on the United States to support Taylor's transfer.[47] The Congressional Black Caucus, which included Democrats and Republicans in the House of Representatives, was receptive to this campaign. Members such as Donald Payne, Ed Royce, Diane Watson, and others were outspoken about the need to prosecute Taylor. In a hearing, Representative Payne, a Democrat who served as chairman of the House Foreign Affairs Subcommittee on Africa, quoted from a letter from the campaign to President Johnson-Sirleaf that stated: "The campaign against impunity looks to you, as Liberia's President, to demonstrate your commitment to fighting impunity and to manifest the leadership necessary to ensure that justice is done." Payne said: "I think they are right, and Mr. Chairman, I am going to ask unanimous request that this letter be placed in the record."[48]

Administration officials, as well as the governments of Sierra Leone and Liberia, however, believed that Taylor's transfer could be a potential source of instability for the region. They were also reticent to renege on the commitment to Nigeria to honor its conditions for accepting Taylor and deferred to Nigeria's views on the matter, given its central role as a regional peacekeeping and political mediating power.[49]

Nevertheless, members of Congress were consistent in their calls for Taylor's transfer to the Special Court. Just after Taylor left for

Nigeria, Republican representative Ed Royce, chairman of the House Subcommittee on Africa, called for Nigeria to hand over Taylor to the court.[50] In the 2004 Appropriations Act, Congress reaffirmed its support for the SCSL and made funds available for "assistance to the central government of a country in which individuals indicted by the SCSL are credibly alleged to be living" if that government cooperated with the court, "including the surrender and transfer of indictees in a timely manner."[51]

By June 2004, US policy was shifting in support of prosecuting Taylor. War crimes ambassador Pierre Prosper stated:

> Justice will not be complete until Charles Taylor finds his way to the Court. The US policy is that Mr. Taylor must be held accountable and must appear before the Court. I personally have shared this policy with President Obasanjo and Chairman Bryant and have asked them for action on this matter. While we understand the need to maintain stability in Liberia, the goal of the US is to work with Nigeria and Liberia to pursue a strategy that will see Charles Taylor face justice before the Special Court for Sierra Leone.[52]

President Obasanjo told Prosper that he "needs to keep his word" in making Nigeria a temporary sanctuary, but that he would defer to the Liberian government after elections had taken place. Prosper asked Obasanjo "to speed up the timetable" and worked on a joint strategy with the head of the Liberian transitional government to transfer Taylor to the Special Court.

Congress reiterated its concerns to Prosper. Republican representative Frank Wolf told Prosper: "Taylor needs to be apprehended and brought to justice before this Administration leaves office, or else you will have failed in your effort." Representative Royce felt that Nigeria should feel justified in turning over Taylor since he had broken the conditions of his asylum by maintaining financial interests and cell phone contacts.[53]

By the spring of 2005, there was a growing recognition within the United States that "the best solution to the Taylor problem" was prosecution before the Special Court.[54] In May 2005, President Obasanjo met with President Bush and Secretary of State Condoleezza Rice to discuss Taylor's status. They agreed that Taylor's interference in Liberia's internal affairs was problematic and that Taylor should be held to account for the crimes he committed.[55] After these meetings, Obasanjo announced that he would turn Taylor over to a newly elected Liberian government if the new administration asked him to do so. It was understood that it would be politically difficult for Nigeria to revoke the asylum it had extended to Taylor until after Liberian elections.

On the same day of these talks, Congress urged Nigeria to "expeditiously transfer" Taylor to the Special Court in a resolution that passed the House by a vote of 421 to 1 and was unanimously endorsed by the Senate.[56] Democrat representative Diane Watson also sponsored an amendment to the 2006 and 2007 Foreign Relations Authorization Acts that restated that it was US policy "to seek the expeditious transfer" of Taylor to the court.[57]

Congress also conditioned future assistance to Nigeria based on the surrender of Taylor to the court. A 2006 Foreign Operations Appropriations bill stated:

> Assistance may be made available for the central Government of Nigeria after 120 days following enactment of this Act only if the President submits a report to the Committees on Appropriations, in classified form if necessary, on: (1) the steps taken in fiscal years 2003, 2004 and 2005 to obtain the cooperation of the Government of Nigeria in surrendering Charles Taylor to the SCSL; and (2) a strategy, including a timeline, for bringing Charles Taylor before the SCSL.[58]

Congress also pressed the Bush administration to act more urgently on the issue. Representative Watson said that the United States had a "duty" to ensure Taylor's transfer.[59] A bipartisan group of 13 House and Senate members wrote Secretary of State Rice, noting: "Should Mr. Taylor continue to evade justice, the international community may show reluctance to continue with its strong support for the reconstruction of Liberia and Sierra Leone."[60]

Despite this pressure, upon taking office in January 2006, Liberian president Ellen Johnson-Sirleaf said that the Taylor issue was not a priority.[61] Her government was gripped by security concerns; Taylor loyalists were still armed and his close associates controlled key positions in the legislature. In a bid to win the second round of the presidential elections, she had sought and received the support of many of Taylor's allies. Newspapers alleged that Sirleaf had promised not to request Taylor's surrender in return for their support.[62]

In response, the Bush administration told Sirleaf that the United States felt the right time had come for Taylor to be sent to Freetown to face justice.[63] Assistant Secretary Frazer said Taylor's prosecution would "bring closure to a tragic chapter in Liberia's history."[64] When it became clear that the grant of much-needed development assistance from the United States and others was linked to bringing Taylor to justice, Sirleaf said, "We also are facing . . . pressure—I must use that word—from the UN, from the United States, from the European Union, who are all our major partners in development, on the need to do something about the Charles Taylor issue."[65]

Despite concerns that Taylor's return would foster unrest, Sirleaf yielded to international pressure. She stated, "the fate of one Liberian should not hold a nation of three million people hostage," and in March 2006, she formally called on Nigeria to transfer Taylor to the custody of the Liberian government.[66] Taylor, however, allegedly tried to flee across the Cameroon border, but strong pressure from the Bush administration on Nigeria to capture him was effective, and Taylor was transferred to the Special Court.[67]

The same day Taylor was surrendered, the Special Court president submitted requests to the Netherlands and the International Criminal Court (ICC) for the trial to be relocated to The Hague. The request cited concerns about stability; however, some speculated a political deal involving Liberia, the United States, the African Union, and ECOWAS was the primary reason for transferring the trial to The Hague.[68] Allegations that Sirleaf had handed Taylor over to the court with the precondition that his trial be held out of the region were subsequently confirmed by senior staff within the Special Court.[69] The Netherlands and the ICC agreed to host the trial, and the United Kingdom agreed to provide detention facilities if Taylor was convicted. Despite the concerns of several international NGOs and others that moving the trial from Sierra Leone would make the justice process less accessible to the communities most affected by the crimes, Taylor was transferred to The Hague in June 2006.[70]

US support for Taylor's move to The Hague contrasted with previous statements in support of "local" justice in Sierra Leone. War crimes ambassador Prosper had said: "We wanted it in Freetown. We wanted it in a place where the atrocities occurred. We wanted it in a place where the population could actually go feel it, smell it, touch it, be part of the process."[71] SCSL attorney Abdul Tejan-Cole said that the continued reference to so-called security threats blurred together political and legal considerations: "The Special Court had indicted others who arguably posed a security threat equal to, if not more serious than, Taylor in terms of the likelihood of causing potential attacks on the court's Freetown premises."[72]

The move of venues also raised discussion about the US position on the ICC, and it was thought by some to signal a change in attitude. Human Rights Watch counsel Elise Keppler thought it was "a more pragmatic approach that could reflect the US prioritizing justice and accountability, and also recognizing the blowback and collateral damage of its policy on the International Criminal Court to date."[73] However, State Department legal advisor John Bellinger said people should not read too much into it:

> The ICC would not be trying Charles Taylor, they would simply be providing their facilities—their bricks and mortar—to the Special Court for Sierra Leone to try Charles Taylor. So we have no problem with that. . . . We don't have a general allergy to the ICC. We are concerned about the ICC's potential coverage of the US government. But we see a role for the ICC and international criminal justice in the world; that's the reason that we did not object to the Security Council Resolution that referred the human rights violations and atrocities in Darfur, Sudan to the ICC.[74]

US officials said they expected other countries to help pay for the move, since the court relied on international donations and it would be costly to bring court officials, witnesses, and Taylor to The Hague.[75]

Taylor made his initial appearance at the Special Court in Freetown in April 2006, where he pled not guilty to all charges. He was then transferred to The Hague in June. A year later, prosecutor Stephen Rapp made his opening statement. However, the trial was delayed until January 2008, partly because Taylor boycotted the proceedings and dismissed his legal team, among other reasons. The prosecution formally closed its case in February 2009 after having presented testimony from 91 witnesses. The defense opened its case in July 2009, and concluded in November 2010 after calling 20 witnesses, including Taylor himself.

When there were court delays in announcing the verdict, a State Department official stated: "The best we can do for Liberia is to see Taylor is put away for a long time and we cannot delay for the results of the present trial to consider next steps."[76] The official added:

> All legal options should be studied to ensure Taylor cannot return to destabilize Liberia. Building a case in the US against Taylor for financial crime such as wire fraud would probably be the best route. There may be other options, such as applying the new law criminalising the use of child soldiers or terrorism statutes.[77]

Thus, even before the verdict was released, the United States was considering additional options to ensure that there would be no possibility that Taylor could return to power. However, in April 2012, the Special Court found Taylor guilty of aiding and abetting, as well as planning war crimes and crimes against humanity committed by Sierra Leonean rebel groups during Sierra Leone's 11-year armed conflict.[78] He was cleared of charges of ordering war crimes, and of joint conspiracy in them. On the day of Taylor's conviction, the State Department stated:

> Today's judgment was an important step toward delivering justice and accountability for victims, restoring peace and stability in the country and the region, and completing the Special Court for Sierra Leone's mandate to prosecute those persons who bear the greatest responsibility for the atrocities committed in Sierra Leone. The Taylor prosecution at the Special Court delivers a strong message to all perpetrators

of atrocities, including those in the highest positions of power, that they will be held accountable.

The trial of Charles Taylor is of enormous historical and legal significance as it is the first of a powerful head of state to be brought to judgment before an international tribunal on charges of mass atrocities and serious violations of international humanitarian law. . . . The successful completion of the Special Court's work remains a top U.S. Government priority.[79]

The prosecution and defense teams filed notices of appeal against the findings of the Trial Chamber on Taylor's conviction and his sentence.[80] However, in September 2013, the Special Court's Appeals Chamber upheld his conviction. Secretary of State John Kerry issued a statement in support of the court's decision.[81]

From 2002 to 2013, the United States contributed $83 million—a third of the court's budget, far surpassing assistance by other donors. Some found that the SCSL prosecutors of American nationality played a role in helping to maintain financial support from the United States. The first prosecutor, David Crane, leveraged US financial support in the court's initial stages. The third prosecutor, Stephen Rapp, who after his tenure at the SCSL was appointed as the fourth war crimes ambassador in September 2009, also played a significant role in securing financial support for the court from the United States, both in his position as prosecutor and as ambassador.

Funding initially came from the Africa Bureau at the State Department. As time passed and as support for the SCSL within the Bush administration diminished, SCSL officials began to directly lobby members of Congress for support. For most years, Congress appropriated funds for the court under the Economic Support Fund (ESF) in the Foreign Operations Budget. The court was funded through the Development Fund for Africa (DFA) one year, and the K Fund for Emergencies in the Diplomatic and Consular Service another year. As a result of Congress directly appropriating funds to the court, the State Department was often left scrambling to find sufficient funds, resulting in the reallocation of funds that would have normally been allocated to USAID projects in Sierra Leone.[82]

Table 4.1 US Assistance for the Special Court for Sierra Leone

Account	Amount ($ millions)	Fiscal year by appropriation and obligation
ESF	2	2000
DFA	3	2001
ESF	5	2002
ESF	10	2003
K Fund	2	2005
ESF	13	2006
ESF	13	2007
ESF	12.4	2008
ESF	9	2009
ESF	7.5	2010
Total through FY 2008	76.9	
ESF	5	Requested 2011 level

Table 4.1 provides the amount of US assistance (in millions) to the Special Court between 2000 and 2010.[83] The United States increased funds significantly the year that Charles Taylor was transferred to the court and for the years that his trial took place.

Since the court was funded by voluntary contributions, a Management Committee was established to oversee the tribunal's efficiency.[84] Four states that served on this committee (the United States, United Kingdom, Canada, and the Netherlands) provided nearly 80 percent of all contributions received.[85] The question of the independence of the court vis-à-vis the Management Committee arose on a number of occasions, including by accused persons arguing that its funding structure undermined its independence. For instance, in one case, the accused argued that the funding arrangements created

a legitimate fear of interference in justice delivered by the Court through economic manipulation since . . . donor States could indicate their displeasure with any decision of the Court by withholding their contributions to the funds of the Court. With basically only three major donor States funding the Court, the ability of the Court to carry out its judicial activities will be impaired, if at least one of them were to withhold voluntary contributions to the funds, thereby bringing the operations of the Court below the standard of judicial independence required of States.[86]

A special advisor in the War Crimes Office explained that although US funding to the tribunal was "without strings attached," they were concerned about how efficiently the money was being spent by the court. In June 2007, the United States requested the court provide a strategy for all ongoing cases, including the Taylor case, to be completed in 18–24 months, which effectively meant an end to additional indictments.[87] Some observers said that since the court was designed to try a very limited number of cases, this may have constituted an interference with the independence of the prosecutor.[88] The Special Court was closed in 2013 with a "residual" court established to oversee witness protection, supervision of prison sentences, and management of SCSL archives.

The Truth and Reconciliation Commission

Although most US attention was on Charles Taylor, during the 2003 peace talks, an additional transitional justice measure was established. The State Department's director for West African Affairs, Michael Arietti, who was present at the talks, said that justice was an important issue in the negotiations, "but not the most important."[89] A war crimes tribunal was first proposed by civil society representatives, as well as rebel factions, who demanded justice for the violations committed by the Taylor government. However, after the Nigerian mediator of the talks reminded rebel factions that they could also be accused of war crimes, "they were much more careful about their call for justice." Prosecutions were also seen as untenable by international actors, due to the presence of rebel groups at the talks and because of significant support for the Special Court in neighboring Sierra Leone. Some factions proposed an amnesty for crimes, but this was not pushed hard, in part because United States and other international delegates insisted that an amnesty for serious crimes was not allowed under international law.[90]

"We were not pushing for a tribunal . . . a TRC was seen as an acceptable alternative," Arietti said.[91] The general agreement to leave a war crimes tribunal and amnesty aside in exchange for a truth commission without prosecutorial powers was made early in the talks and was not returned to in detail. Some said that civil society groups present at the talks proposed the establishment of a truth and reconciliation commission.[92] An international delegate said that international actors present were responsible for the inclusion of a TRC in the agreement:

> It was really, primarily put in by the international community. I don't think any of the parties to the fighting really wanted [a TRC]. So it was almost forced onto them. But they accepted it and it was part of the peace agreement.[93]

After the success of the South African TRC, truth commissions had become "quite fashionable around that time" and international delegates believed that a TRC would help address the fundamental problems that led to the turmoil in Liberia.[94]

The truth commission proposal was accepted fairly quickly, with discussion taking less than a week in the plenary session.[95] Article 13 of the Comprehensive Peace Agreement (CPA) established the TRC in order "to respond to the ardent desire of the people of Liberia for genuine lasting peace, national unity and reconciliation."[96] The provision states:

1. A Truth and Reconciliation Commission shall be established to provide a forum that will address issues of impunity, as well as an opportunity for both the victims and perpetrators of human rights violations to share their experiences, in order to get a clear picture of the past to facilitate genuine healing and reconciliation.
2. In the spirit of national reconciliation, the Commission shall deal with the root causes of the crises in Liberia, including human rights violations.

3. This Commission shall, among other things, recommend measures to be taken for the rehabilitation of victims of human rights violations.

4. Membership of the Commission shall be drawn from a cross-section of Liberian society. The Parties request that the International Community provide the necessary financial and technical support for the operations of the Commission.

To execute the dictates of the peace agreement, the transitional government created a nine-member panel of TRC commissioners in January 2004. Civil society groups opposed the process, however, because they felt it lacked clear objectives, mandate, jurisdiction, and legal status outside the peace agreement. They held a conference of Liberian stakeholders in April 2004 to consolidate perspectives on the TRC process and to draft a TRC act to submit as a proposal to the legislature.[97]

Prior to this conference, USAID's Office of Transition Initiatives (OTI) began working with the Transitional Justice Working Group (TJWG), a consortium of Liberian human rights groups that had been created to press the government to carry out the terms of the peace accord. One grant managed by Creative Associates (OTI's implementing partner) provided for a nationwide survey to collect citizen views on transitional justice.[98]

Civil society efforts were successful and their proposal became law in June 2005.[99] The TRC act gave a two-year mandate to commissioners to investigate human rights violations from 1979 to 2003; provide a forum to address impunity and allow victims and perpetrators to share their experiences; investigate the antecedents of the crises; conduct a critical review of Liberia's historical past; and compile a report of its findings.[100]

The TRC was officially launched in June 2006, but limitations of infrastructure, human resources, criticism of the commissioners, and other basic structural and organizational demands compounded what was already a large task of investigations, statement taking, and public hearings. TRC commissioners and staff pointed to delays in funding as a principal explanation for its difficulties. A US official said that the funding constraints in

Liberia were real, but that part of the problem was that donors had to wait for the TRC to complete basic financial reporting so that funds could be released.[101] Others felt that the TRC's challenges were "a question of focus, unity of purpose, and an ambitious mandate."[102]

With limited progress by the beginning of 2007, international actors felt they needed to step in or the TRC would fail. As the "moral guarantors of the CPA," ECOWAS, the UN, the African Union, and the International Contact Group on Liberia (ICGL), which consisted of Nigeria, Ghana, the United States, and the United Kingdom, began to more actively support the TRC.[103] An ICGL member said:

> After a year, it became evident that little progress was going to be made. . . . There was no proper administration, no permanent staff, no budget, nothing. So the ICGL, which was meant to meet monthly, decided to establish a joint working group with the TRC.[104]

The TRC/ICGL working group was created in February 2007 and met intensely for several months. During this time, committees were set up to discuss the TRC's work plan and budget, interpreting its mandate, organizational structure, and planning for statement taking and public hearings. Eventually, a new budget was adopted, renewed outreach took place, new statement-takers were hired, and international donors began to contribute funds.

The ICGL intervention was a turning point, and the work of the TRC essentially began again. According to a member of the ICGL, the working relationship between the TRC and the ICGL was positive in part because they "scrupulously did not get involved in the content. This was *their* process."[105] A US official said, however, that there was "a lot of handholding from the international community."[106] A senior member of the TRC staff said that although "donors were overbearing," he acknowledged that the working group helped to source funding and that ICGL technical assistance was effective.[107] The Liberian government provided nearly 60 percent of the commission's resources. Contributing just 8 percent made Sweden the largest individual country donor, closely followed

Table 4.2 International Assistance to the TRC

Donor	Amount (in USD)	Percentage
Liberia	4,427,466	59
UNDP	796,544	11
Sweden	576,213	8
United States	439,148	6
Others	1,209,702	16
Total	7,560,635	100

by the United States with 6 percent. These figures are illustrated in table 4.2.[108]

By 2008, the TRC had collected more than 17,000 statements and conducted public hearings throughout the 15 counties of Liberia, as well as from Liberians living in the United States, United Kingdom, and Ghana. The State Department contributed a small amount of funding to Benetech's Human Rights Data Analysis Group, which assisted the TRC in coding the majority of statements.[109] The Minnesota-based NGO Advocates for Human Rights (AHR), along with Northwestern University's Center for Human Rights Law, coordinated the work of the TRC with the Liberian diaspora. AHR published a report based on an analysis of more than 1,600 statements, fact-finding interviews, and witness testimony at public hearings held in the United States.[110] Other US-based NGOs, such as the Carter Center, supported certain aspects of the TRC, such as statement taking with religious leaders, thematic hearings on the role of the media, and diaspora work, including statement taking in Atlanta.[111] The US Embassy followed the TRC process closely throughout its operations, and there was at least one official whose main function was to report on the commission.

Once statement taking and public hearings were complete, the TRC was required to compile a report of its findings. The report examined the root causes and social effects of armed conflict in Liberia, and presented findings regarding violations of international human rights and humanitarian law and egregious domestic law violations. It laid out recommendations for public sanctions, including lists of alleged perpetrators of human rights violations and economic crimes whom the TRC recommended for prosecution or further investigation, and for nonjudicial public sanctions, such as a prohibition on holding public office for a period of 30 years.[112] The latter included a list of 49 individuals named for their role in "supporting, financially and otherwise, various warring factions."[113] Other recommendations in the report related to diverse issues, including public integrity, corruption, human rights, economic empowerment, good governance, national identity, reparation, among others "intended to resolve past conflicts as part of a national progression towards lasting peace and reconciliation."[114]

The final report was written and released in several stages. A preliminary report was submitted to the National Legislature in December 2008 (volume 1); an unedited version of volume 2 was released in July 2009; and the edited version was released in December 2009. Since TRC operations extended into 2009, all versions of the report were written in a short time period. The TRC mandate was supposed to expire in September 2008, but the TRC act allowed for four three-month extensions. Instead, however, the legislature gave the TRC one nine-month extension ending in July 2009. The United States was concerned that anything submitted after the first three months might face legal challenges, so it pressured the TRC to submit a report by December 2008.[115]

Consensus among commissioners to release volume 1 of the report was not reached, yet the chairman decided to do so anyway in December, as suggested by the ICGL. One commissioner said that this decision further divided the commissioners.[116] A staff member of the International Center for Transitional Justice (ICTJ) said:

> I didn't really ever get a sense of what those legal challenges were, especially when the report only offered recommendations and a prosecutor could pursue prosecutions with or without a set of TRC recommendations. From a technical, though admittedly not political, standpoint, there was little chance that a report that came out at that time was going to be of any value to the process.[117]

A US official said that the ICGL ultimately wanted to ensure that the TRC submitted a report and was unsure if delaying its release would have made a difference in the report's contents.[118]

Once the report was released, the TRC's decision to recommend certain individuals for prosecution and public sanctions was surprising for many Liberians and international actors alike, and stimulated significant debate. The decision to include President Sirleaf's name on the list to be banned from public office for 30 years, however, was seen as "the single greatest thing [to] influence how the report [was] handled."[119] the basis for the recommendation was not explained in detail in the report, but appears to have been rooted in the president's support for Taylor at the start of his effort to oust Doe.[120]

A US official said that the recommendation came "out of the blue" and felt that the TRC did not have the mandate to tell people they could not run for public office.[121] Another US official said: "It was unfortunate that Sirleaf was named in such a public way because it took away from the real issues. The report named names, but didn't achieve reconciliation." Nevertheless, "the US didn't feel overly close to the process." The official added, "The US just didn't want the report to be a destabilizing factor. There was so much progress since 2003. We don't want to move backwards."[122] US officials also felt that other recommendations in the report that were important to building a sustainable peace—such as the reparations fund for victims, alternative justice processes, and the idea that perpetrators could "pay their way off the prosecutions list" by giving money to the general budget—were ignored because of the controversial ones.[123]

The recommendation to sanction the president made it more difficult for the United States and others to support the report and its recommendations. A staff member from the ICTJ stated:

Everybody that's in a position to support the recommendations is supporting this country because of Sirleaf's Administration. . . . If the US comes out in support of the report, it will be understood as coming out against her, something they just cannot do. On the other hand, if they condemn the report, then they are seen as coming out against impunity, something they also cannot do . . . they just can't touch it.[124]

Similarly, the Liberia country director of the American Bar Association Rule of Law Initiative said:

> The TRC shot itself in the foot by mentioning Ellen. They equated alleged perpetrators with the President. The TRC Chairman felt they had to do it—and I agree—yet the TRC should have made a clearer distinction between personal and financial involvement. They could have done it more subtly.[125]

President Sirleaf questioned the recommendation's constitutionality because of the TRC's failure to take into account the due process rights of those to whom the recommendation pertained. Despite the recommendation, she announced that she would seek re-election to a second term in 2011, as many observers had expected. In the same message, she proposed amendments to the Independent National Human Rights Commission Act of 2005 to enable it to work in collaboration with the Ministry of Justice in order to determine which of the recommendations that had been the "subject of great debate since the TRC Report was made public" were "implementable or enforceable." She specifically mentioned the recommendations for a criminal tribunal, criminal and public sanctions, and investigations into economic crimes.[126]

After the release of the final report, the US Embassy took the lead in drafting an ICGL statement that commended the work of the TRC and said, "It is now up to the Liberian people to decide how to implement the recommendations of the TRC, in accordance with Liberian law."[127] Shortly after this statement was released, Secretary of State Hillary Clinton made an official visit to Liberia, where she reiterated US support and deference to the Liberian government:

> I am very supportive of actions that will lead to the peace, reconciliation, and unity of Liberia. And I believe that President Sirleaf has been a very effective leader . . . the US officially supports what this government is doing.[128]

Civil society groups felt that international actors should have taken a stronger position on the TRC report.[129] A member of the

Transitional Justice Working Group (TJWG) said: "If the US speaks on the report, this will send a strong signal. They are the moral guarantors, along with other ICGL members."[130] A youth leader expressed his frustration with the role of the international community:

> I feel terrible about the role of the international community . . . [They] invested a lot of money into it . . . UNMIL, Europe and the US guid[ed] and monitor[ed] the whole process. No Liberian is neutral when it comes to a Liberian process . . . [The international community] should implement it no matter how it goes. But UNMIL said, "We will go by what the Liberians say." And Secretary of State Clinton said, "America will go by what the Liberian people say." But who are the Liberian people? The majority of Liberian people do not have a voice. Our voices are not being heard.[131]

Another youth leader said that the international community did not want to do anything to undermine the government after investing so heavily in it.[132] Others felt that the international community should have established a court in Liberia, as it did in Sierra Leone.[133] Others raised the historic relationship between the United States and Liberia as justification for greater involvement. One civil society leader said: "The US must be a peacemaker for Liberia. Liberia is their brainchild."[134]

ICGL members responded to the criticism in different ways. Some felt it was not their place to make a pronouncement on the report and that it was a sovereignty issue.[135] Others acknowledged civil society concerns: "If we don't believe in the rule of law, then who is going to believe in it?"[136] Another international observer said that the ICGL would have to analyze all of the TRC recommendations in order to know how to proceed. He doubted, however, that there would be consensus among all the international donors on the recommendations.[137] Another international observer said:

> What has made the decision more difficult, even on a personal level, is that you have the president on the list of those who should be

sanctioned and banned from public office. Formally or informally, you cannot avoid taking this into consideration, which is why the international group is trying to be more neutral. That is why the position is "up to Liberia" . . . You have to look at the TRC process within the Liberian context of 2009 and looking to the future.[138]

There was also an acknowledgment of resource constraints and the need to prioritize. "It's all about choices," a US official said; funds contributed to the Special Court for Sierra Leone "could have gone to development."[139] Another international observer added that with limited resources and immense economic, social, political, and justice challenges, "they are expecting too much from the donors."[140] The Liberia country director of the American Bar Association Rule of Law Initiative did not think there would be US funding for the implementation of recommendations because "the US wants to put forth the idea that Liberia is on the road to recovery."[141] The Liberian government has also done little to address the recommendations thus far.[142]

Conclusions

Similar to Cambodia, the United States was not willing to respond to atrocities while they were being committed in Liberia. This policy of noninterference ended toward the end of the second civil war when Congress and the administration decided to get involved due to the deteriorating situation and view that Taylor was a key problem to stability. Congressional and presidential support for the establishment of the Special Court for Sierra Leone was strong, and was viewed as one way to remove Taylor from power. The State Department drafted the UN proposal for the court, ensured that its mandate would allow for Taylor's prosecution, selected an American chief prosecutor who had worked at the DOD, and contributed over a third of the court's budget.

Yet when the court threatened to undermine an option that administration officials and the State Department viewed as a more expedient solution to the Taylor problem, they were furious and temporarily cut political support to the court. After orchestrating a deal with Nigeria that it believed would end the war and prevent regional instability, the administration had no interest in prosecuting Taylor.

Here, internal interests within the US foreign policy bureaucracy diverged: the administration and the State Department wanted Taylor removed by the most readily available means, while Congress wanted Taylor transferred to the Special Court. This internal tension lasted for three years as Congress used a variety of mechanisms to apply pressure on the administration to transfer Taylor to the court. Congress called for Taylor to "face justice" and stated that his prosecution would "bring closure" to the past and would have "enormous historical and legal significance." The calls came from both Democrats and Republicans from the House and Senate Africa Subcommittees and Congressional Black Caucus. Supporting Taylor's prosecution "appealed to the moral instincts" of Congress and was aided by an active civil society campaign specifically focused on Taylor's prosecution.[143] This consistent pressure, along with threats to reduce assistance to Nigeria, eventually paid off when the Bush administration moved forward on crafting a deal with Nigeria and Liberia to facilitate Taylor's transfer to the court.

The TRC got nowhere near the same attention as Taylor's prosecution. State Department officials at the peace talks opposed amnesties for war crimes, but did not push for prosecution. It was clear that the United States was unwilling to support another tribunal considering its extensive support for the Special Court. However, there was a sense that some form of accountability should be included in the peace agreement, and for this reason, the truth commission proposal was viewed as an acceptable alternative.

The United States provided technical and financial support to the commission to get it off the ground. But after the TRC submitted its final report, which included a recommendation to sanction President Sirleaf, the United States said that TRC follow-up was "up to the Liberian people." Because the United States had firmly supported her election and presidency, US officials were unwilling to take a stronger stance on the report or assist in the implementation of TRC recommendations.

The next chapter undertakes the third and final case study, which examines US involvement in the justice and peace process in Colombia. This chapter provides another opportunity to explore the forces that drive US foreign policy on transitional justice.

Notes

1   US Public Papers of the Presidents, "Meeting With Samuel K. Doe, Head of State of Liberia," *Weekly Compilation of Presidential Documents*, 17 August 1982.

2   James Brooke, "Mission to Liberia Evidently Fails," *New York Times*, 5 December 1988. The United States contributed $402 million in aid between the 1980 coup and 1985 elections, accounting for more than one-third of the country's operating budget. See Advocates for Human Rights, "A House with Two Rooms: Final Report of the Truth and Reconciliation Commission of Liberia Diaspora Project," Dispute Resolution Institute at Hamline University School of Law, Saint Paul, MN, 2009; and Reed Kramer, "A Casualty of the Cold War's End," *CSIS Africa Notes*, July 1995. For data on US assistance to Liberia from 1945 to 2001, see USAID, "Overseas Loans and Grants, Obligations and Loan Authorizations July 1, 1945–September 30, 2001," no date.

3   Herman Cohen, US Assistant Secretary of State for African Affairs, 1989–93, stated that "[Doe] should have lost, but he rigged the election. But at that time all West African elections were rigged. It was a very normal thing to do, for the government to win the election even though they had less than the majority of the vote. So it did not trouble us at all." See Nancee Oku Bright, "Liberia: America's Stepchild," transcript of PBS documentary, 10 October 2002; and David B. Ottaway, "Shultz Sees Liberian Doe, Cites 'Genuine Progress,'" *Washington Post*, 15 January 1987.

4   Ian Fisher, "Heart of Greed," *New York Times*, 10 June 2001.

5   BBC News, "Charles Taylor—Preacher, Warlord, President," 13 July 2009.

6   Some reports say he managed to escape the prison by sawing through the bars; others that there was some collusion in his departure from Americans who wanted him to help overthrow Doe. In January 2012, the *Boston Globe* reported that Charles Taylor had ties with US intelligence agencies. The newspaper issued a correction, however, since there was inadequate evidence for this claim. See *Boston Globe*, "Former Liberian Dictator Charles Taylor Had US Spy Agency Ties," 17 January 2012.

7   Carl Ek, "Liberia: Issues for the United States," Congressional Research Service Issue Brief, 21 November 1996.

8   At one point there were discussions that Taylor might be the lesser of two evils and the United States could quietly cooperate with him. Opponents of this approach within the administration "quickly reminded everyone that Taylor was actually an escaped convict from a Massachusetts prison," and wanted in the United States for embezzlement. See Walter H. Kansteiner, "U.S. Policy in Africa in the 1990s," in *U.S. and Russian Policymaking with Respect to the Use of Force*, ed. Jeremy R. Azrael and Emil A. Payin (Santa Monica, CA: Rand, 1996).

9   Advocates for Human Rights, "A House with Two Rooms," 289.

10 Walter H. Kansteiner, "U.S. Policy in Africa in the 1990s."

11 See Appendix 1 for interview list.

12 Judd Gregg, "A Graveyard Peace," *Washington Post*, 9 May 2000.

13 See Cerone, "Dynamic Equilibrium," 306; and Michelle Sieff, "A 'Special Court,'" Global Policy Forum, 2001. Regarding the media, Cerone finds that the "sensationalism" of Sierra Leonean amputees "appealed to the camera-chasing members of Congress." For more on congressional discussion of the amputee issue, see US Congressional Record, "Proceedings and Debates of the 106th Congress, May 24, 2000 to June 12, 2000, V. 146, Pt. 7," 2000, 21850–51.

14 For more on Senator Gregg's interest in Taylor's prosecution, see Chris Mahony, "Judd Gregg's War against Liberia's Charles Taylor," *Fair Observer*, 30 May 2012.

15 Human Rights Watch, "Weapons Sanctions, Military Supplies, and Human Suffering: Illegal Arms Flows to Liberia and the June–July 2003 Shelling of Monrovia," *A Briefing Paper*, 3 November 2003.

16 US State Department, "Clinton Proclamation Regarding Sierra Leone," 11 October 2000; US White House, "Statement by the President," Office of the Press Secretary, 11 October 2000.

17 Scheffer writes: "Holbrooke's bottom line was to maintain the international jurisdiction of the Security Council over whatever was built." Scheffer, *All the Missing Souls*, 326.

18 Scheffer, *All the Missing Souls*, 329–30.

19 UN Security Council Resolution 1315, 14 August 2000.

20 Mahony, "Judd Gregg's War against Liberia's Charles Taylor," 14.

21 Ibid., 17.

22 Cerone, "Dynamic Equilibrium," 306.

23 Ibid.

24 Mahony, "Judd Gregg's War against Liberia's Charles Taylor," 19.

25 David Scheffer, interview, 12 March 2012.

26 Ibid.

27 Priscilla Hayner, "Negotiating Peace in Liberia: Preserving the Possibility for Justice," Centre for Humanitarian Dialogue and the International Center for Transitional Justice, November 2007, 28.

28 Frazer went on to serve as assistant secretary of state for African affairs from 2005 to 2009.

29 Michael Arietti, interview, 9 May 2011.

30 Abdul Tejan-Cole, "A Big Man in a Small Cell: Charles Taylor and the Special Court for Sierra Leone," in *Prosecuting Heads of State*, ed. Ellen L. Lutz and Caitlin Reiger (New York: Cambridge University Press, 2009), 213.

31 Taylor was indicted under seal by the Special Court for Sierra Leone on 7 March 2003 on a 17-count indictment for crimes against humanity, violations of Article 3 common to the Geneva Conventions and of Additional Protocol II (commonly known as war crimes), and other serious violations of international humanitarian law. On 16 March 2006, a judge of the Special Court approved an amended indictment reducing the number of counts to 11. The indictment was ordered to be kept under seal.

32 Cerone, "Dynamic Equilibrium," 309.

33 Ibid.

34 Hayner, "Negotiating Peace in Liberia," 8.

35 Cerone, "Dynamic Equilibrium," 309.

36 Hayner, "Negotiating Peace in Liberia," 10.

37 Ibid.

38 Michael Arietti, interview, 9 May 2011.

39 Cerone, "Dynamic Equilibrium," 309.

40 David Crane, interview, 19 April 2010.

41 Kirk Semple and Somini Sengupta, "Pushing Peace in Africa, Bush Tells Liberian President to Quit," *New York Times*, 26 June 2003.

42 Nicolas Cook, "Liberia's Post-war Recovery: Key Issues and Developments," Congressional Research Service, 13 December 2005, 14.

43 US House of Representatives, "US Policy toward Liberia," Hearing before the Subcommittee on Africa, Committee on International Relations, 2 October 2003, 12.

44 US House of Representatives, "Confronting War Crimes in Africa," Hearing before the Subcommittee on Africa, Committee on International Relations, 24 June 2004, 19.

45 Ibid.

46 By mid-2005, persistent claims were emerging that Taylor was violating the terms of his Nigerian asylum deal to refrain from political interference in West Africa, including that he had been involved in an attempt to assassinate Guinean president Lansana Conteh in January 2005, that he continued to back armed groups, and that he attempted to influence the forthcoming post-transition Liberian elections. Special Court investigators accused him of backing a coup plot in Ivory Coast. See Craig Timberg, "A Warlord's Exile Divides His Hosts: Liberian Ex-President Charles Taylor Doing Business

as Usual in Nigeria," *Washington Post*, 9 October 2005, A22. However, it is unclear the extent to which these allegations were fueled by those who wanted to make it possible for Taylor to be transferred to the SCSL, including Special Court officials. See Thierry Cruvelier, email communication, May 31, 2014.

47 See Campaign Against Impunity, "Civil Society Coalition Letter to New Liberian President Johnson-Sirleaf," 26 January 2006; Amnesty International, "Nigeria: Surrender Charles Taylor to Special Court for Sierra Leone," 11 August 2005; Human Rights Watch, "Civil Society Efforts to Bring Charles Taylor to Justice," 23 April 2012.

48 US House of Representatives, "The Impact of Liberia's Election on West Africa," Hearing before the Subcommittee on Africa, Global Human Rights and International Operations, Committee on International Relations, 8 February 2006.

49 See, for example, Ambassador Jeter's comments in US House of Representatives, "Confronting War Crimes in Africa."

50 US House of Representatives, "US Policy toward Liberia," 12.

51 US Public Law 108-199, Consolidated Appropriations Act, 2004, 23 January 2004, 206.

52 US House of Representatives, "Confronting War Crimes in Africa."

53 Ibid., 29.

54 Cerone, "Dynamic Equilibrium," 309.

55 US White House, Press Briefing, 5 May 2005.

56 See US H. Con. Res. 127, "Calling on the Government of the Federal Republic of Nigeria to transfer Charles Ghankay Taylor, former President of the Republic of Liberia, to the Special Court for Sierra Leone to be tried for war crimes, crimes against humanity, and other serious violations of international humanitarian law," 5 May 2005. Ron Paul was the only member who voted against the resolution. On 24 February 2005, the European Parliament unanimously passed a resolution calling for Nigeria to transfer Taylor to the Special Court.

57 See US H. Amdt. 480, An Amendment to H.R. 2601 [109th]: Foreign Relations Authorization Act, Fiscal Years 2006 and 2007, 20 July 2005. Meanwhile, court officials hoped that the congressional resolutions would bolster their efforts to win a Security Council Chapter VII resolution that would legally require Nigeria to transfer Taylor to Freetown for trial. See Victor Peskin, *International Justice in Rwanda and the Balkans: Virtual Trials and the Struggle for State Cooperation* (New York: Cambridge University Press, 2008), 249–50. In November 2005, the Security Council expanded UNMIL's mandate to include the ability to apprehend and detain Taylor in the event of a return to Liberia and to transfer him to the SCSL. See UN Security Council Resolution 1638, 11 November 2005.

58 US P.L. 109-102, Foreign Operations, Export Financing, and Related Programs Appropriations Act, 2006, 67.

59 US House of Representatives, "The Impact of Liberia's Election on West Africa," 33.

60 Ibid., 30.

61 BBC News, "Taylor 'Not' a Priority for Liberia," 27 January 2006.

62 Tejan-Cole, "Big Man in a Small Cell," 217.

63 Ibid.; Cook, "Liberia's Post-war Recovery," 13.

64 US House of Representatives, "The Impact of Liberia's Election on West Africa," 47.

65 Jim Lehrer, "Liberia's New President," *Newshour with Jim Lehrer*, transcript of interview, 23 March 2006.

66 Ibid.

67 Tejan-Cole, "Big Man in a Small Cell," 218.

68 Thierry Cruvellier, "Why Try Taylor in the Hague?" *International Justice Tribune*, 10 April 2006.

69 Craig Timberg, "Liberian President Backs Bid to Move Taylor Trial to Hague," *Washington Post*, 31 March 2006, A15.

70 See International Center for Transitional Justice (ICTJ), "Taylor Trial Should Be Moved from Sierra Leone Only as Last Resort," Press Release, 3 April 2006; Human Rights Watch, "Trying Charles Taylor in The Hague: Making Justice Accessible to Those Most Affected," June 2006, 2.

71 Michele Keleman, "Taylor War Crimes Trial Worries West Africa," *NPR News*, 6 April 2006.

72 Tejan-Cole, "Big Man in a Small Cell," 219.

73 Keleman, "Taylor War Crimes Trial Worries West Africa."

74 Ibid.

75 Ibid. In 2009, the trial was moved from the ICC premises to the Special Tribunal for Lebanon, also based in The Hague.

76 See Afua Hirsch, "WikiLeaks Cables Reveal US Concerns over Timing of Charles Taylor Trial," *Guardian*, 17 December 2010. A State Department cable revealed concerns about the Taylor trial. Allegedly, Special Court judge Julia Sebutinde slowed proceedings while she waited for her turn at the court's rotating presidency so that she could personally give the verdict in the case.

77 Ibid.

78 The Special Court found Taylor guilty of the war crimes of terrorizing civilians, murder, outrages on personal dignity, cruel treatment, looting, and recruiting and using child soldiers; and the crimes against humanity of murder, rape, sexual slavery, mutilating and beating, and enslavement. See SCSL Judgement, *Prosecutor v. Charles Ghankay Taylor*, Trial Chamber II, Special Court for Sierra Leone, 26 April 2012.

79 US State Department, "The Verdict in the Charles Taylor Trial at the Special Court for Sierra Leone," 26 April 2012.

80 The prosecution appealed the conviction on the Chamber's failure to find
    Taylor liable for ordering and instigating the commission of crimes, and other
    grounds. The defense disagreed with findings about Taylor's involvement
    in planning attacks in certain locations, the jail sentence, and other issues.
    See Taegin Reisman, "Appeals Chamber Upholds Taylor's Jail Sentence,"
    International Justice Monitor, 26 September 2013.

81 US State Department, "State Dept. on Sierra Leone Court Upholding Taylor
    Conviction," 26 September 2013.

82 See Wierda and Triolo, "Resources," 147–50; Muck and Wiebelhaus-Brahm,
    "Patterns of Transitional Justice Assistance among the International
    Community."

83 Nicolas Cook, "Liberia's Post-war Development: Key Issues and U.S.
    Assistance," Congressional Research Service, 25 May 2010, 54–55.

84 Article 7 of the Agreement for and Statute of the Special Court for Sierra Leone
    (16 January 2002) states: "It is the understanding of the Parties that interested
    States will establish a management committee to assist the Secretary-General
    in obtaining adequate funding, and provide advice and policy direction on
    all non-judicial aspects of the operation of the Court, including questions of
    efficiency, and to perform other functions as agreed by interested States. The
    management committee shall consist of important contributors to the Special
    Court. The Government of Sierra Leone and the Secretary-General will also
    participate in the management committee." The Management Committee
    consists of the four major donors (US, UK, the Netherlands, and Canada), two
    regional donors (Sierra Leone and Liberia), and the Office of the Legal Adviser
    at the UN.

85 Wierda and Triolo, "Resources," 147.

86 See Appeals Chamber Decision on Preliminary Motion Based on Lack of
    Jurisdiction (Judicial Independence), *Prosecutor v. Sam Hinga Norman*,
    SCSL-2004-14-AR72(E), 13 March 2004, para. 18.

87 Annie Frank, "Taylor Trial: U.S. Fears Delay, but Control Limited," *World
    Politics Review*, 22 June 2007.

88 Wierda and Triolo, "Resources," 160.

89 Michael Arietti, interview, 9 May 2011.

90 See Hayner, "Negotiating Peace in Liberia," 15; and Michael Arietti,
    interview, 9 May 2011. Hayner found that this position was based on an
    oversimplified understanding of the amnesty issue, but she was unclear
    about the ultimate role international voices played in the conversation
    about amnesty. The final language in the accord left the subject for future
    consideration by the transitional government. See Comprehensive Peace
    Agreement between the Government of Liberia and the LURD and the
    MODEL and Political Parties (CPA), Accra, Ghana, 18 August 2003,
    Article 34. For a description of the current state of the law on amnesties
    and other aspects of accountability, see Diane Orentlicher, "Independent

Study on Best Practices, Including Recommendations, to Assist States in Strengthening their Domestic Capacity to Combat All Aspects of Impunity," UN Doc. E/CN.4/2004/88, 27 February 2004; Orentlicher, "Updated Set of Principles."

91   Michael Arietti, interview, 9 May 2011.

92   Representatives of civil society and political parties also put forward a proposal for a TRC in 2002. See "Position Statement on Security, Reconciliation and Peace in Liberia, Presented to the Authority of ECOWAS and the Government of the Federal Republic of Nigeria," 15 March 2002, 3.

93   ICGL member, interview, 28 November 2009.

94   Ibid.

95   Hayner, "Negotiating Peace in Liberia," 15.

96   Comprehensive Peace Agreement between the Government of Liberia and the LURD and the MODEL and Political Parties (CPA), Accra, Ghana, Preamble.

97   TRC Consolidated Final Report (unedited), vol. 2, 29 June 2009, 175.

98   See Creative Associates, "The Road to Peace in Liberia: Citizens Views on Transitional Justice," Transitional Justice Working Group Initiative, August–September 2004. TJWG and Greenberg Quinlan Rosner (a research and strategic consulting firm) led focus groups and the survey to gauge Liberian attitudes about justice and reconciliation. The study found, among other things, that Liberians wanted faction leaders and commanders to be prosecuted for war crimes and human rights abuses, and supported the creation of a special court made up of Liberian and international jurists to prosecute the combatants and commanders accused of war crimes. See Mark Feierstein and John Moreira, "National Consensus on Dealing with War Crimes Report on the Baseline Survey and Focus Groups," Greenberg Quinlan Rosner, 16 November 2004, 2.

99   An international observer closely engaged with the process felt that the powers of the TRC act "far superseded" the ability to implement it and that it had become a way for civil society groups to "get back" at the warlords who crafted the CPA with "an obvious bias to accepting impunity." See International actors had encouraged civil society groups to draft a more realistic act; however, the same observer stated: "No law here in Liberia is more a product of the people of Liberia than that particular act. No internationals tampered with the content and therefore it is very originally Liberian." International observer 1, interview, 30 November 2009.

100   Act that established the Truth and Reconciliation Commission (TRC) of Liberia, enacted by the National Transitional Legislative Assembly, 12 May 2005, Article 4.

101   US official 2, interview, 25 January 2010.

102   International NGO staff member, interview, 9 December 2010.

103 Article XXXIII of the CPA called on ECOWAS, the United Nation, the African Union, and the ICGL (Nigeria, Ghana, United States, and United Kingdom) "to ensure that the spirit and content of this Peace Agreement are implemented in good faith and with integrity by the Parties."

104 ICGL member, interview, 28 November 2009.

105 Ibid.

106 US official 2, interview, 25 January 2010.

107 Senior TRC staff member, interview, 3 December 2009.

108 TRC, "Consolidated Final Report (unedited)," 40.

109 In FY2006, USAID provided $.5 million in support to the TRC. See Nicolas Cook, "Liberia's Post-war Development: Key Issues and U.S. Assistance," Congressional Research Service, 25 May 2010, 54–55.

110 Advocates for Human Rights, "House with Two Rooms."

111 Project Officer, Carter Center, interview, 8 December 2009.

112 TRC, "Consolidated Final Report (unedited)."

113 Ibid.

114 TRC press release, 11 December 2009.

115 US official 1, interview, 10 December 2009.

116 TRC Commissioner, interview, 10 December 2009.

117 ICTJ staff member, interview, 2 December 2009.

118 US official 1, interview, 10 December 2009.

119 ICTJ staff member, interview, 2 December 2009.

120 In early 2009, President Sirleaf testified to the TRC that she had not been party to any armed group during Liberia's civil wars. She said that while she was an early supporter of Taylor and provided funds to him in light of his role in opposing Doe, she later became disillusioned with Taylor and the National Patriotic Front of Liberia and had never joined it as a member. President Sirleaf attributed her initial support for the NPFL to being "fooled by" Taylor, which she implied was a lapse in judgment for which she had "to apologize to this nation." TRC, "Consolidated Final Report (unedited)"; and Boakai Fofana, "Sirleaf Testifies to Truth Commission," AllAfrica.com, 13 February 2009. The TRC chairman felt that naming the president in the report proved that the commission had not been politically compromised. "We didn't see Ellen as president and discuss what extra privileges should be accorded [to her]. The same way we invited everyone to appear, we invited the president." TRC chairman, interview, 9 December 2009.

121 US official 1, interview, 10 December 2009.

122 US official, interview, 16 March 2010.

123 US official 1, interview, 10 December 2009.

124 ICTJ staff member, interview, 2 December 2009.

125 Liberia Country Director, American Bar Association Rule of Law Initiative, interview, 7 December 2009.

126   Ellen Johnson-Sirleaf, "Annual Message to the Legislature," President of the Republic of Liberia, 25 January 2010.

127   ICGL, "ICGL Statement," on file with author (2009). Also, US official 1, interview, 10 December 2009.

128   US State Department, "Secretary of State Hillary Clinton, Address to Joint Session of Liberian National Legislature," 13 August 2009.

129   The TRC act stated that "civil society organizations and moral guarantors of the CPA [i.e., the ICGL] shall have the responsibility to monitor, and campaign for the scrupulous implementation of all recommendations contained in the report." See TRC, "Consolidated Final Report (unedited)."

130   TJWG member, interview, 7 December 2009.

131   Youth leader 1, focus group, 26 November 2009.

132   Youth leader 2, focus group, 26 November 2009.

133   Ibid.

134   Civil society leader 2, focus group, 4 December 2009.

135   US official 1, interview, 10 December 2009; and international rule of law advisor, interview, 8 December 2009.

136   ICGL member, interview, 28 November 2009.

137   International observer 2, interview, 28 November 2009.

138   Ibid.

139   US official 1, interview, 10 December 2009.

140   International observer 2, interview, 28 November 2009.

141   Liberia Country Director, American Bar Association Rule of Law Initiative, interview, 7 December 2009.

142   Ellen Johnson-Sirleaf, "The Challenges of Post-war Reconstruction: The Liberian Experience," President of the Republic of Liberia, Chatham House 13 June 2011. At this event, Sirleaf said the government would support one of the TRC recommendations to set up "palava huts" for less serious crimes, a traditional reconciliation measure where individuals can admit their wrongful acts and seek pardon from the people of Liberia.

143   Tom Malinowski, interview, 15 March 2010.

5 :: US Involvement in the Colombian Justice and Peace Process

When Colombian president Álvaro Uribe initiated a justice and peace process with paramilitary groups, President Bush, who saw Uribe as a strong ally, offered US support. During the negotiations of the "Justice and Peace Law", Congress advocated for strengthening the provisions on accountability for paramilitary leaders who had committed serious human rights violations, while the Department of Justice (DOJ) pushed to maintain its ability to extradite those leaders who were also top drug traffickers, to the United States. The law was passed in 2005, and stipulated that in exchange for truth-telling, reparations to victims, and a promise not to return to lawlessness, paramilitaries would receive reduced sentences. DOJ and USAID—both of which had been in Colombia for years—provided extensive support to operationalize the law. A few years into the process, Uribe decided to extradite several paramilitary leaders to the United States, which some observers believed undermined the justice and peace process. Before looking more closely at this process, this chapter begins with a review of the Colombian conflict and US-Colombia relations since the 1960s.

Colombia continues to experience the longest-running armed conflict in the world today.[1] The intensity of the fighting and the range and organization of the actors involved has fluctuated over nearly half a century of hostilities, yet the Revolutionary Armed Forces of Colombia (FARC), the National Liberation Army (ELN), the United Self-Defense Forces (AUC), and the Colombian government have been key actors. Huge numbers of Colombians, both civilians and fighters, have been killed since the violence began in 1963.[2] One exhaustive study claims that nearly four million people have been the direct victims of armed violence from 1964 to 2004, and that 40 to 50 percent of the population have been injured or are direct family members of victims.[3] The conflict has internally displaced approximately three million people, and has resulted in over 80,000 refugees in Ecuador.[4]

The United States became a close partner to the Colombian government in developing its internal security apparatus to counter insurgent forces. This cooperation dates back to 1961, when the United States shipped $1.5 million worth of military hardware to enable public order missions by Colombian military forces. These efforts led to a vastly expanded internal security effort under Military Assistance Program support. A clear distinction was made between criminally motivated violence and the more complex phenomena of violence posed by insurgent groups.[5]

Despite US military support, FARC and ELN continued to expand operations to such an extent that they influenced or controlled local government in over half the country's 1,000 municipalities by the 1990s.[6] In order to finance its political and military operations, FARC was involved in most phases of cocaine production and trafficking. In response to FARC gains, Governor Álvaro Uribe (who would be elected president of Colombia just a few years later) promoted the establishment of civilian rural defense groups called *Convivir* in the northern state of Antioquia. Over 400 *Convivir* groups were created, until the Constitutional Court declared them unlawful in 1997. *Convivir* groups were accused of committing human rights abuses; some were also believed to have served as fronts for, or were otherwise linked to, paramilitary groups.[7]

Paramilitary groups had emerged during this period to provide private security for important economic and political sectors in Colombia, who used them to protect their interests from non-state armed groups.[8] The Autodefensas Campesinas de Córdoba y Urabá (ACCU) was formed in 1994 in order to defeat non-state armed groups, recruit new members, and expand its control of territory throughout the 1990s.[9] These various, scattered paramilitary groups consolidated in 1997 with the creation of an umbrella body called the United Self-Defense Forces of Colombia (Autodefensas Unidas de Colombia—AUC). The AUC's foundational document stated that the group was a politico-military movement based upon the right of legitimate defense. The AUC had an antisubversive character and called for transformations within the state but did not seek to threaten its integrity.[10] The AUC comprised nearly 4,000 fighters organized into military and vigilante units, death squads, and logistic and intelligence units.[11] From 1998 to 2001, the AUC's strategy comprised a terror campaign against the alleged "social bases" of FARC and ELN, in collusion with the public forces. The focus was thus on civilians, and not on attempting to defeat non-state armed groups.[12] By 2002, it was estimated that there were approximately 12,000 fighters in the AUC that were operating in the majority of Colombia's provinces.[13] The AUC became increasingly involved in drug trafficking, eventually deriving 70 percent of its income from this activity.[14]

Colombia's coca and poppy production became a major source of cocaine and heroin in the United States. The Clinton administration declared drug trafficking a threat to national security and Colombia became the number one recipient of US military aid in the Americas.[15] Plan Colombia was announced in September 1999, which increased US aid from $50 million to $1 billion; 80 percent of the aid went to Colombia's armed forces, and most of that support was for aerial spraying of coca and poppy crops.

When President Bush entered office in 2001, US policy shifted from counternarcotics to counterterrorism. Marine commander James Jones explained: "Counterterrorism was a more palatable mantle than counternarcotics for waging counterinsurgency, which many in Washington feared after Vietnam. And it was easy to make the case for drugs as a terrorist threat."[16] With his peace process failing, Colombian president Andres Pastrana asked Bush in November 2001 to include Colombia in the global war on terrorism.[17]

President Uribe's election in 2002 brought US and Colombian foreign policies even closer together.[18] Uribe was a strong proponent of Plan Colombia and moved the country to the front lines of the global war on terror.[19] Between fiscal years 2000 and 2008, the United States provided over $6 billion to support Plan Colombia, making Colombia a top foreign aid recipient with one of the largest US embassies in the world.[20]

During this period, Uribe made talks with the AUC the foundation of his government's peace policy. The United States played an important role in this process. This chapter first looks at the US role in the negotiations of the Justice and Peace Law and then explores US assistance to the process, focusing on the Justice Department's support of the Justice and Peace Unit (JPU) and USAID's support of the National Commission for Reparations and Reconciliation (CNRR). It then examines the extradition of paramilitary leaders to the United States. The chapter draws on 58 Colombia-specific interviews with officials from the US and Colombian governments, international organizations, as well as Colombian and international NGOs.[21]

Negotiating the Justice and Peace Law

On the day Álvaro Uribe was inaugurated as president of Colombia, FARC launched an attack on the presidential palace, killing 20 civilians. As a result, Uribe began a vigorous campaign to defeat FARC and other non-state armed groups, receiving generous US support for his offensive.[22] Due to this approach with the FARC, Uribe decided to focus on demobilizing the AUC as his contribution toward ending the armed conflict.[23] Although the alleged links between the AUC and the Colombian government made many skeptical of Uribe's and AUC's motives for engaging in the talks, the Colombian government and the AUC signed a framework peace accord at Santa Fé de Ralito in July 2003 committing the paramilitaries to full demobilization by the end of 2005.[24]

President Bush warmed to Uribe's talks with the AUC, even though the AUC, along with the FARC and ELN, was on US terrorist lists.[25] Although this complicated contributing funds for the demobilization process, a US official said: "This is the first semi-serious show of intent on the part of one of these armed groups. I don't think it matters [that they are on the terrorist list]."[26] The State Department's narcotics chief, Robert Charles, said: "A window of opportunity has opened that will not always remain open. President Uribe has taken a huge risk, and we must do everything in our power to facilitate these peace efforts."[27]

The Bush administration got around terrorism-financing laws by providing support to the Organization of American States (OAS) Mission to Support the Peace Process, an organization that the United States said could receive funds without infringing on US laws.[28] The United States supported the collective demobilization of over 32,000 AUC members. In addition, more than 20,000 members of FARC, AUC, ELN, and other illegal armed groups individually surrendered their arms. Despite major concerns about the demobilization process, in April 2006, the high commissioner for peace announced that the process was complete.[29]

One obligation in the demobilization agreement was that some form of judicial treatment be accorded to demobilized AUC members for their responsibility in committing atrocities. Between January 1994 and December 2003, the Colombian government found that paramilitaries were responsible for the majority of 1,969 massacres, resulting in 10,174 deaths.[30] To comply with this obligation, the Uribe administration introduced the draft Alternative Penalty Law in August 2003. This draft law pardoned AUC members who demobilized if they agreed to a set of minimal conditions.

The draft was heavily criticized in domestic and international arenas, including in the United States, for being too lax and not dealing adequately with victims' rights to justice, truth, and reparations.[31] Fifty-seven members of the US Congress sent a letter to Uribe expressing their concerns:

We have doubts about your government's willingness to prosecute AUC
members, including Carlos Castaño and Salvatore Mancuso, for their
gross violations of human rights and drug trafficking in Colombia.
Recent public statements made by Colombia's High Commissioner
for Peace, Luis Carlos Restrepo, indicate that your government may
consider allowing these criminals to receive suspended sentences and
pay reparations in lieu of jail time. We believe that such an exchange
would amount to impunity for serious human rights violations and
would erode the rule of law in Colombia, encourage further violence,
and establish an undesirable template for future negotiations with the
guerrillas. Instead, we encourage you to ensure that an eventual peace
agreement with the AUC includes accountability for human rights
violations, excludes the possibility of cash-for-justice swaps, provides
for the rapid disarmament, demobilization, and reintegration of the
AUC combatants, and requires that your government control disarmament and demobilization zones.[32]

While members of Congress were concerned about impunity for
serious human rights violations, the State and Justice departments were primarily concerned that the law would exclude
the possibility of extraditing top drug traffickers to the United
States. A letter was sent to the peace commissioner, asking that
the draft Alternative Penalty Law not affect the extradition of
paramilitary leaders accused of narcotrafficking.[33] US ambassador to Colombia William Wood met with proponents of the draft
law and "insisted" that the benefits being debated not allow nar-
cotraffickers "to use the façade of the armed conflict in order to
evade justice."[34]

AUC leaders were resolute about their patriotic service to the
nation, and pledged never to serve jail time in Colombia or accept
a peace deal allowing for their possible extradition to the United
States.[35] The second in command of the AUC, Salvatore Mancuso,
invited the United States "to participate directly" in the peace
negotiations in an attempt to trade a promise not to extradite for
information on the drug trade.[36] Both Ambassador Wood and
Assistant Secretary of State Roger Noriega rejected this request and
reiterated US insistence on the extradition of Colombians indicted

in the United States and on the need to bring gross violators of human rights and major drug traffickers to trial.[37]

The Colombian government was divided on the issue. Some members of the Colombian Congress felt that a promise not to extradite was essential in order for the process to move forward. In a press release, however, Uribe said, "Extradition is not negotiable," noting that "if extradition was prohibited, Colombia would suffer international discredit." But his statement also left open the possibility that extradition could be suspended in exchange for an individual's cooperation with the process: "He who wants to avoid [extradition] has to show to the international community his good will and readiness to rectify."[38]

In May 2004, it was decided that AUC paramilitary commanders would not be detained or extradited if they moved to a zone subject to OAS verification in the northern province of Cordoba and complied with agreements within the peace process.[39] Four days later, however, US deputy attorney general Mary Lee Warren submitted an extradition request to Colombian authorities for six paramilitary leaders, including AUC leader Salvatore Mancuso, based on DOJ information about their alleged narcotrafficking activity.[40] Ambassador Wood said that there were not clear signs the AUC wanted to break its connections with drug trafficking, and that the United States was waiting for the AUC to comply with the government's requirements.[41] Uribe suspended the extradition requests as long as AUC leaders agreed to cooperate, and US pressure decreased.

Meanwhile, debate continued for another year within the Colombian Congress, which had rejected a second draft of the Alternative Penalty Law. USAID contributed some funding to Fundación Social, an organization that advised the drafting of legislation by Senator Rafael Pardo and a multiparty group in Congress. Fundación Social provided members of the Colombian Congress with tools and documents about transitional justice, victims' rights, and international standards. Paula Gaviria, then director of public policy at Fundación Social, felt their impact was sizable in changing the discussion about the law.[42] The Pardo draft legislation was widely viewed as the most rigorous in terms of international standards and victims' rights.[43]

Gaviria mentioned that the relationship with USAID was positive and noted that during intense negotiations of the law from January to June 2005, USAID followed the process closely. Due to the detail of the requests for information being made, Gaviria had the sense that there must have been calls for information from the ambassador or State Department.[44] The director of USAID's DDR program said that every provision of the law was discussed in USAID.[45]

Just before a third draft of the law was presented, US members of Congress continued to express their concerns. Republican senator Richard Lugar said he was concerned that the law "would leave intact the complex mafia-like structures" by failing to require commanders to disclose knowledge of the organization's operations or financing.[46] The letter also said that paramilitary leaders requested for extradition in the United States would receive extremely short sentences compared to the crimes committed.[47] In another letter to Uribe, six Democratic senators expressed similar concerns. They felt the terms agreed thus far could have an extremely negative impact on peace, justice, and the rule of law in Colombia, in addition to the fight against drug trafficking and terrorism.[48] The House International Relations Committee said that State Department funding would be rejected unless a legal framework in accordance with human rights, truth, reparations, and justice, as well as the extradition of paramilitary leaders, was adopted.[49] Congress also required the State Department to certify that the Colombian government had severed links with paramilitary organizations and dismantled their networks before the provision of financial assistance.[50] This pressure reportedly resulted in a longer investigation time frame of AUC members and the loss of benefits if members did not provide all information known about the group's structure.[51]

In June 2005, Law 975/05 was adopted and came to be known as the "Justice and Peace Law" (JPL). The law mandated punishment for those individuals who committed war crimes or serious human rights violations, but offered reduced sentences of five to eight years if the ex-combatant gave testimony about his illicit acts. The law also required victims to be informed of judicial findings and allowed them to claim reparations from the perpetrator. The law passed without a promise not to extradite, but AUC leaders were under the impression that this would not take place.[52]

Upon passage, the Justice and Peace Law was hailed by Colombian government officials as groundwork for removing one of the three illegal armed groups battling in Colombia. "We are proud of this instrument," said Luis Carlos Restrepo, the country's peace commissioner.[53] Government officials felt the law reflected a viable balance between victims' rights and political necessity.[54]

However, the law continued to be heavily criticized. "This law tries to simulate truth, justice and reparations, but what it really offers is impunity," said Iván Cepeda, whose father, Senator Manuel Cepeda, was killed by paramilitary gunmen in 1994.[55] Human rights groups condemned the law, stating it favored the perpetrators of human rights violations over their victims. A *New York Times* opinion piece called it the "Impunity for Mass Murderers, Terrorists and Major Cocaine Traffickers Law."[56] Some concerns were addressed by Colombia's Constitutional Court, which, immediately after ratification, reviewed and strengthened components of the law, increasing the criteria paramilitaries needed to meet to obtain reduced prison sentences and inserting language ensuring the rights of victims to participate in all stages of the criminal process.[57]

Implementing the Law

The Justice and Peace Unit (JPU) and the National Commission for Reparations and Reconciliation (CNRR) were two institutions created to implement the Justice and Peace Law. In response to Uribe's requests for international assistance, the United States was one of the first foreign governments to support the law's implementation. Support came primarily from the Department of Justice (DOJ) and the US Agency for International Development (USAID).

Justice Department Support of the Justice and Peace Unit

The Justice Department has a long history of involvement in Colombia. Since the 1990s, the Office of Overseas Prosecutorial

Development Assistance and Training (OPDAT) and the International Criminal Investigative Training Assistance Program (ICITAP) have worked in Bogotá, helping to shift Colombia's legal system from an inquisitorial to an adversarial one.[58] The DOJ got involved in the justice and peace process because, as one official noted, it was "fundamental to the development of the Colombian justice system." But he also placed DOJ's involvement within the broader goals of US foreign policy:

> Colombia is very strategic to the USG in terms of where it sits geographically but also politically, historically as a close ally of the US and from a law enforcement perspective given the criminal and terrorist organizations and years of being a central focus of cocaine trafficking.[59]

More specifically, he spoke about DOJ's long-standing relationship with the Colombian Prosecutor General's Office, and with Luis Gonzales Leon, whom the DOJ had worked closely with before his appointment as head of the JPU. Failure to support the newly created unit within the Prosecutor General's Office, the official added, would have been "irresponsible" considering the unit was in charge of much of the law's requirements.

Initially, DOJ was the only international actor working with the Justice and Peace Unit. DOJ's approach was to look at the law from the optics of the accusatory system and to focus on obtaining information. DOJ therefore focused its assistance on helping build the unit's capacity to aid in the investigation and prosecution of crimes committed by former paramilitary members.[60] Between 2005 and 2010, DOJ contributed over $10 million in funding to the Justice and Peace Unit for the development of hearing rooms, forensic equipment and training, vehicles, training for data management and analysis, and technical assistance to Colombian prosecutors and investigators.[61]

A DOJ official explained how paramilitaries "ran" initial sessions with JPU prosecutors who were mandated to take the testimony of ex-combatants about the illicit acts they perpetrated as a member of an illegal armed group. To respond to this problem, DOJ arranged proffer sessions with prosecutors and investigators in order to help them "think" like prosecutors.[62] DOJ was also involved in training exhumation units, and arranged closed-circuit sessions with paramilitaries.

The Justice Department influenced interpretations of the Justice and Peace Law and its implementation. DOJ's emphasis on the judicial aspect of the law meant that issues relating to victims' rights and truth-telling did not receive as much attention, despite provisions for these components in the law. A DOJ official felt that the law, by including judicial and truth components, had two aims that were in conflict with each other. He admitted that DOJ's focus was on prosecutorial and investigative capacities, adding, "If that happens to mean the prosecution of human rights abuses and the inclusion of victims, that's not a problem," but "DOJ sees its role as different from a human rights agenda."[63]

According to the same official, the justice and peace process in Colombia was the first transitional justice mechanism the DOJ had been involved in, which may explain the agency's unfamiliarity with the ways in which a legal process may also be used to benefit victims.[64] He explained that DOJ's role in Colombian transitional justice is unique because the Justice and Peace Law is "so unique." He said that DOJ colleagues in Eastern Europe and Africa have asked DOJ-Colombia for advice on assistance, specifically about their work on plea bargaining and exhumations. He noted:

> DOJ is underutilized in foreign assistance efforts and has a significant contribution to make given DOJ's expertise and unique perspective in the area of criminal justice development. Our efforts in Colombia have clearly demonstrated that. The Department of State has traditionally looked to contractors rather than working with DOJ and using existing USG resources. What we have done in Colombia demonstrates a more effective foreign assistance approach with respect to justice development including your focus: transitional justice. As we discussed, development of effective criminal investigation and prosecution capabilities are essential to any transitional justice effort.[65]

He felt that DOJ's relationship with Colombian prosecutors is an example of US foreign policy working right—since the two have worked "hand in hand" for many years.

USAID Support of the National Commission for Reparations and Reconciliation

Like the Justice Department, USAID has also been active in Colombia for many years. It has supported government agencies and civil society groups, and views itself as a facilitator between the two.[66] USAID created the Demobilization and Reintegration program within its Office for Vulnerable Populations in 2005. The program's focus was on supporting the reintegration of demobilized ex-combatants, which helped to implement Colombia's Demobilization and Reintegration Law, and to support conflict victims' guarantees of truth, justice, judicial reparations, and no repetition, which helped to implement the Justice and Peace Law.

The Justice and Peace Law mandated the establishment of the National Commission for Reparations and Reconciliation (CNRR) to ensure victim participation in the judicial process, recommend criteria for reparations, and advance reconciliation projects, along with a range of other tasks. The CNRR comprised government officials, representatives of civil society, and victims. It was given an ambitious mandate that included monitoring and reporting on key aspects of DDR and reparations processes.

USAID was the first international donor to the CNRR. When asked if and how USAID assistance had impacted the commission, CNRR president Eduardo Pizarro said it had changed the commission's priorities.[67] From 2006 to 2010, USAID supported the design of a victims' reparations fund, a victims' database, and an asset identification database in order to monitor reparations. It also supported the regulatory framework for implementing reparations and pilot reparations projects. It strengthened judicial counseling and representation for victims, and provided support to field offices and their outreach activities to build a service network for victims.[68]

USAID contributed nearly $3 million for these activities with the greatest contribution for CNRR regional offices and a pilot project on

Table 5.1 USAID Contribution to the CNRR

Activities	Amount (in USD)
Reconciliation	
International experiences on reconciliation	392,581
Database of victims	43,589
Workshops on reconciliation and reparations	275,589
Reparations	
CNRR regional offices: Medellín, Bucaramanga, Bogotá	1,232,868
Assistance to victims and collective reparations	
Questionnaire	89,325
Awareness workshops	6,453
Pilot project on collective reparations	921,378
Total	2,961,783

collective reparations. Table 5.1 illustrates the activities and amount of USAID assistance to the CNRR between 2006 and 2009.[69]

Pizarro explained how USAID's confidence in the process generated a snowball effect where other international donors became involved.[70] Nevertheless, in the initial years of the commission's operations, US assistance far surpassed that of other donors, as depicted in table 5.2.[71]

UNDP coordinated all international assistance to the process, except for assistance from the United States. An OAS official speculated that USAID did not participate in the UNDP process because USAID knew more about the topic than other donors and wanted to maintain its autonomy.[72] USAID did take part in an inter-institutional committee on transitional justice led by the Colombian Ministry of the Interior and Justice.

In order to determine its funding priorities, USAID held consultative meetings every two months with a range of Colombian government agencies responsible for implementing the justice and peace process (i.e., Acción Social, CNRR, Fiscalía, Procuraduría,

Table 5.2 International Assistance to the CNRR

Donor	Amount (in millions of pesos)	Percentage
United States	7.247	29
Netherlands	4.820	19
Spain	3.111	12
Sweden	2.997	12
UNDP	2.432	10
Canada	1.818	7
Others	1.671	7
Switzerland	0.983	4

Ministry of Interior and Justice). The principal organizations that implemented USAID programs for the CNRR were the International Organization for Migration (IOM) and Management Sciences for Development, Inc. (MSD).[73]

A CNRR director said that USAID was the most flexible and comprehensive donor with a coherent approach at the political and technical levels.[74] Acción Social's director of international cooperation, Viviana Tamayo, said that USAID shifted its funding approach based on consultative meetings with Colombian government agencies.[75]

From 2010 to 2013, USAID continued to support CNRR reconciliation work, as well as collective, judicial, and administrative reparations. The reparations work involved strengthening processes to search out and identify the remains of the "disappeared," assistance for the accelerated adjudication of victims' applications, and formalizing collective reparations measures undertaken in pilot sites. USAID supported the National Land Fund and Regional Commissions for Restitution of Goods, as well as the CNRR's work on historical memory. USAID worked to strengthen victims' defense through the national ombudsman and by direct institutional support to victims' organizations, and to re-establish socioeconomic security for victim populations through income generation, training, and psychosocial attention.

USAID also funded civil society organizations working on the justice and peace process. For example, MSD gave one-year contracts to organizations working with victims who were bringing cases before the JPU.[76] One grantee said USAID/MSD was the first donor with interest in the justice and peace process. His organization, País Libre, received MSD funding from 2007 to 2009 for work accompanying victims through the justice and peace process and providing judicial representation, which Sweden then decided to fund.[77] Another grantee said that MSD had been an important facilitator between civil society and government agencies: "MSD presence helps make things happen at the Ministry of Interior."[78] The main criticism of civil society groups supported by USAID was that one-year grants were not renewed or took a long time to receive, which meant that these organizations had to stop services for victims. USAID grants also did not include funds for administrative costs, unlike most other donor grants.

Some NGOs working on the justice and peace process refused to accept US assistance because of US support for Plan Colombia. The Colombian Commission of Jurists (CCJ), for example, does not accept US funds for reasons of security and credibility. CCJ president Gustavo Gallón explained that because US funds go to the military, those who accept them can become mixed up with the war and subject to guerilla attacks.[79]

Paramilitary Extraditions to the United States

There was no discussion about extradition for the first two years of the justice and peace process. In May 2008, however, Uribe requested that 14 AUC leaders be extradited to the United States. DOJ was not initially prepared to accept these leaders since Uribe gave the United States under 48 hours' advance notice. The Colombian government argued that the extraditions relieved the justice and peace process of the negative influence exercised by the paramilitary leaders, who allegedly continued to commit crimes from jail and were contributing very little to the process of truth and reparations. Even worse, said the government, these commanders were trying to control the testimony of other former combatants who had taken advantage of the Justice and Peace Law.[80] CNRR president Eduardo Pizarro said: "The justice and peace process began the day the paramilitaries were extradited to Washington."[81]

Some believed that Uribe went through with the extraditions because AUC leaders were revealing sensitive information about the nexus between the paramilitaries and the state. The "parapolitics" scandal had erupted in 2006, where AUC leader Mancuso publicly claimed that the AUC had secured the electoral success of 35 percent of congressional members.[82] By April 2008, just a month before Uribe announced the extraditions, nearly 100 government officials had either been sentenced or were being investigated for colluding with paramilitaries, including 62 members of Congress, President Uribe's cousin, the former president of Congress, the army chief general, the former head of the Colombian Intelligence and Security Service, and the former president of the Superior Council of the Judicature.[83] Post-demobilization investigations and trials also found department governors, former and current legislators, and other senior government and military figures guilty of collusion with paramilitary groups.[84] Colombia expert Adam Isacson said "it became far more convenient for Uribe to get them out of the country incommunicado."[85]

US ambassador William Brownfield pledged that the extraditions would not interfere with Colombia's efforts to hold paramilitaries accountable for their crimes in Colombia. The United States would try to "facilitate all access, all of the information, and all of the opportunities to the victims, the victims' representatives and to the [Colombian] prosecutors."[86]

Despite this pledge, some believed that, since the extraditions, the paramilitary leaders' cooperation with Colombian investigators had ceased. A UC Berkeley report said that logistical difficulties were compounded by the absence of a written agreement between the United States and Colombia to coordinate judicial cooperation. The report discussed the limited access of Colombian prosecutors and judges to defendants in US custody and the rejection of efforts of Colombian victims by US prosecutors to divulge information about their crimes. The report also talked about how plea agreements that DOJ reached with the extradited defendants did not contain incentives for defendants to cooperate with Colombian law enforcement or to reveal details of their human rights crimes.[87]

Colombian and international NGOs also expressed concern about the impact of the extradition on the justice and peace process. Paula Gaviria of Fundación Social said:

> The justice and peace process is a domestic process, but it went out of the government's hands when the extraditions took place. JPL had no institutions or processes in place. When the [paramilitary] leaders didn't comply with the requirements of the law, the government always had the option of extradition. The government took this decision late and the result had huge consequences for thousands of victims. In addition, the impact on the collective imagination of Colombians was very negative. It sent the message: We're not capable of undertaking this process. [The decision to extradite] showed deeper problems of incapacity, fear, and dependence on the US.[88]

Gustavo Gallón, president of the Colombian Commission of Jurists, stated: "The US is far from Colombia legally, culturally, and geographically"—now that the leaders are there, he said, there is no access to them.[89] Colombia expert Michael Reed said: "Extraditions have been an obstacle to peace. The FARC has slowed down demobilization, now that it has seen how the paramilitaries were betrayed."[90] Both felt that there should have been better sequencing, trying leaders for human rights abuses in Colombia first and then for drug charges in the United States. Luis Carlos Restrepo, Colombia's peace commissioner, said: "US interest was always based on the extradition of AUC leaders."[91]

In response to the debate, a DOJ official said: "On what basis do you say no to the biggest drug traffickers in the world?" He expressed frustration with NGO criticism of the extraditions and felt that an "honest discussion" should take place: "It's clear that the only place that these leaders would serve a stiff sentence is in the United States. Sentences would be close to 30 years in the United States, as opposed to eight years under the Justice and Peace Law." The same official spoke about how the justice and peace process had not been taken seriously by paramilitary leaders:

> Mancuso used to come to the justice and peace process with his Gucci shoes and a nice suit, and completely control the process. Now you see him in his prison outfit. This is an important change.

He believed that the argument that leaders had started talking had been distorted in the press, and that they were actually talking very little.[92]

In order to fulfill the US pledge to facilitate access to those extradited, US and Colombian authorities began to identify legal procedures for this access. AUC leaders were moved to Miami, Florida, and Great Neck, Virginia. JPU prosecutors were given access to leaders held in Miami for three days a week, 9:00 a.m. to 5:00 p.m., and five days a week, 9:00 a.m. to 5:00 p.m., to those in Virginia. In addition, DOJ paid for 10 JPU prosecutors to meet with DC prosecutors in April 2010 in order to share information about the Justice and Peace Law and the importance of paramilitary cooperation with the process.[93]

The issue of offering incentives for continued participation in the justice and peace process was complicated by protections in US laws, which did not obligate the leaders to participate in the process. However, the Colombian government told the extradited paramilitaries that if they participated, any sentence given under the justice and peace process would run concurrently with their sentence in the United States. This meant that after they completed their sentences in the United States, they would not face additional jail time upon return to Colombia.[94] A DOJ official referred to Rule 35 of the US Federal Rules of Criminal Procedure and mentioned that leaders may be able to receive a reduced sentence if they cooperate with the justice and peace process.[95] However, this was at the discretion of the court, and because plea agreements are sealed, it is not possible to know who ultimately cooperated with the process.

According to the State Department, as of July 2009, all 15 extradited paramilitary members had elected to resume participation in the justice and peace process.[96] On approximately 36 occasions, the DOJ facilitated the transmittal of approximately 10 voluntary confessions, and conducted interviews with about 12 former paramilitary leaders, in cooperation with the relevant Colombian authority.[97] A DOJ official said that he believed the extraditions were helping the justice and peace process and wanted them to contribute to revealing the truth. "DOJ philosophy is that extraditions should be a vehicle of truth," he said. "DOJ wants the justice and peace process to be a success; our prosecution goal is transnational justice for human rights and drug cases."[98]

Efforts undertaken by DOJ were not well known by observers and are difficult to verify. Colombia expert Adam Isacson said: "We're all trying to figure this out. We're in new legal ground here and it's very hard to get information from DOJ."[99] Despite the report that extradited leaders had resumed participation in the justice and peace process, one source reported that at least three leaders (Salvatore Mancuso, Diego Murillo Bejarano, alias "Don Berna," and Ramiro Vanoy, alias "Cuco Vanoy") had discontinued their cooperation with the process, claiming that their families had not received the security promised to them.[100]

A consequence of the extradition was the Colombian Supreme Court decision to ban future extraditions of paramilitary leaders participating in the justice and peace process. The court found that the extraditions of AUC members adversely impacted "the rights of victims and the Colombian public" by leaving them "without the possibility of knowing the truth and obtaining reparation for the crimes committed by paramilitary groups."[101] The court further reasoned that extradition would "violate Colombia's international obligations to combat impunity with regard to crimes against humanity" and undermine victims' rights. It found that "recent experience" proves that extraditions "paralyze" the justice and peace process because extradited leaders were unable to continue their confessions from the United States.[102] The Supreme Court concluded that individuals should complete their confessions in Colombia before being extradited to the United States. When the United States requested the extradition of additional AUC leaders participating in the justice and peace process, in accordance with the Supreme Court's ruling, Colombia denied these requests.[103] A 2011 OAS study on the justice and peace process, led by Judge Baltazar Garzon, recommended that extradited leaders serve the remainder of their sentences in Colombia.[104]

Conclusions

This chapter examined US involvement in the negotiations of the Justice and Peace Law, its implementation, and the extradition of several paramilitary leaders to the United States who had been participating in the justice and peace process. Although this process was by no means a major component of US foreign policy on Colombia, the Bush administration supported President Uribe's decision to focus on the AUC as the foundation of his peace policy.

Negotiations for the Justice and Peace Law took two years. During this time, members of Congress were consistent in their calls for a law that ensured adequate investigation of the demobilized and the rights of victims. DOJ, in contrast, was insistent that the law not infringe on the ability to extradite top drug traffickers to the United States, and even submitted extradition requests for several paramilitary leaders while the law was being negotiated. Ultimately, both congressional and DOJ interests were met: the investigation component of the law was strengthened, and it did not prohibit extraditions.

The Justice and Peace Law provided reduced sentences in return for truth-telling, reparations to victims, and a promise not to return to lawlessness. In order to implement the law, two institutions were established: the Justice and Peace Unit and the National Commission for Reparations and Reconciliation. The United States was the first international donor to support the two bodies, with DOJ providing key support to the JPU and USAID supporting the CNRR.

When Uribe extradited 14 paramilitary leaders to the United States two years into the justice and peace process, observers felt that this decision undermined the process. The State Department pledged to allow JPU access to the extradited leaders, and DOJ made arrangements for JPU prosecutors to continue to take testimony. Although some leaders continued to participate, others did not.

This concludes examination of US involvement in transitional justice in the three case studies. The final chapter provides a summary of the book's findings, the broader implications of the study, and avenues for further research.

Notes

1   The Santos administration began peace talks with the FARC in 2012, which, if successful, may lead to the end of the conflict.

2   The Colombian conflict has its roots in the assassination of the Liberal Party's presidential candidate, Jorge Eliécer Gaitán, in 1948, which sparked riots in Bogotá. The riots gave rise to *"La Violencia,"* a 10-year period of civil conflict in the countryside between supporters of the Liberal and Conservative parties, which resulted in between 200,000 to 300,000 deaths. *La Violencia* ended in 1957 with an agreement between the Liberals and the Conservatives to take turns to govern the country. Nevertheless, the conflict continued in rural areas, where peasant armies joined with leftist guerrillas to gain or retain possession of land. The 1960s saw the emergence of several non-state armed groups in remote areas of the country, in particular the National Liberation Army (ELN) and the Revolutionary Armed Forces of Colombia (FARC). FARC remains the largest and oldest insurgent group in the Americas. It claims to be a revolutionary, agrarian, anti-imperialist Marxist-Leninist organization of Bolivarian inspiration that represents the rural poor in a struggle against Colombia's wealthier classes. ELN was formed in 1963 by "Catholic radicals and left-wing intellectuals," and ideologically was influenced by the Cuban Revolution. See S. Hansom, "FARC, ELN: Colombia's Left-Wing Guerillas," Council on Foreign Relations, 2009; J. F. G. Forero, "Colombia in Armed Conflict? 1946–1985," Papel Político, Universidad Javeriana, 2005.

3   El Instituto de Estudios para el Desarrollo y la Paz (INDEPAZ), "Las Cifras del Conflicto," *Comunicaciones*, 22 March 2007.

4   UN High Commissioner for Refugees, "2008 Global Trends: Refugees, Asylum-seekers, Returnees, Inter-nally Displaced and Stateless Persons," 16 June 2009.

5   D. M. Rempe, "The Past as Prologue? A History of US Counterinsurgency Policy in Colombia, 1958–66," US Army War College, Strategic Studies Institute, 2002, 4, 31.

6   Congressional Research Service, "Colombia: Conditions and US Policy Options," 12 February 2001, 1.

7   Congressional Research Service, "Colombia: The Uribe Administration and Congressional Concerns," 14 June 2002, 3; US State Department, "Country Reports: Colombia," 1997, 462.

8   See A. Carrillo-Suarez, "Hors de logique: Contemporary Issues in International Humanitarian Law as Applied to Internal Armed Conflict," *American University International Law Review* 15, no. 1 (1999): 7. The emergence of paramilitaries was part of the state's counterinsurgency strategy, but the involvement of paramilitaries themselves in drug trafficking

progressively located them outside the orbit of state control. See Mariana Escobar, "Seize the State, Seize the Way: State Capture as a Form of Warlords Politics in Colombia," PhD thesis, London School of Economics, 2011.

9 International Crisis Group (ICG), "Colombia's New Armed Groups," Latin American Reports No. 20, 2007, 3.

10 Escobar, "Seize the State."

11 ICG, "Colombia's New Armed Groups," 3.

12 It has been argued that the AUC facilitated the paramilitaries' transition from private drug-barons' armies to political actors, and represented finding a "public objective" to cover their "private goal" of increasing territorial expansion. See F. Cubides, "Los paramilitares como agentes organizados de violencia: Su dimensión territorial," in *Violencia y desarrollo municipal*, ed. F. Cubides, C. Olaya, and C.M. Ortiz (Bogotá: Centro de Estudios Sociales, Universidad Nacional de Colombia, 1995); F. Cubides, "De lo privado y de lo público en la violencia colombiana: Los paramilitares," in *Las violencias: Inclusión creciente*, ed. J. Arocha, F. Cubides, and M. Jimeno (Bogotá: Centro de Estudios Sociales, Universidad Nacional de Colombia, 1998); F. Cubides, "Narcotráfico y paramilitarismo ¿Matrimonio indisoluble?" in *El poder paramilitar*, ed. A. Rangel (Bogotá: Planeta, 2005); F. Cubides, *Burocracias armadas: El problema de la organización en el entramado de las violencias colombianas* (Bogotá: Norma, 2005). The AUC had access to a variety of financial resources, mainly through the cocaine and heroin markets, assisted by complex regional and/or local alliances with elites and organized crime. So, although the AUC allied itself with the Colombian government against other non-state armed groups, it was simultaneously at loggerheads with the state in the fight against drugs. See F. Gutiérrez and M. Barón, "Estado, control territorial paramilitar y orden político en Colombia: Notas para una economía política del paramilitarismo," in *Nuestra guerra sin nombre: Transformaciones del conflicto en Colombia*, ed. F. Gutiérrez, M. E. Wills, and G. Sánchez (Bogotá: Norma, 2006), 272.

13 See Presidencia de la República, "Proceso de paz con las autodefensas," Oficina Alto Comisionado para la Paz, Informe Ejecutivo, December 2006, 8; ICG, "Colombia's New Armed Groups," 4.

14 ICG, "Colombia's New Armed Groups," 3.

15 Congressional Research Service, "Colombia: Summary and Tables on U.S. Assistance, FY1989–FY2003," 3 May 2002.

16 James C. Jones, "US Policy and Peace in Colombia: Lost in a Tangle of Wars," in *Colombia: Building Peace in a Time of War*, ed. Virginia Bouvier (Washington, DC: US Institute of Peace, 2009), 358.

17 Juan Forero, "Asking for Aid, Colombians Cite Terror; US Demurs," *New York Times*, 11 November 2001.

18 Rodrigo Pardo, "Changes in the Andean Region and Foreign Policy Alternatives for Colombia," Peace Initiatives and Colombia's Armed Conflict,

Woodrow Wilson Center and Fundación Ideas Para La Paz, September 2009.

19   Colombia was one of the few Latin American countries to support the war in Iraq. See J. Forero, "Hard-Liner Elected in Colombia with a Mandate to Crush Rebels," *New York Times*, 27 May 2002.

20   The embassy has 2,000 employees, 450 of which are military; and 32 US agencies. See Virginia Bouvier, "Evaluating US Foreign Policy in Colombia," Policy Report for the International Relations Center, Americas Program, 11 May 2005; and William Wood, "U.S. Policy in Colombia: Current and Future Challenges," Woodrow Wilson Center, 14 June 2005. See also US Government Accountability Office (GAO), "Plan Colombia: Drug Reduction Goals Were Not Fully Met, but Security Has Improved; U.S. Agencies Need More Detailed Plans for Reducing Assistance," Report to the Honorable Joseph R. Biden, Jr., Chairman, Committee on Foreign Relations, U.S. Senate, October 2008.

21   See Appendix 1 for full interview list.

22   In 2004, President Uribe received generous US support for *Plan Patriota*, which created mobile military units to launch an offensive against FARC in its southern Colombian strongholds. See A. Isacson, "The End of the 'Plan Colombia' Era," Just the Facts Blog, 26 October 2010; International Crisis Group (ICG), "The History and Current State of FARC," March 2009.

23   Arturo Carrillo, "Truth, Justice and Reparations in Colombia: The Path to Peace and Reconciliation?" in Bouvier, *Colombia*, 134.

24   In addition to whatever deals were offered by the Colombian government, the threat of extradition to the United States was also viewed as an important motive for the AUC's sudden desire to negotiate its demobilization and reintegration. See International Crisis Group (ICG), "Demobilizing the Paramilitaries in Colombia: An Achievable Goal?" Latin American Report no. 8, 5 August 2004. See also Adam Isacson, interview, 2 March 2010; and Carrillo, "Truth, Justice and Reparations in Colombia," 150.

25   President Bush designated the FARC and the AUC organizations as "Specially Designated Global Terrorists" in October 2001 and as "Significant Foreign Narcotics Traffickers" in May 2003. Eighteen AUC members were also added to a list of foreign narcotics trafficking "kingpins," which applied economic sanctions under the Kingpin Act. A US Treasury press release stated: "These Kingpin Act designations reinforce the reality that the FARC and the AUC are not simply terrorist/guerrilla organizations fighting within Colombia to achieve political agendas. They are part and parcel of the narcotics production and export threat to the United States, as well as Europe and other countries of Latin America." See US Department of Treasury, "Treasury Takes Action against FARC/AUC Narco-Terrorist Leaders in Continued Effort to Halt Narcotics Trafficking," Press Release, 19 February 2004.

26   Jones, "US Policy and Peace in Colombia," 362.

27   Sergio Gómez Maseri, "EU y el mundo deben apoyar con vigor y cuanto antes la desmovilización de los grupos paramilitares," *El Tiempo*, 16 December 2004.

28   See Center for International Policy, "Paramilitary Talks (6): Extradition and the U.S. Role," 15 December 2004. This announcement did not indicate resolution of the question whether the United States could provide direct funding to the Colombian government or even NGOs if this were to benefit the AUC or its members. See ICG, "Demobilizing the Paramilitaries in Colombia."

29   Some paramilitaries did not demobilize; others demobilized, only to re-emerge some time later to take up arms once more, claiming that the Colombian government had broken its promises to them. Other demobilized paramilitaries later became involved with drug-trafficking organizations. See International Crisis Group (ICG), "Colombia Conflict History," Background Piece, June 2011; and ICG, "Colombia's New Armed Groups."

30   *El Tiempo*, "Así ha sido el recorrido, en cifras, del horror 'para' durante 3,650 días," 26 September 2004.

31   Carrillo, "Truth, Justice and Reparations in Colombia," 135.

32   US Letter to President Uribe, Organized by Rep. Tom Lantos, Ranking Member of House International Relations Committee, 23 September 2003.

33   *El Tiempo*, "EEUU se opone a que beneficios de la ley de excarcelación cobijen a 'narcos' pedidos en extradición," 10 October 2003.

34   *El Tiempo*, "EU pide no tocar extradición," 5 November 2003.

35   Cynthia Arnson, "The Peace Process in Colombia with the Autodefensas Unidas de Colombia–AUC," Woodrow Wilson Center Report on the Americas no. 13, 2005.

36   *El Tiempo*, "Negociaciones, AUC invitan a negociar a EU," 23 March 2004.

37   *Semana*, "Los paras perdieron su disfraz," 7 May 2004; William Wood, "The Peace Process in Colombia with the Autodefensas Unidas de Colombia–AUC," Woodrow Wilson Center seminar, 28 June 2004.

38   Comunicado Casa de Nariño, 28 April 2004.

39   BBC News, "U.S. Seeks Colombian Extraditions," 18 May 2004; *El Tiempo*, "No extraditarán a ningún paramilitary que esté en zona de ubicación en Córdoba," 14 May 2004.

40   BBC News, "U.S. Seeks Colombian Extraditions"; *El Tiempo*, "Vicefiscal de Estados Unidos formalizó la solicitud de extradición de seis jefes paramilitares," 18 May 2004.

41   *El Tiempo*, "Embajador de Estados Unidos, William Wood, cuestiona proceso de diálogo con las autodefensas," 31 May 2004.

42   Paula Gaviria, interview, 8 September 2010.

43   Carrillo, "Truth, Justice and Reparations in Colombia," 143.

44 Paula Gaviria, interview, 8 September 2010.

45 Director, USAID Demobilization and Reintegration Program, interview, 31 August 2010.

46 Juan Forero, "New Colombia Law Grants Concessions to Paramilitaries," *New York Times*, 23 June 2005.

47 US Letter to President Uribe from Senator Lugar, 22 May 2005.

48 US Letter to President Uribe from several Democratic senators, 3 June 2005.

49 *El Tiempo*, "Sin extradición no habría ayuda," 12 June 2005.

50 This determination and certification is pursuant to Section 7046(b) of the Department of State, Foreign Operations, and Related Programs Appropriations Act, 2009. This law requires the State Department to certify that the government of Colombia is prosecuting members of the armed forces who have committed human rights violations; severing links with paramilitary organizations or successor armed groups; dismantling paramilitary networks and returning illegally acquired land to its rightful occupants; and respecting the rights of Colombia's indigenous and Afro-Colombian communities.

51 *El Tiempo*, "Desmovilizados perderían beneficios si omiten intencionalmente participación en crímenes," 13 June 2005.

52 Constanza Vieira, "US Supervision of Colombian Paramilitary Demobilization Becomes Evident," Antiwar.com, 19 August 2006; and Stanford University, "United Self-Defense Forces of Colombia," Mapping Militant Organizations, 2012.

53 Forero, "New Colombia Law Grants Concessions to Paramilitaries."

54 Carrillo, "Truth, Justice and Reparations in Colombia" 135.

55 Forero, "New Colombia Law Grants Concessions to Paramilitaries."

56 *New York Times*, "Colombia's Capitulation," 6 July 2005.

57 Jaime Cordoba Triviño, "Comunicado de la Corte Constitucional sobre la sentencia que declaró ajustada a la Constitución la Ley 975 de 2005," President of the Colombian Constitutional Court, 19 May 2006.

58 USAID's Justice Program in Colombia was also involved in this work from 1995 to 2005. The USAID Justice Reform and Modernization Program (2006–10) was established to train judicial operators in the new accusatory system; create "justice houses," virtual hearing rooms in remote, conflict-prone areas, and public defender offices; and support civil society organizations to promote justice reform and expand justice services. See US Foreign Operations and Related Programs Appropriations Act, 2009, § 7046(b).

59 DOJ official 1, email communication, 8 September 2010.

60 US State Department, "Memorandum of Justification concerning Human Rights Conditions with Respect to Assistance for the Colombian Armed Forces," Foreign Operations, and Related Programs Appropriations Act, 2 September 2010.

61   US State Department, "Memorandum of Justification," note 9.

62   DOJ official 1, interview, 6 September 2010.

63   Ibid.

64   For example, see Priscilla Hayner, *Unspeakable Truths: Facing the Challenge of Truth Commissions* (New York: Routledge, 2002).

65   DOJ official 1, email communication, 7 September 2010.

66   USAID official 1, interview, 18 August 2010.

67   Eduardo Pizarro, interview, 7 September 2010.

68   USAID, "USAID-Colombia Fact Sheet," April 2010.

69   Data provided by CNRR executive director, 4 September 2010.

70   Eduardo Pizarro, interview, 7 September 2010.

71   Data provided by CNRR executive director, 4 September 2010.

72   Daniel Millares, interview, 23 August 2010.

73   When asked why IOM was chosen as the primary US operator, IOM project coordinator Maria Mejia discussed IOM's long history in Colombia (nearly 60 years), its close relationship with the US and Colombian governments, and its expertise in the field (i.e., experience with DDR in 20 countries and work on reparations). IOM project coordinator, interview, 9 September 2010.

74   Executive Director, National Commission for Reparations and Reconciliation, interview, 26 August 2010.

75   Assessor, Office of International Cooperation, Acción Social, interview, 20 September 2010.

76   For example, MSD works with Fundación País Libre, Fundación Infancia, Corporación Nación, Corporación por Pública, and Fundación Dos Mundos. These organizations provide psychosocial support and legal support for victims bringing cases before the JPU.

77   Coordinator of Victims' Attention Center, País Libre, interview, 7 September 2010.

78   Angela Ceron, interview, 1 September 2010.

79   Gustavo Gallón, interview, 10 September 2010.

80   Woodrow Wilson Center and Fundación Ideas Para La Paz, "Peace Initiatives and Colombia's Armed Conflict," September 2009, preface.

81   Eduardo Pizarro, interview, 7 September 2010.

82   C. W. Cook, "Colombia: Issues for Congress," Congressional Research Service, 9 November 2007.

83   ICG, "Colombia's New Armed Groups," 5; *Guardian*, "Colombia's 'Para-politics' Scandal Casts Shadow Over President," 23 April 2008.

84   ICG, "Colombia Conflict History."

85   Adam Isacson, interview, 2 March 2010.

86   William Brownfield, "Remarks of US Ambassador at a Press Conference in Bogota," 13 May 2008.

87   UC Berkeley School of Law, "Truth behind Bars: Colombian Paramilitary Leaders in US Custody," International Human Rights Law Clinic, February 2010.

88   Paula Gaviria, interview, 8 September 2010.

89   Gustavo Gallón, interview, 10 September 2010.

90   Michael Reed, interview, 27 August 2010.

91   Luis Carlos Restrepo, email communication, 21 September 2010.

92   DOJ official 1, interview, 6 September 2010.

93   US State Department, "Determination and Certification of the Colombian Government and Armed Forces with Respect to Human Rights Related Conditions," 11 September 2009; US State Department, "Determination and Certification of the Colombian Government and Armed Forces with Respect to Human Rights Related Conditions," 15 September 2010.

94   US State Department, "Memorandum of Justification concerning Human Rights Conditions with Respect to Assistance for the Colombian Armed Forces," 8 September 2009, 37.

95   DOJ official 2, interview, 27 August 2010.

96   See Chris Kraul, "Colombia hands ex-paramilitary leader over to U.S." Los Angeles Times, 6 March 2009. In March 2009, paramilitary leader Hebert Veloza Garcia, better known as "HH," was extradited to the US on drug-trafficking charges. Uribe postponed Veloza's original extradition date by six months so he could have more time to confess his misdeeds.

97   US State Department, "Memorandum of Justification," 8 September 2009, 37.

98   DOJ official 2, interview, 27 August 2010.

99   Adam Isacson, interview, 2 March 2010.

100 Travis Mannon, "Committee to Interrogate Extradited Paramilitaries Leaders in US," Colombia Reports, 16 August 2011.

101 Supreme Court, "Aprobada Acta No. 260," 19 August 2009, 44.

102 Ibid., 38.

103 US v. Diego Vecino, "Superseding Indictment," No. 05-00967 (S.D.N.Y.) (3 March 2009); US v. Rendon-Herrera et al., "Superseding indictment," No. 04-962 (S.D.N.Y.) (16 April 2009).

104 Travis Mannon, "Extradited Paramilitaries Should Serve Sentence in Colombia: OAS," Colombia Reports, 21 October 2011.

Conclusion

The United States is a leading supporter of transitional justice. It is often one of the first—and largest—donors to fund transitional justice measures. It contributes detailed, technical expertise to a range of mechanisms, and offers crucial political support at key moments in the lifespan of measures. Without US support, many transitional justice measures would not have been established. Considering the extent of US involvement, and the lack of attention in the literature to its role, this empirical, systematic account of US foreign policy on transitional justice offers an important contribution to scholarship, policy, and practice.

By tracing the development of US foreign policy on transitional justice, and through the examples outlined in the three case studies, this book argues that the US approach is symbolic, retributive, and strategic. We saw how US support for transitional justice is affected by the powerful, symbolic role that a specific and limited concept of "justice" plays in American society. Trials are seen as an enactment of justice in which a simplified version of what happened is told and an alleged perpetrator is deemed responsible. A "get the bad guy" narrative allows the US to perceive itself as the "good guy"—an idea that resonates with dualistic good-versus-evil narratives prevalent in the American psyche. These preconceptions contribute to greater support for and a stronger commitment from policymakers to transitional justice.

We also saw how the United States prefers retributive mechanisms such as trials over restorative ones like truth commissions. This stems in part from greater familiarity with this form of justice, and in part from pride in the US justice system and a desire to "export" it abroad. The composition of the foreign policy bureaucracy, along with the outlook and biases of individuals within it, also support a retributive approach to the field.

Finally, we saw how strategic US interests explain fluctuations in US support to transitional justice. The range of stakeholders in the US foreign policy bureaucracy, their diverse interests, and constantly evolving priorities all contribute to how transitional justice is viewed, and whether it is seen to advance or impede strategic interests. These interests will almost always influence decisions to establish measures, the design of measures, and their operations.

This book's findings contribute to the long-standing interests-versus-values debate in the foreign policy literature.[1] Some scholars believe that interests take precedence over values; some take the opposite view. Others regard the debate as a false dichotomy. Few, however, provide an empirical account of how the conflation of and competition between interests and values plays out in practice. This research contributes to this debate through its three case studies.

In Cambodia, members of Congress and the State Department pressed the UN and Cambodian government to establish a tribunal, but also worked to ensure that the tribunal's jurisdiction was limited to a small number of top leaders responsible for certain crimes during a specific timeframe. After pushing for the establishment of the tribunal, Congress then refused to fund it because of its distrust of the Cambodian prime minister. Eventually, the funding block was lifted, and the United States provided funding and technical assistance to the court.

In Liberia, prosecuting Liberian President Charles Taylor offered one way to achieve the US objective to remove him from power. This idea was dismissed when the option to grant him asylum in Nigeria appeared to be a more expedient way to achieve this goal. Congress, however, kept the idea of prosecution alive and pushed the Bush administration and the State Department to transfer Taylor to the Special Court for Sierra Leone to be tried for war crimes. The United

States contributed a third of the court's budget, far surpassing that of other donors. It provided some technical assistance to the truth commission established in Liberia, but decreased support when the commission recommended sanctioning President Ellen Johnson-Sirleaf, a leader the United States strongly supported.

In Colombia, Congress advocated for strengthening the provisions on accountability for perpetrators in the Colombian justice and peace law, while the Department of Justice pushed to maintain its ability to extradite top drug traffickers that would participate in the justice and peace process. Nevertheless, the United States was the first international donor to support the bodies created by the law, with significant financial and technical assistance provided by the Justice Department and USAID.

The cases do not show that interests take precedence over values, or vice versa, but instead depict how the two are in constant tension with one another, and how this tension, reflected by the diverse and changing interests within the bureaucracy, shapes US policy. Members of Congress can be forceful and effective advocates for transitional justice, but they can also block support for reasons that may be disconnected from the original aims of a measure. Presidential administrations support transitional justice when a measure helps to advance or hinders another key foreign policy objective, or when a president or key members of his administration are personally invested in a particular case. The State Department and other federal agencies, as well as individuals within these agencies, can also have a significant impact on whether and how the United States chooses to support a specific measure. This study's empirical illustration of how interests and values interact with one another to shape US foreign policy may help contribute to a better understanding of US involvement in other areas as well.

A second contribution involves the attention this study pays to the retributive approach of US foreign policy. Scholars have discussed the US "propensity toward a lawyerly foreign policy" and the export of domestic legal norms abroad,[2] but have not highlighted the US preference for criminal prosecutions in transitional justice mechanisms. In Cambodia, we saw the United States focused solely on a criminal tribunal. In Liberia, we saw much greater US attention to and support for prosecuting Taylor than for the establishment of a truth commission. In Colombia, we saw more attention and resources to investigations of paramilitary leaders than the truth-seeking and reparative functions of the justice and peace process. The question of whether the US preference for criminal prosecutions may have broader implications for other areas of US foreign policy merits further study.

A third contribution of this study is its analysis of the multiple sources—including the external, societal, bureaucratic, and individual sources—that underpin the complex reality of US foreign policy. The external, global environment influences how the United States uses fields like transitional justice as a way to increase its power in the international system, how it responds to the behaviors of other state and non-state actors, and how international norms influence US policymaking. The societal environment within the United States influences how deeply rooted American traditions and ideas affect foreign policymaking, as well as the prominent role that domestic interest groups play in lobbying the United States to get involved in a particular issue area. The bureaucratic setting in which policymaking occurs is also of fundamental importance, as this is where foreign policy decisions are actually made and implemented. Lastly, individuals within the US foreign policy bureaucracy play a key role, since even one well-placed individual who takes an interest in a particular issue can have a significant impact on US foreign policy.

Due to the significant role that the United States plays in transitional justice, its choices and attention have broader implications for the field. The US preference for criminal prosecutions of major perpetrators of atrocities has contributed to the spread and prominence of the "justice cascade"—the new trend in world politics toward holding individual state officials criminally accountable for human rights violations.[3] US advocacy of this approach has arguably provided the political backing as well as the technical and financial assistance needed to strengthen this global norm. US conceptions and models of justice have thus influenced this global trend to individualize responsibility and deliver "justice" within the confines of a trial.

The US preference for criminal prosecutions of major perpetrators of atrocities has also meant that other measures of transitional justice receive less support. Considering that the aims of transitional justice are usually broader than holding high-profile perpetrators accountable, a focus on punishing these individuals may be too narrow of an approach, or even viewed as counterproductive for societies that prioritize truth-seeking, reparations, or other measures that promote reconciliation. US prescriptions for transitional justice that fail to consider the populations that have experienced abuse may fail to achieve the underlying purpose of the field to deter the recurrence of violence.

It would be useful to study other cases of US involvement in transitional justice to further test the findings of this research and to assess any changes over time. Considering that the US approach has remained relatively consistent across three administrations, it is likely to remain intact in the years to come. Recent bureaucratic developments support this claim. In 2012, the mandate of the State Department's Office of War Crimes Issues was broadened to include support for a range of tools "to help expose the truth, judge those responsible, protect and assist victims, enable reconciliation, and build the rule of law"—goals similar to those of transitional justice. However, the office's new name—the Office of Global Criminal Justice—clearly suggests its focus and priorities. Also in 2012, President Obama established an interagency Atrocities Prevention Board (APB) to improve the US policy response to genocide and mass atrocities. However, a focus on criminal accountability again appears to be the focus. The White House stated that the United States commits to supporting

> national, hybrid, and international mechanisms (including, among other things, commissions of inquiry, fact finding missions, and tribunals) that seek to hold accountable perpetrators of atrocities when doing so advances US interests and values, consistent with the requirements of US law.[4]

The White House also made specific mention of the role that the Departments of State, Justice, and Homeland Security play in

providing technical assistance to foreign and international prosecutions. With the emphasis on prosecuting perpetrators when it
advances US interests and values, this new initiative appears to reinforce the US approach to transitional justice put forward in this study.

Despite the clear emphasis on criminal accountability, a call for
proposals by the State Department's Bureau of Democracy, Human
Rights, and Labor in 2014 illustrates an attempt to broaden under-
standings of transitional justice. The bureau's "Transitional Justice
Global Initiative" requested proposals from NGOs that

> utilize a range of restorative and retributive approaches to justice and
> accountability for gross human rights violations, including truth-telling,
> reconciliation, memorialization, and other forms of historical memory,
> reparative justice initiatives, legal processes and institutional reform.[5]

Nevertheless, a funding initiative does not indicate the endorsement
of a policy shift. Broadening the US approach to transitional justice
will require a high-level commitment from individuals across the
US foreign policy bureaucracy and time for any significant change
to take root.

It would also be important to compare the US approach to that
of other international actors. A comparative study between the US
and other major donors of transitional justice, such as Canada,
the Netherlands, the United Kingdom, and Japan,[6] would likely
raise interesting results, as would a comparison with the approach
taken by the Swiss and the European Union.[7] Comparative
research on the approach of the UN and international NGOs like
the International Center for Transitional Justice would also be
valuable because of their focus on recognizing victims, fostering
trust, and facilitating the rule of law through the establishment of
particular measures, including trials, truth-seeking, reparations,
and institutional reform. In addition, a comparison with those
organizations In addition, a comparison with those organizations
that emphasize local, traditional, or informal justice processes,[8] or
economic and social justice would also be worthwhile.[9]

A study of the impact of the US approach to transitional justice on the populations that have experienced atrocities, however, is

most pressing. The degree to which the views of victims are absent in this study is revealing, since they do not appear to be a significant factor in US calculations. If the United States aims to support transitional justice mechanisms that help deter the recurrence of violence, the US approach will need to take into account the preferences and needs of these populations.

Notes

1   For example, see Kegley, Wittkopf, and Scott, *American Foreign Policy*, 25–26.
2   Bass, *Stay the Hand of Vengeance*.
3   Sikkink, *Justice Cascade*, 5.
4   US White House, "Fact Sheet: A Comprehensive Strategy and New Tools to Prevent and Respond to Atrocities," *Office of the Press Secretary*, 23 April 2012.
5   US State Department Bureau of Democracy, Human Rights, and Labor, "Request for Proposals: Transitional Justice Global Initiative," 7 March 2014.
6   Muck and Wiebelhaus-Brahm, "Patterns of Transitional Justice Assistance Among the International Community," 31–34.
7   For more on the Swiss model, see the Directorate of Political Affairs, "Introduction," in *Politorbis* (Bern: Federal Department of Foreign Affairs, 2010); and Swiss Peace/FDFA, "Dealing with the Past: Conceptual Framework," 2006. For more on the EU, see Laura Davis, *EU Foreign Policy, Transitional Justice and Mediation: Principle, Policy and Practice* (New York: Routledge, 2014).
8   See, for example, Luc Huyse and Mark Salter, eds., *Reconciliation and Traditional Justice after Violent Conflict: Learning from African Experiences* (Stockholm: International Institute for Democracy and Electoral Assistance, 2008); Lars Waldorf, "Mass Justice for Mass Atrocity: Rethinking Local Justice as Transitional Justice," *Temple Law Review* 79, no. 1 (2006): 1–87; and Kieran McEvoy and Lorna McGregor, *Transitional Justice from Below: Grassroots Activism and the Struggle for Change* (Portland, OR: Hart, 2008).
9   Lisa Hecht and Sabine Michalowski, "Economic and Social Dimensions of Transitional Justice," Essex Transitional Justice Network; Louise Arbour, "Economic and Social Justice for Societies in Transition," *New York University Journal of International Law and Politics* 40 (2007): 1–27; De Greiff and Duthie, *Transitional Justice and Development*.

APPENDIX 1: INTERVIEW DATA

In addition to extensive background research of US government documents, UN and NGO reports, academic sources, and the media, this book drew on 190 semistructured interviews conducted with members of key stakeholder groups in the United States and the case study countries. Fieldwork in Washington, DC, from January to April 2010 was possible because of financial support from the Marshall Commission. While in DC, I was a visiting researcher at Georgetown University. Fieldwork in Liberia was undertaken while carrying out an impact assessment of the TRC for Benetech in November–December 2009. Fieldwork in Cambodia undertaken in June–July 2010 and The Hague in January 2012 was possible due to funding from LSE's International Relations Department. Fieldwork in Colombia was undertaken in July–August 2010 and was possible due to funding from the Abbey Santander Grant.

A cross section of views from key stakeholder groups was taken in order to ensure a mix between case study country actors and international actors. A mix between government and nongovernmental actors was also achieved. Additionally, within each stakeholder group, a variation of views was sought. For example, within the US government, officials from the State Department, USAID, and Congress were interviewed. Interviews with a range of national and international NGOs were conducted. In addition, different perspectives within these groups were sought.

Interviewees were initially identified through personal contacts knowledgeable about transitional justice. Each interviewee was asked if he or she could suggest other possible interviewees, which created a "snowball effect." The same individuals would often be recommended numerous times, and served as a useful cross-check to ensure that key persons were interviewed.

Semistructured interviews were conducted with an interview guide prepared beforehand that provided a framework for the interview. All interviewees were first explained the purpose of the project and asked if the interview could be recorded. They were also asked whether or not the interview could be attributed to the individual. Those interviews conducted on a nonattributable basis were attributed in the way the interviewee requested. Interviews lasted from one to two hours.

Each interview covered similar topics, but left room for certain areas to be explored more thoroughly. Depending on the interviewee's position and perspective, some issues were more relevant than others. Generally speaking, however, each interview solicited views about US involvement in the development of transitional justice more generally, or more specifically, about the establishment and operations of the transitional justice processes explored in this study. Interviews were then analyzed in order to draw out trends and divergences within and across stakeholder groups.

Interviews generated a wealth of material in terms of background information, confirmation of perceptions and views, and usable quotes. The quotations used in this book have been chosen to characterize or typify views or perceptions that have been commonly articulated by interviewees. Only a small proportion of the transcribed material from interviews is reproduced in quote format in this book. Nevertheless, the richness of material gathered through the many interviews and discussions underpins much of the analysis and conclusions reached in this research.

Interview List

Types of Interviews Conducted

	Number
Total interviews conducted	190
Total related to case studies	147
Cambodia	38
Liberia	55
Colombia	58
Total other/general	39
US government	55
Cambodia	6
Liberia	15
Colombia	16
Other	18
Transitional justice measures	23
Cambodia	4
Liberia	9
Colombia	4
Other	6
Case study governments	11
Cambodia	0
Liberia	2
Colombia	9
International organizations	16
Cambodia	4
Liberia	7
Colombia	4
Other	1
International NGOs	34
Cambodia	8
Liberia	11

(continued)

(Continued)

	Number
Colombia	9
Other	6
Local NGOs	19
Cambodia	6
Liberia	10
Colombia	7
Academia	19
Cambodia	9
Liberia	0
Colombia	2
Other	8
Media	3
Cambodia	1
Liberia	0
Colombia	2
US implementing partners (Colombia)	5
Foreign state government	1

Cambodia Interviews

Types of Interviews Conducted for Cambodia Case Study

	Number
Total interviews conducted	**38**
US government	6
State Department	6
Transitional justice measure	4
Extraordinary Chambers in the Courts of Cambodia (ECCC)	4
International organizations	4
United Nations	4
International NGOs	8

(*continued*)

(Continued)

	Number
Open Society Justice Initiative	3
Human Rights Watch	2
International Center for Transitional Justice	1
National Endowment Democracy	2
Cambodian NGOs	6
Documentation Center of Cambodia	3
Cambodian Human Rights and Development Association	1
Cambodian Human Rights Action Committee	1
Center for Justice and Reconciliation	1
Academia	9
Media	1

Cambodia Interview List

Name and Position	Organization	Date
Kent Wiedemann, former US Ambassador to Cambodia	State Department	21 July 2010
US official 1	State Department	4 August 2010
US official 2	State Department	4 April 2010
US official 3	State Department	23 February 2010
State Department official	State Department	18 March 2010
State Department official	State Department	14 April and 4 August 2010
Craig Etcheson, Lead Investigator, Office of Co-Prosecution; Khmer Rouge scholar	ECCC	20 July 2010
Bophal Keat, former head of Victims' Unit (2008–9)	ECCC	23 July 2010
Richard Rogers, Chief of Defence Support Section	ECCC	8 August 2010

(continued)

Name and Position	Organization	Date
Steve Heder, Investigator, ECCC/ Lecturer, SOAS	ECCC / School of Oriental and Asian Studies	28 October 2009
Ton Vong, Legal Associate	UN Office of the High Commissioner for Human Rights	14 July 2010
David Tolbert, former UN Special Expert on UN Assistance to the Khmer Rouge Trials	UN	10 May 2010
UN official	UN	17 June 2010
UN official	UN Office of the High Commissioner for Human Rights	13 November 2009
Long Panhavuth, Program Officer	Open Society Justice Initiative	19 July 2010
Heather Ryan, Monitor of the Khmer Rouge Tribunal	Open Society Justice Initiative	29 July 2010
James Goldston, Executive Director	Open Society Justice Initiative	23 February 2010
Cambodia expert		28 April 2010
Sophie Richardson, Asia Advocacy Director	Human Rights Watch	17 March 2010
Caitlin Reiger, Director, International Policy Relations	International Center for Transitional Justice	3 November 2009
John Knaus, Senior Program Officer for Asia	National Endowment for Democracy	13 April 2010
Lynn Lee, Program Officer for East Asia	National Endowment for Democracy	13 April 2010
Youk Chhang, Director	Documentation Center of Cambodia	15 July 2010
Anne Heindel, Legal Advisor	Documentation Center of Cambodia	15 July 2010

(continued)

(Continued)

Name and Position	Organization	Date
John Ciorciari, Legal Advisor / Assistant Professor	Documentation Center of Cambodia / University of Michigan	10 March and 27 July 2010
President	Cambodian Human Rights and Development Association	19 July 2010
Program Officer	Cambodian Human Rights Action Committee	20 July 2010
Theary Seng, Founder and President	Center for Justice and Reconciliation	8 August 2010
Fred Z. Brown, Lecturer / former US foreign service officer	Johns Hopkins University	6 November 2009
Kenton Clymer, Professor	Northern Illinois University	22 July 2010
David Chandler, Professor	Monash University	24 July 2010
Ben Kiernan, Professor and Director of the Genocide Studies Program	Yale University	20 February 2010
Jaya Ramji-Nogales, Assistant Professor of Law	Temple University	2 November 2009
Pamela Sodhy, Visiting Associate Professor	Georgetown University	1 March 2010
David Steinberg, Professor / former USAID official	Georgetown University / USAID	18 February 2010
Robert Sutter, Visiting Professor	Georgetown University	18 February 2010
Beth Van Schaack, Associate Professor of Law	Santa Clara University	31 October 2009
Journalist		17 July 2010

Liberia Interviews

Types of Interviews Conducted for Liberia Case Study

	Number
Total interviews conducted	**55**
US government	15
State Department	9
USAID	3
Congress	2
Department of Justice	1
Transitional justice measures	9
Special Court for Sierra Leone	3
Liberian Truth and Reconciliation Commission (TRC)	6
Liberian government	2
Executive	1
Legislature	1
Foreign state government	1
International Contact Group on Liberia	1
International organizations	7
UN Mission in Liberia	6
UNDP-Monrovia	1
International NGOs	11
International Center for Transitional Justice	2
Carter Center	3
American Bar Association	1
Search for Common Ground	1
Open Society Initiative of West Africa	1
Human Rights Watch	1
US Institute of Peace	1
Benetech	1
Liberian NGOs	10
Justice and Peace Commission	1
Liberian Council of Churches	1

(continued)

(Continued)

	Number
Transitional Justice Working Group	2
Women's NGO Secretariat of Liberia	1
Civil society and youth leaders	5

Liberia Interview List

Name and Position	Organization	Date
Jendayi Frazer, Assistant Secretary of State for African Affairs (2005–9)	State Department	9 April 2010
Pamela Bridgewater, Deputy Assistant Secretary for African Affairs (2002–4)	State Department	21 April 2010
Chester Crocker, Assistant Secretary of State for African Affairs (1981–89)	State Department	16 February 2010
Michael Arietti, Director, Office of West African Affairs (2001–4)	State Department	9 May 2011
US official	State Department	16 March 2010
US official	State Department	18 May 2010
US official 1	State Department	10 December 2009
US official	State Department	10 December 2009
US official 2	State Department	25 January 2010
US official	USAID	3 December 2009
DOJ official	Department of Justice	8 December 2009

(continued)

(Continued)

Name and Position	Organization	Date
USAID official, Office of Transition Initiatives	USAID	7 April 2010
USAID official	USAID	13 April 2010
Congressional staff member	Senate	24 March 2010
Congressional staff member	House of Representatives	12 April 2010
David Crane, Chief Prosecutor	Special Court for Sierra Leone	19 April 2010
Gregory Townsend, Senior Legal Officer	Special Court for Sierra Leone	12 January 2012
Chris Mahony, Consultant	Special Court for Sierra Leone and Truth and Reconciliation Commission for Sierra Leone	29 January 2012
Jerome Verdier, TRC Chairman	Liberian Truth and Reconciliation Commission	9 December 2009
Gerald B. Coleman, TRC Commissioner	Liberian Truth and Reconciliation Commission	10 December 2009
Pearl Brown Bull, TRC Commissioner	Liberian Truth and Reconciliation Commission	7 December 2009
Salif Massalay, statement coder	Liberian Truth and Reconciliation Commission	23 November 2009
TRC staff member	Liberian Truth and Reconciliation Commission	26 January 2010
Senior TRC staff member	Liberian Truth and Reconciliation Commission	3 December 2009

(continued)

Name and Position	Organization	Date
Natty Davis, Minister of State Development and Reconstruction	Office of the President, Liberia	2 December 2009
Rep. G. Wesseh Blamoh, Chairman, Standing Committee on Peace and National Reconciliation	Legislature of Liberia	3 December 2009
Member	International Contact Group on Liberia	28 November 2009
International rule of law advisor	UNMIL	8 December 2009
International observer 1	UNMIL	30 November 2009
International observer 2	UNMIL/OHCHR	28 November 2009
International observer	UNMIL	26 November 2009
International observer	UNMIL	26 November 2009
International observer	UNDP, Monrovia	30 November 2009
Macdonald Metzger, Media Consultant for ICTJ / Radio Producer for UNMIL	International Center for Transitional Justice / UNMIL	28 November 2009
International NGO staff member	International NGO	9 December 2010
ICTJ staff member	International Center for Transitional Justice	2 December 2009
Liberia Country Director	American Bar Association, Rule of Law Initiative	7 December 2009
Staff member	Search for Common Ground / Talking Drums	7 December 2009

(continued)

Name and Position	Organization	Date
Staff member	Open Society Initiative of West Africa	27 November 2009
Tom Crick, Associate Director	Carter Center	28 June 2009
Project Officer	Carter Center	8 December 2009
Pewee Flomoku, Project Coordinator	Carter Center	8 December 2009
Elise Keppler, Senior Counsel, International Justice Program	Human Rights Watch	23 February 2010
Abiodun Williams, Vice President of the Centre for Conflict Analysis and Prevention	US Institute of Peace	26 February 2010
Kirsten Cibelli, Program Manager	Benetech	21 November 2009
Augustine Toe, National Director	Justice and Peace Commission	2 December 2009
Benjamin Lartey, General Secretary	Liberian Council of Churches	3 December 2009
James Yarsiah, Coordinator of the Transitional Justice Working Group and Executive Director of Rights and Rice Foundation	Transitional Justice Working Group/ Rights and Rice Foundation	28 November 2009
Kanio Gbala, Coordinator of the Transitional Justice Working Group and Programme Manager of the PRS Tracking Network	Transitional Justice Working Group / PRS Tracking Network	27 November 2009
Staff member	Women NGO Secretariat of Liberia	27 November 2009

(continued)

Name and Position	Organization	Date
Alex Ballo, community leader	Sinje, Grand Cape Mount	1 December 2009
Civil society leader 1	Focus group in Buchanan, Grand Bassa	4 December 2009
Civil society leader 2	Focus group in Buchanan, Grand Bassa	4 December 2009
Youth leader 1	Focus group in Kakata, Margibi	26 November 2009
Youth leader 2	Focus group in Kakata, Margibi	26 November 2009

Colombia Interviews

Types of Interviews Conducted for Colombia Case Study

	Number
Total interviews conducted	**58**
US government	16
State Department	7
USAID	6
Senate	1
Department of Justice	2
US implementing partners	5
International Organization of Migration	2
Management Sciences for Development	3

(*continued*)

(Continued)

	Number
Transitional justice measures	4
Justice and Peace Unit	2
National Commission for Reparation and Reconciliation	2
Colombian government	9
Prosecutor-General	1
Acción Social	3
National Planning Department	2
Office of the High Commissioner for Reintegration	1
Office of the High Commissioner for Peace	1
Ministry of the Interior and Justice	1
International organizations	4
Organization of American States	1
United Nations	2
World Bank	1
International NGOs	9
International Center for Transitional Justice	3
Center for International Policy	1
Washington Office on Latin America	2
Human Rights First	1
Woodrow Wilson Center	1
US Institute of Peace	1
Colombian NGOs	7
Colombia Commission of Jurists	1
Fundación Ideas para la Paz	1
Arco Iris	1
Fundación Social	1
País Libre	1
Iniciativa de Mujeres Colombianas por la Paz	1
Independent consultant	1
Academia	2
Media	2

Colombia Interview List

Name	Organization	Date
Director, Demobilization and Reintegration Program	USAID/Colombia	31 August 2010
Sandra Pabón, Assistant Director, Demobilization and Reintegration Program	USAID/Colombia	31 August 2010
USAID official 1	USAID/Colombia	18 August 2010
USAID official	USAID/Colombia	18 August 2010
USAID official	USAID	9 March 2010
USAID official	USAID	9 March 2010
Myles Frechette, US Ambassador to Colombia (1983–87)	US Embassy in Colombia	7 April 2010
Embassy official	US Embassy in Colombia	23 August 2010
State Department official	State Department	23 March 2010
State Department official, Bureau of Democracy, Human Rights and Labor	State Department	12 March 2010
State Department official, Office of the Coordinator for Reconstruction and Stabilization	State Department	12 April 2010
State Department official, Office of the Coordinator for Reconstruction and Stabilization	State Department	22 March 2010
State Department official, Office of the Coordinator for Reconstruction and Stabilization	State Department	22 March 2010

(*continued*)

Name	Organization	Date
Janet Drew, staff member	Senate Caucus on International Narcotics Control	24 March 2010
DOJ official 1	Department of Justice	6 September 2010 (interview) / 7–8 September 2010 (email communication)
DOJ official 2	Department of Justice	27 August 2010
Project Coordinator	International Organization of Migration	9 September 2010
Staff member	International Organization of Migration	7 September 2010
Staff member	Management Sciences for Development	1 September 2010
Staff member	Management Sciences for Development	1 September 2010
Staff member	Management Sciences for Development	31 August 2010
Luis González León, Director, Justice and Peace Unit	Prosecutor General's Office	3 September 2010
Loreley Oviedo, staff member, International Cooperation, Justice and Peace Unit	Prosecutor General's Office	3 September 2010
Eduardo Pizarro, President	National Commission for Reparations and Reconciliation	7 September 2010

(continued)

Name	Organization	Date
Executive Director	National Commission for Reparations and Reconciliation	26 August 2010
Patricia Linares Prieto, former delegate of the Procuradora to CNRR	Procuradora	26 August 2010
Sandra Alzate, Director	Acción Social	25 August 2010
Viviana Cañon Tamayo, Assessor, Office of International Cooperation	Acción Social	20 September 2010
Gloria Gomez, Assessor, Office of International Cooperation	Acción Social	3 September 2010
Luis Carlos Restrepo, High Commissioner for Peace	Office of the High Commissioner for Peace	21 September 2010
Paola Buendia, Director of the Justice and Security Unit	National Planning Department	19 August 2010
Paula Aponte, staff member, Justice and Security Unit	National Planning Department	19 August 2010
Heidi Abuchaibe, Director of Transitional Justice	Ministry of the Interior and Justice	1 September 2010
Colombian government official	Office of the High Commissioner for Reintegration	10 September 2010
Daniel Millares, Justice and Peace Manager, Mission to Support the Peace Process in Colombia	Organization of American States	23 August 2010
Veronica Hinestroza, Consultant	World Bank	20 August 2010

(continued)

(Continued)

Name	Organization	Date
UN official	UN Department of Peacekeeping Operations	22 February 2010
UN official	UN Department of Political Affairs	23 February 2010
Michael Reed, Colombia expert	Independent	27 August 2010
Angelica Zamora, staff member, Colombia office	International Center for Transitional Justice	19 March 2010
Cristina Rivera, Communications Associate, Colombia office	International Center for Transitional Justice	25 August 2010
Adam Isacson, Director	Center for International Policy	2 March 2010
Gimena Sanchez, Senior Associate for the Andes	Washington Office on Latin America	18 March 2010
Anthony Dest, Intern	Washington Office on Latin America	18 March 2010
Andrew Hudson, Senior Associate	Human Rights First	8 September 2009
Colombia expert	Woodrow Wilson Center	10 March 2010
Virginia Bouvier, Senior Program Officer for Latin America	US Institute of Peace	25 February 2010
Gustavo Gallón, President	Colombia Commission of Jurists	10 September 2010
Maria Victoria Llorente, Director	Fundación Ideas para la Paz	24 August 2010

(continued)

Name	Organization	Date
Lucho Celis, Coordinator	Arco Iris	24 August 2010
Paula Gaviria, Director of Public Policy	Fundación Social	8 September 2010
Coordinator of Victims' Attention Center	País Libre	7 September 2010
Angela Cerón, Director	Iniciativa de Mujeres Colombianas por la Paz	1 September 2010
Álvaro Cordoba, Consultant	UNDP/USAID/CNRR	25 October 2009
Florian Huber, Doctoral Candidate	University of Göttingen	16 October 2009
Lerber Lisandro, Investigator	National University of Colombia	6 September 2010
Marta Ruiz, Editor, Security and Justice Section	Semana	24 August 2010
Toby Muse, Independent Media Consultant	Independent	28 August 2010

General Interviews

Types of General Interviews

	Number
Total interviews conducted	**39**
US government	18
Transitional justice measures	6
International organizations	1
NGOs	6
Academia	8

List of General Interviewees

Name	Organization	Date
David Scheffer, Ambassador-at-Large for War Crimes Issues (1997–2001)	State Department	12 March 2012
Pierre Prosper, Ambassador-at-Large for War Crimes Issues (2001–5)	State Department	22 April 2010
Clint Williamson, Ambassador-at-Large for War Crimes Issues (2006–9)	State Department	21 April 2010
Stephen Rapp, Ambassador-at-Large for War Crimes Issues (2009–)	State Department	26 July 2010
Anne-Marie Slaughter, Head of Policy Planning (2009–11) / Professor	State Department / Princeton University	23 May 2012
Donald McHenry, former US Ambassador to the UN / Professor	USUN / Georgetown University	1 March 2010
Anthony Lake, former National Security Council Advisor / Professor	National Security Council / Georgetown University	18 February 2010
Victor Cha, Former Asian Affairs Director / Professor	National Security Council / Georgetown University	1 March 2010
US official	National Security Council	20 April 2010
Senate staff member	Senate	8 January 2010

(continued)

(Continued)

Name	Organization	Date
David Hodgkinson, Director, Office of Human Rights and Transitional Justice, Coalition Provisional Authority	State Department	8 April 2010
Andy Loomis, Senior Conflict Prevention Officer	State Department	12 March 2010
Lisa Chandonnet-Bedoya, Program Analyst, Office of Conflict Management & Mitigation	USAID	6 April 2010
Marie Pace, Democracy Specialist, Office of Civilian Response	USAID	20 April 2010
Andrew Natsios, Administrator	USAID	22 March 2010
Grant Harris, Senior Policy Advisor	USUN	24 February 2010
Professional staff member	House Foreign Affairs Committee	16 April 2010
State Department official	State Department	14 April 2010
ICTY Special Advisor to the Prosecutor	International Criminal Tribunal for the Former Yugoslavia	13 January 2012
Matias Hellman, External Relations Advisor, Office of the President	International Criminal Court	13 January 2012
Rod Rastan, Legal Advisor, Office of the Prosecutor	International Criminal Court	13 January 2012
Court official	Special Tribunal for Lebanon	12 January 2012
Court official	Special Tribunal for Lebanon	12 January 2012
Court official	International Criminal Tribunal for Rwanda	13 January 2012

(continued)

Name	Organization	Date
Kaoru Okuizumi, transitional justice focal point in the judicialof section	UN Department Peacekeeping Operations	4 March 2010
Tom Melia, Senior Advisor	Freedom House	9 March 2010
Tom Malinowski, Washington Advocacy Director	Human Rights Watch	15 March 2010
Paige Arthur, Deputy Director, Institutional Development	International Center for Transitional Justice	22 February 2010
Juan Mendez, President Emeritus	International Center for Transitional Justice	9 April 2010
Morton Halperin, Senior Advisor	Open Society Foundations	19 March 2010
Neil Kritz, Senior Scholar in Residence	US Institute of Peace	16 March 2010
Charles Kupchan, Professor	Georgetown University	16 February 2010
Lynn C. Ross, Professor	Georgetown University	19 February 10
Pauline Baker, Adjunct Professor / Director of Fund for Peace	Georgetown University	4 November 2009
Erik Voeten, Associate Professor	Georgetown University	17 March 2010
Julie Shackford-Bradley, Lecturer	UC Berkeley	2 November 2009
Richard Wilson, Professor of Law / Director of the International Human Rights Law Clinic	American University	4 November 2009
Victor Peskin, Associate Professor	Arizona State University	30 June 2009
Eric Stover, Adjunct Professor of Law and Public Health; Faculty Director, Human Rights Center	UC Berkeley	12 February 2009

APPENDIX 2: CASE STUDY TIMELINES

Cambodia Timeline

1969–73	President Nixon approves covert bombing of Cambodia.
1975–79	Khmer Rouge in power.
1979–89	Vietnamese control of Cambodia.
1991	Paris Peace Accords; establishment of UN Transitional Authority.
1993	Elections in Cambodia; UN withdraws.
1994	United States passes Cambodian Genocide Justice Act.
1997	Cambodian request to UN for assistance with a tribunal; Hun Sen stages coup.
1997–2001	David Scheffer serves as first US ambassador for war crimes issues.
1998	Hun Sen wins elections in Cambodia; United States circulates draft for an international criminal tribunal; UN Group of Experts commissioned.
1999	UN Group of Experts release their report; Cambodia rejects report; mixed tribunal is proposed by the United States.
2001	Cambodia passes the law to establish the Extraordinary Chambers in the Courts of Cambodia.

2002	UN withdraws from court negotiations with Cambodia.
2003	UN resumes negotiations and signs an agreement with Cambodia on the court's establishment.
2004	UN/Cambodia Agreement approved by Cambodia's National Assembly.
2004–7	US Congress blocks funding for the court.
2008	United States announces $1.8 million for the tribunal.
2009	Court's first trial begins.
2010	First defendant convicted; former US war crimes ambassador Clint Williamson appointed as UN special expert to ECCC.
2011	Court's second trial begins.

Liberia Timeline

1821	African Americans establish settlements in Liberia.
1847	Liberia achieves independence.
1971	Liberian president William Tubman dies while in office. Tubman's vice president, William Tolbert, assumes the presidency.
1980–89	Samuel Doe leads a coup and assumes power. Doe wins elections in 1985.
1989–97	Liberia's first civil war between Charles Taylor's National Patriotic Front of Liberia (NPFL) and six other major factions.
1997	Charles Taylor wins the presidential election.
1999–2003	Liberia's second civil war.
2001	The UN Security Council imposes sanctions on Liberia because of Taylor's support of the Revolutionary United Front (RUF) in Sierra Leone.
2002	The Special Court for Sierra Leone established to address serious crimes against civilians during the country's civil war.
2003	Liberian peace talks in Ghana. The Special Court for Sierra Leone unseals an indictment against Taylor. Taylor resigns and accepts asylum in Nigeria. A peace

agreement is signed, which establishes a two-year transitional government. The UN Mission in Liberia (UNMIL) takes over peacekeeping operations.

2005   The Truth and Reconciliation Commission (TRC) Act is passed. Ellen Johnson-Sirleaf wins the presidential election.

2006   Charles Taylor is arrested and transferred to the Special Court for Sierra Leone. The work of the TRC begins.

2007   Taylor's trial begins.

2008   Volume 1 of the TRC's final report is released.

2009   Complete TRC final report released.

2011   Johnson-Sirleaf is re-elected as president of Liberia.

2012   Taylor found guilty by the Special Court for Sierra Leone for war crimes and crimes against humanity.

Colombia Timeline

1948   Riots in Bogota give rise to a 10-year period of civil conflict.

1960s   The emergence of several non-state armed groups in remote areas of the country, in particular, the ELN and FARC, that ignite the current conflict.

1980s   The emergence of paramilitary groups to provide private security for important economic and political sectors in Colombia.

1997   Various paramilitary groups consolidate with the creation of an umbrella body—the United Self-Defense Forces of Colombia (AUC).

1999   Clinton administration announces Plan Colombia.

2002   Álvaro Uribe is elected as president of Colombia.

2003   The Colombian government and the AUC sign a framework peace accord committing paramilitaries to full demobilization by the end of 2005.

2005   The Justice and Peace Law is passed.

2008   14 AUC leaders are extradited to the United States.

2010   Juan Manuel Santos is elected as president of Colombia.

APPENDIX 3: LIST OF TRANSITIONAL JUSTICE ACTORS

Note: This is an illustrative list, not a comprehensive one.

International organizations

Office for the High Commissioner of Human Rights

UN Department of Peacekeeping Operations

UN Development Programme (UNDP)

UNICEF

World Bank

International NGOs

International Center for Transitional Justice

Amnesty International

Center for Justice and International Law (CEJIL)

Human Rights Watch

Humanitarian Law Center

Open Society Justice Initiative

International Coalition of Sites of Conscience

Local NGOs

The Arab Institute for Human Rights

The Association for Human Rights (APRODEH)

The Association for Truth and Reconciliation

The Burma Lawyers' Council (BLC)

The Center for Human Rights Legal Action (CALDH)

The Center for Legal and Social Studies (CELS)

The Centre for Democracy and Development (CDD)

The Centre for the Study of Violence and Reconciliation

The Commission on Involuntary Disappearances and Victims of Violence (KONTRAS)

Conflict Management and Development Associates (CMDA)

The Congolese Coalition for Transitional Justice (CCJT)

Documentation Center of Cambodia (DC-Cam)

The East Timor Steering Committee on the Truth Commission

The Foundation Ideas for Peace

The Ghana Center for Democratic Development

The Greensboro Truth and Community Reconciliation Project

Groupe Lotus

Guatemalan Forensic Anthropology Foundation (FAFG)

The Healing Through Remembering Project

Human Rights Education Institute of Burma (HREIB)

The Human Rights Information and Documentation Center (INDOK)

The Human Rights Office of the Social Foundation

The Institute for Justice and Reconciliation (IJR)

Institute for Policy Research and Advocacy (ELSAM)

The International Centre for Ethnic Studies

Iraq Memory Foundation

The Kenya Human Rights Commission

The Khulumani Support Group (KSG)

The Kosovar Research and Documentation Institute (KODI)

The Law & Society Trust

The Lebanese Center for Policy Studies

Legal Aid Foundation (YLBHI)

The Liberia National Law Enforcement Association (LINLEA)

The Mexican Commission for the Defense and Promotion of Human Rights (CMDPDH)

The Moroccan Center for Documentation, Information and Training in Human Rights

The National Forum for Human Rights, Sierra Leone

The National Human Rights Coordinating Group (CNDDHH)
The NGO Follow-up Committee, Morocco
Peace Advocates for Truth and Healing (PATH)
The Post-conflict Reintegration Initiative for Development and
Empowerment (PRIDE)
The Research and Documentation Center (Sarajevo)
The Sierra Leone Court Monitoring Programme (SLCMP)
The Sustainable Democracy Center (SDC), Lebanon
The Task Force Detainees of the Philippines (TFDP)
The Transitional Justice Working Group in Liberia
The Transitional Justice Working Group in Sri Lanka
UMAM Documentation & Research

Universities

The Centre for the Study of Human Rights (CSHR), University of
Colombo, Sri Lanka
Essex Transitional Justice Network, University of Essex, UK
The Human Rights Center, University of California, Berkeley, United
States
The Human Rights Center of the University of Chile Law School, Chile
Katholieke Universiteit Leuven, Belgium
London Transitional Justice Network, UK
Oxford Transitional Justice Research, UK
Transitional Justice Institute, University of Ulster, UK
Transitional Justice Project at the Center for Civil and Human Rights,
University of Notre Dame, United States
New York University Law School's Justice in Transition Program, United
States
Columbia Law School, United States
Transitional Justice Database Project, University of Wisconsin, United
States

Foundations

Ford Foundation
MacArthur Foundation

BIBLIOGRAPHY

Adams, Brad. "No Pass for the Khmer Rouge." *Washington Post*, 18 April 2000.
———. "Snatching Defeat from the Jaws of Victory?" *Phnom Penh Post*, 25 January 1999.
Adler, E. "Constructivism and International Relations." In *Handbook of International Relations*, edited by W. Carlnaes, T. Risse, and B. Simmons. London: Sage, 2002.
Advocates for Human Rights. "A House with Two Rooms: Final Report of the Truth and Reconciliation Commission of Liberia Diaspora Project." Dispute Resolution Institute at Hamline University School of Law, Saint Paul, MN, 2009.
Agence France-Presse. "Cambodia Lauds Fresh US Proposal to Break Khmer Rouge Trial Deadlock." 17 April 2000.
———. "Khmers Rouges: Védrine favorable à un procès au Cambodge." 14 January 2000.
Agreement Between the United Nations and the Royal Government of Cambodia on the ECCC. 2004.
Agreement on a Comprehensive Political Settlement of the Cambodia Conflict. 23 October 1991.
Alexander, J. "A Scoping Study of Transitional Justice and Poverty Reduction." Final Report for DFID. 2003.
Alexander, Jeffrey C. *Remembering the Holocaust: A Debate*. New York: Oxford University Press, 2009.
Alfaro, Richard J., Special Rapporteur. "Report on the Question of International Criminal Jurisdiction." A/CN.4/15. *Yearbook of the International Law Commission* 2 (1950).
Allison, Graham T. *Essence of Decision: Explaining the Cuban Missile Crisis*. Boston: Little, Brown, 1971.
Alvarez, Jose E. "Trying Hussein: Between Hubris and Hegemony." *Journal of International Criminal Justice* 2 (2004): 319–29.

Amann, Diane Marie, and M. N. S. Sellers. "United States of America and the International Criminal Court." *American Journal of Comparative Law* 50 (supplement) (2002): 381–404.

American Society of International Law. "Transitional Justice, Rule of Law and the Creation of the Civilian Response Corps." 22 January 2009. http://www.crs.state.gov/index.cfm?fuseaction=public.display&shortcut=C4MB.

Amnesty International. "Nigeria: Surrender Charles Taylor to Special Court for Sierra Leone." 11 August 2005.

Appeals Chamber Decision on Preliminary Motion Based on Lack of Jurisdiction (Judicial Independence). *Prosecutor v. Sam Hinga Norman.* SCSL-2004-14-AR72(E). 13 March 2004.

Arbour, Louise. "Economic and Social Justice for Societies in Transition." Annual Lecture on Transitional Justice, New York University School of Law. 25 October 2006.

———. "Economic and Social Justice for Societies in Transition." *New York University Journal of International Law and Politics* 40 (2007): 1–27.

Arnold, Thurman. *The Symbols of Government.* New Haven: Yale University Press, 1935.

Arnson, Cynthia. "The Peace Process in Colombia with the Autodefensas Unidas de Colombia-AUC." Woodrow Wilson Center Report on the Americas, no. 13. 2005.

Arthur, Paige. "How 'Transitions' Reshaped Human Rights: A Conceptual History of Transitional Justice." *Human Rights Quarterly* 31 (2009): 321–67.

Arthur, Paige, and Debbie Sharnak. "Data Collected on Transitional Justice Funding." Forthcoming.

Arthur, W. Brian. *Increasing Returns and Path Dependence in the Economy.* Ann Arbor: University of Michigan Press, 1994.

Asian Wall Street Journal. "The Growing Cambodia-China Alliance." 28 July 2000.

Askin, Kelly. "The Quest for Post-conflict Gender Justice." *Columbia Journal of Transnational Law* 41 (2003): 509–21.

Associated Press. "Clinton to Pursue Khmer Leaders." 17 April 1998.

———. "Progress for Khmer Rouge Trial Seen." 10 January 2000.

———. "U.S. Envoy Backs Cambodia Tribunal." 9 March 2000.

———. "UN Pressured over Cambodia Tribunal." 14 March 2000.

Bali, Ash U. "Justice under Occupation: Rule of Law and the Ethics of Nation-Building in Iraq." *Yale Journal of International Law* 30 (2005): 431–72.

Bangkok Post. "Column Reports Interview with Hun Sen." 3 May 1991.

———. "Politicians Still at Play in 'Killing Fields.'" 29 April 2000.

Barnett, Michael, and Raymond Duvall. "Power in International Politics." *International Organization* 59 (2005): 39–75.

Bass, Gary Jonathan. *Stay the Hand of Vengeance.* Princeton, NJ: Princeton University Press, 2002.

Bassiouni, M. Cherif. "Post-conflict Justice in Iraq: An Appraisal of the Iraq Special Tribunal." *Cornell International Law Journal* 38 (2005): 327–90.

BBC News. "Charles Taylor: Preacher, Warlord, President." 13 July 2009.

———. "Taylor 'Not' a Priority for Liberia." 27 January 2006.

———. "U.S. Seeks Colombian Extraditions." 18 May 2004.

Becker, Elizabeth. *When the War Was Over: The Voices of Cambodia's Revolution and Its People.* New York: Simon and Schuster, 1986.

Bennett, W. Lance, and David L. Paletz. *Taken by Storm: The Media, Public Opinion, and U.S. Foreign Policy in the Gulf War.* Chicago: University of Chicago Press, 1994.

Bernstein, Richard. "As Notorious Khmer Figure Is Tried, Few in U.S. Take Notice." *New York Times,* 3 December 2009.

Bird, Annie. "The Development of US Foreign Policy on Transitional Justice: The Role of the US War Crimes Ambassadors." International Studies Association Annual Convention, San Diego, CA, 2012.

Boraine, Alex, Janet Levy, Ronel Scheffer, and Institute for a Democratic Alternative for South Africa. *Dealing with the Past: Truth and Reconciliation in South Africa.* Cape Town: IDASA, 1994.

Boston Globe. "Former Liberian Dictator Charles Taylor Had US Spy Agency Ties." 17 January 2012.

Boulding, Kenneth. "National Images and International Systems." *Journal of Conflict Resolution* 3, no. 2 (1959): 120–31.

Bouvier, Virginia. "Evaluating US Foreign Policy in Colombia." Policy Report for the International Relations Center Americas. 11 May 2005.

Bravin, Jess. "U.S. Warms to Hague Tribunal: New Stance Reflects Desire to Use Court to Prosecute Darfur Crimes." *Wall Street Journal,* 14 June 2006.

Bright, Nancee Oku. "Liberia: America's Stepchild." Transcript of PBS documentary, 10 October 2002.

Brogan, D. W. *America in the Modern World.* New Brunswick, NJ: Rutgers University Press, 1960.

———. *Politics in America.* Rev. ed. Garden City, NY: Doubleday, 1972.

Brooke, James. "Mission to Liberia Evidently Fails." *New York Times,* 5 December 1988.

Broomhall, Bruce. *International Justice and the International Criminal Court: Between Sovereignty and the Rule of Law.* New York: Oxford University Press, 2003.

Brown, Bartram. "U.S. Objections to the Statute of the International Criminal Court: A Brief Response." *New York University Journal of International Law and Politics* 31 (1999): 855.

———. "Unilateralism, Multilateralism, and the International Criminal Court." In *Multilateralism and US Foreign Policy: Ambivalent Engagement,* edited by Stewart Patrick and Shepard Forman. Boulder, CO: Lynne Rienner, 2002.

Brown, Chris. "Ethics, Interests and Foreign Policy." In *Ethics and Foreign Policy*, edited by Karen Elizabeth Smith and Margot Light. New York: Cambridge University Press, 2001.

Brown, Fred Z. *Second Chance: The United States and Indochina in the 1990s*. New York: Council on Foreign Relations Press, 1989.

Brownfield, William. "Remarks of US Ambassador at a Press Conference in Bogota." 13 May 2008.

Bryce, James. *The American Commonwealth*. London: Macmillan, 1888.

Bryden, Alan, and Heiner Hänggi, eds. *Security Governance in Post-conflict Peacebuilding*. Münster: LIT; Piscataway, NJ: distributed in North America by Transaction Publishers, 2005.

Buckley-Zistel, Susanne, and Ruth Stanley, eds. *Gender in Transitional Justice*. New York: Palgrave Macmillan, 2012.

Cambodia Tribunal Monitor. "Composite Chronology of the Evolution and Operation of the Extraordinary Chambers in the Courts of Cambodia." No date.

Campaign Against Impunity. "Civil Society Coalition Letter to New Liberian President Johnson-Sirleaf." 26 January 2006.

Campbell, Kirsten. "The Gender of Transitional Justice: Law, Sexual Violence and the International Criminal Tribunal for the Former Yugoslavia." *International Journal Transitional Justice* 1, no. 3 (2007): 411–32.

Carrillo, Arturo. "Truth, Justice and Reparations in Colombia: The Path to Peace and Reconciliation?" In *Colombia: Building Peace in a Time of War*, edited by Virginia Bouvier. Washington, DC: US Institute of Peace, 2009.

Carrillo-Suarez, A. "*Hors de logique*: Contemporary Issues in International Humanitarian Law as Applied to Internal Armed Conflict." *American University International Law Review* 15, no. 1 (1999): 1–150.

Center for International Policy. "Paramilitary Talks (6): Extradition and the U.S. Role." 15 December 2004.

Cerone, John P. "Dynamic Equilibrium: The Evolution of US Attitudes toward International Criminal Courts and Tribunals." *European Journal of International Law* 18, no. 2 (2007): 277–315.

———. "U.S. Attitudes toward International Criminal Courts and Tribunals." In *The Sword and the Scales: The United States and International Courts and Tribunals*, edited by Cesare P. R. Romano. New York: Cambridge University Press, 2009.

Chandler, David, and Volker Heins. *Rethinking Ethical Foreign Policy: Pitfalls, Possibilities and Paradoxes*. New York: Routledge, 2007.

Chang, Chih-Hann. *Ethical Foreign Policy? US Humanitarian Interventions*. Burlington, VT: Ashgate, 2011.

Chapman, Audrey R. "Approaches to Studying Reconciliation." In *Assessing the Impact of Transitional Justice: Challenges for Empirical Research*, edited by Hugo Van Der Merwe, Victoria Baxter, and Audrey R. Chapman. Washington, DC: United States Institute of Peace Press, 2009.

Checkel, Jeffrey. "Constructivism and Foreign Policy." In *Foreign Policy: Theories, Actors, Cases,* edited by Steve Smith, Amelia Hadfield, and Tim Dunne. New York: Oxford University Press, 2008.

Clinton, William J. "Remarks at the University of Connecticut." 31 *Weekly Compilation of Presidential Documents* 1840, 1842. 23 October 1995.

———. "Remarks to the 52nd Session of the United Nations General Assembly in New York City." 33 *Weekly Compilation of Presidential Documents* 1386, 1389. 29 September 1997.

Clymer, Kenton. *The United States and Cambodia, 1969-2000: A Troubled Relationship.* New York: Routledge, 2004.

Colby, William, and Jeremy Stone. "Thailand Can Become the Key to Restraining the Khmer Rouge." *Los Angeles Times,* 23 October 1989.

Commission on the Responsibilities of the Authors of the War and on the Enforcement of Penalties. "Report Presented to the Preliminary Peace Conference, March 29, 1919, Annex II: Memorandum of Reservations Presented by the Representatives of the United States to the Report of the Commission on Responsibilities." *American Journal of International Law* 14 (1920): 95–154.

Comprehensive Peace Agreement Between the Government of Liberia and the LURD and the MODEL and Political Parties (CPA). Accra, Ghana. 18 August 2003.

Comunicado Casa de Nariño. 28 April 2004.

Congressional Research Service. "Colombia: Conditions and US Policy Options." 12 February 2001.

———. "Colombia: Summary and Tables on U.S. Assistance, FY1989–FY2003." 3 May 2002.

———. "Colombia: The Uribe Administration and Congressional Concerns." 14 June 2002.

Cook, C. W. "Colombia: Issues for Congress." Congressional Research Service. 9 November 2007.

Cook, Christopher R. "A Question of Intervention: American Policymaking in Sierra Leone and the Power of Institutional Agenda Setting." *African Studies Quarterly* 10, no. 1 (2008): 1–33.

Cook, Nicolas. "Liberia's Post-war Development: Key Issues and U.S. Assistance." Congressional Research Service. 25 May 2010.

———. "Liberia's Post-war Recovery: Key Issues and Developments." Congressional Research Service. 13 December 2005.

Creative Associates. "The Road to Peace in Liberia: Citizens Views on Transitional Justice." Transitional Justice Working Group Initiative. August–September 2004.

Cruvellier, Thierry. "Why Try Taylor in the Hague?" *International Justice Tribune*, 10 April 2006.

Cubides, F. *Burocracias armadas: El problema de la organización en el entramado de las violencias colombianas.* Bogotá: Norma, 2005.

———. "De lo privado y de lo público en la violencia colombiana: Los paramilitares." In *Las violencias: Inclusión creciente*, edited by J. Arocha, F. Cubides, and M. Jimeno. Bogotá: Centro de Estudios Sociales, Universidad Nacional de Colombia, 1998.

———. "Los paramilitares como agentes organizados de violencia: Su dimensión territorial." In *Violencia y Desarrollo Municipal*, edited by F. Cubides, C. Olaya, and C. M. Ortiz. Bogotá: Centro de Estudios Sociales, Universidad Nacional de Colombia, 1995.

———. "Narcotráfico y paramilitarismo ¿Matrimonio Indisoluble?" In *El Poder Paramilitar*, edited by A. Rangel. Bogotá: Planeta, 2005.

David, Paul A. "Clio and the Economics of QWERTY." *American Economic Review* 75 (1985): 332–37.

Davis, Laura. *EU Foreign Policy, Transitional Justice and Mediation: Principle, Policy and Practice.* New York: Routledge, 2014.

De Greiff, Pablo, and Roger Duthie. *Transitional Justice and Development: Making Connections.* New York: Social Science Research Council, 2009.

"Demand on Genocide Reference Reiterated." FBIS EAS-91-174. 9 September 1991.

Dermody, John. "Beyond Good Intentions: Can Hybrid Tribunals Work after Unilateral Intervention?" *Hastings International and Comparative Law Review* 30 (2006–7): 77–102.

Directorate of Political Affairs. "Introduction." In *Politorbis*. Bern: Federal Department of Foreign Affairs, 2010.

Donnelly, Jack. *Realism and International Relations.* New York: Cambridge University Press, 2000.

Doyle, Michael W. "Liberalism and Foreign Policy." In *Foreign Policy: Theories, Actors, Cases*, edited by Steve Smith, Amelia Hadfield, and Tim Dunne. New York: Oxford University Press, 2008.

———. *Ways of War and Peace: Realism, Liberalism, and Socialism.* New York: Norton, 1997.

Drezner, Daniel. "The Future of U.S. Foreign Policy." *Internationale Politik und Gesellschaft* 15 (January 2008): 11–35.

Dubiel, Helmut. "The Remembrance of the Holocaust as a Catalyst for a Transnational Ethic?" *New German Critique* 90 (Autumn 2003): 59–70.

Earl, Hilary. *The Nuremberg SS-Einsatzgruppen Trial, 1945–1958: Atrocity, Law, and History.* New York: Cambridge University Press, 2009.

Ek, Carl. "Liberia: Issues for the United States." Congressional Research Service Issue Brief. 21 November 1996.

El Instituto de Estudios para el Desarrollo y la Paz (INDEPAZ). "Las cifras del conflicto." *Comunicaciones*, 22 March 2007.

El Tiempo. "Así ha sido el recorrido, en cifras, del horror 'para' durante 3,650 días." 26 September 2004.

———. "Desmovilizados perderían beneficios si omiten intencionalmente participación en crímenes." 13 June 2005.

———. "EEUU se opone a que beneficios de la ley de excarcelación cobijen a 'narcos' pedidos en extradición." 10 October 2003.

———. "Embajador de Estados Unidos, William Wood, cuestiona proceso de diálogo con Las Autodefensas." 31 May 2004.

———. "EU pide no tocar extradición." 5 November 2003.

———. "Negociaciones, AUC invitan a negociar a EU." 23 March 2004.

———. "No extraditarán a ningún paramilitary que esté en zona de ubicación en Córdoba." 14 May 2004.

———. "Sin extradición no habría ayuda." 12 June 2005.

———. "Vicefiscal de Estados Unidos formalizó la solicitud de extradición de seis jefes paramilitares." 18 May 2004.

Escobar, Mariana. "Seize the State, Seize the Way: State Capture as a Form of Warlords Politics in Colombia." PhD thesis, London School of Economics, 2011.

Etcheson, Craig. *After the Killing Fields: Lessons from the Cambodian Genocide.* Westport, CT: Praeger, 2005.

———. "'The Number': Quantifying Crimes against Humanity in Cambodia." Documentation Center of Cambodia, 2000.

Far Eastern Economic Review. "Cambodia: The Price of Justice." 17 February 2000.

Farah, Douglas. "A Protected Friend of Terrorism." *Washington Post*, 25 April 2005.

Fawthrop, Tom, and Helen Jarvis. *Getting Away with Genocide? Elusive Justice and the Khmer Rouge Tribunal.* London: Pluto Press, 2004.

Feierstein, Mark, and John Moreira. "National Consensus on Dealing with War Crimes Report on the Baseline Survey and Focus Groups." Greenberg Quinlan Rosner. 16 November 2004.

Festinger, Leon. *A Theory of Cognitive Dissonance.* Stanford, CA: Stanford University Press, 1957.

Finnemore, Martha, and Kathryn Sikkink. "Taking Stock: The Constructivist Research Program in International Relations and Comparative Politics." *Annual Review of Political Science* 4 (2001): 391–416.

Fisher, Ian. "Heart of Greed." *New York Times*, 10 June 2001.

Fletcher, Laurel E., and Harvey M. Weinstein. "Violence and Social Repair: Rethinking the Contribution of Justice to Reconciliation." *Human Rights Quarterly* 24, no. 3 (2002): 573–639.

Flockhart, Trine. "Constructivism and Foreign Policy." In *Foreign Policy: Theories, Actors, Cases*, edited by Steve Smith, Timothy Dunne, and Amelia Hadfield. New York: Oxford University Press, 2012.

Fofana, Boakai. "Sirleaf Testifies to Truth Commission." AllAfrica.com. 13 February 2009.

Ford, Stuart. "How Leadership in International Criminal Law Is Shifting from the United States to Europe and Asia: An Analysis of Spending on and Contributions to International Criminal Courts." *Saint Louis University School of Law* 55 (2011): 953–99.

Forero, J. F. G. "Colombia in Armed Conflict? 1946–1985." Papel político, Universidad Javeriana, 2005.

Forero, Juan. "Asking for Aid, Colombians Cite Terror; US Demurs." *New York Times*, 11 November 2001.

———. "New Colombia Law Grants Concessions to Paramilitaries." *New York Times*, 23 June 2005.

Forges, Alison Des. *"Leave None to Tell the Story": Genocide in Rwanda*. New York: Human Rights Watch, 1999.

Frank, Annie. "Taylor Trial: U.S. Fears Delay, but Control Limited." *World Politics Review*, 22 June 2007.

Garfinkle, Adam. "Be Careful Which Graves We Exhume." *Los Angeles Times*, 24 January 1999.

Gersh, David M. "Poor Judgment: Why the Iraqi Special Tribunal Is the Wrong Mechanism for Trying Saddam Hussein on Charges of Genocide, Human Rights Abuses, and Other Violations of International Law." *Georgia Journal of International and Comparative Law* 33 (2004–5): 273–302.

Gheciu, Alexandra. "Security Institutions as Agents of Socialization? NATO and the 'New Europe.'" *International Organization* 59 (2005): 973–1012.

Goldsmith, Jack. "The Self-Defeating International Criminal Court." *University of Chicago Law Review* 70, no. 1 (2003): 89–104.

Goldstein, Judith, and Robert O. Keohane, eds. *Ideas and Foreign Policy: Beliefs, Institutions, and Political Change*. Ithaca, NY: Cornell University Press, 1993.

Goldstone, Jack A. "Initial Conditions, General Laws, Path Dependence, and Explanation in Historical Sociology." *American Journal of Sociology* 104 (1998): 829–45.

Goldstone, Richard J. *For Humanity: Reflections of a War Crimes Investigator*. New Haven, CT: Yale University Press, 2000.

Gray, Jerry. "At Rwanda Border, Mass Graves and the Start of a Journey Home." *New York Times*, 26 July 1994.

Greenberg, Melanie C., John H. Barton, and Margaret E. McGuinness. *Words over War: Mediation and Arbitration to Prevent Deadly Conflict*. Lanham, MD: Rowman & Littlefield, 2000.

Gregg, Judd. "A Graveyard Peace." *Washington Post*, 9 May 2000.

Guardian. "Colombia's 'Parapolitics' Scandal Casts Shadow over President." 23 April 2008.

Gutiérrez, F., and M. Barón. "Estado, control territorial paramilitar y orden político en Colombia: Notas para una economía política del paramilitarismo." In *Nuestra guerra sin nombre: Transformaciones del conflicto en Colombia*, edited by F. Gutiérrez, M. E. Wills, and G. Sánchez. Bogotá: Norma, 2006.

Guzzini, Stefano, and Anna Leander. *Constructivism and International Relations: Alexander Wendt and His Critics*. London: Routledge, 2006.

Haas, P. "Introduction: Epistemic Communities and International Policy Coordination."*International Organization* 46, no. 1 (1992): 1–35.

Hafner, Gerhard, Kristen Boon, Anne Rübesame, and Jonathan Huston. "A Response to the American View as Presented by Ruth Wedgwood." *European Journal of International Law* 10, no. 1 (1999): 108–23.

Halperin, Morton H., Priscilla Clapp, and Arnold Kanter. *Bureaucratic Politics and Foreign Policy*. Washington, DC: Brookings Institution Press, 2006.

Hamber, Brandon. "Masculinity and Transitional Justice: An Exploratory Essay." *International Journal of Transitional Justice* 1, no. 3 (2007): 375–90.

Hammarberg, Thomas. "How the Khmer Rouge Tribunal Was Agreed: Discussions between the Cambodian Government and the UN." Searching for the Truth. Documentation Center of Cambodia. 2001.

Hansom, S. "FARC, ELN: Colombia's Left-Wing Guerilla." Council on Foreign Relations. 2009.

Hayner, Priscilla. *Unspeakable Truths: Facing the Challenge of Truth Commissions*. New York: Routledge, 2002.

———. "Negotiating Peace in Liberia: Preserving the Possibility for Justice." Centre for Humanitarian Dialogue and the International Center for Transitional Justice. November 2007.

Hecht, Lisa, and Sabine Michalowski. "Economic and Social Dimensions of Transitional Justice." Essex Transitional Justice Network.

Heder, Steve. "Politics, Diplomacy, and Accountability in Cambodia: Severely Limiting Personal Jurisdiction in Prosecution of Perpetrators of Crimes against Humanity." In *Historical Justice in International Perspective: How Societies Are Trying to Right the Wrongs of the Past*, edited by Manfred Berg and Bernd Schaefer. Washington, DC: German Historical Institute; New York: Cambridge University Press, 2009.

———. "A Review of the Negotiations Leading to the Establishment of the Personal Jurisdiction of the Extraordinary Chambers in the Courts of Cambodia." 1 August 2011.

Hirsch, Afua. "Wikileaks Cables Reveal US Concerns over Timing of Charles Taylor Trial." *Guardian*, 17 December 2010.

Hogan, Robert, and Nicholas P. Emler. "Retributive Justice." In *The Justice Motive in Social Behavior: Adapting to Times of Scarcity and Change*, edited by Melvin J. Lerner and Sally C. Lerner. New York: Plenum Press, 1981.

Hollis, Martin, and Steve Smith. "Roles and Reasons in Foreign Policy Decision Making." *British Journal of Political Science* 16 (1986): 269–86.

Holsti, Ole. "Public Opinion and Foreign Policy." *International Studies Quarterly* 36 (1992): 439–66.

Houghton, David Patrick. "Reinvigorating the Study of Foreign Policy Decision Making: Toward a Constructivist Approach." *Foreign Policy Analysis* 3, no. 1 (2007): 24–45.

Hughes, Barry. *The Domestic Context of American Foreign Policy*. San Francisco: W. H. Freeman, 1978.

Human Rights Watch. "Civil Society Efforts to Bring Charles Taylor to Justice." 23 April 2012.

———. "Trying Charles Taylor in the Hague: Making Justice Accessible to Those Most Affected." June 2006.

Huntington, Samuel P. *American Politics: The Promise of Disharmony*. Cambridge: Harvard University Press, 1981.

Huyse, Luc, and Mark Salter, eds. *Reconciliation and Traditional Justice after Violent Conflict: Learning from African Experiences*. Stockholm: International Institute for Democracy and Electoral Assistance, 2008.

ICGL. "ICGL Statement." On file with author. 2009.

International Center for Transitional Justice (ICTJ). "Taylor Trial Should Be Moved from Sierra Leone Only as Last Resort." Press release. 3 April 2006.

International Crisis Group (ICG). "Colombia Conflict History." Background piece. June 2011.

———. "Colombia's New Armed Groups." Latin American Reports no. 20. 2007.

———. "Demobilizing the Paramilitaries in Colombia: An Achievable Goal?" Latin American Reports no. 8. 5 August 2004.

———. "The History and Current State of FARC." March 2009.

Isacson, A. "The End of the 'Plan Colombia' Era." Just the Facts Blog. 26 October 2010.

Jaime Cordoba Triviño. "Comunicado de la Corte Constitucional sobre la sentencia que declaró ajustada a la constitución la ley 975 de 2005." President of the Colombian Constitutional Court. 19 May 2006.

Janis, Irving. *Groupthink: Psychological Studies of Policy Decisions and Fiascos*. Boston: Houghton Mifflin, 1982.

———. *Personality and Persuasibility*. Westport, CT: Greenwood Press, 1982.

Janis, Irving Lester, and Leon Mann. *Decision Making: A Psychological Analysis of Conflict, Choice, and Commitment*. New York: Free Press; London: Collier Macmillan, 1977.

Jennings, Peter. "From the Killing Fields," Peter Jennings Reporting (1990).

Jervis, Robert. *Perception and Misperception in International Politics*. Princeton, NJ: Princeton University Press, 1976.

Jones, James C. "US Policy and Peace in Colombia: Lost in a Tangle of Wars." In *Colombia: Building Peace in a Time of War*, edited by Virginia Bouvier. Washington, DC: US Institute of Peace, 2009.

Kansteiner, Walter H. "U.S. Policy in Africa in the 1990s." In *U.S. and Russian Policymaking with Respect to the Use of Force*, edited by Jeremy R. Azrael and Emil A. Payin. Santa Monica, CA: Rand, 1996.

Karadžic Indictment. "Prosecutor v. Karadžić et al. (It-95-5-I), Indictment." 14 July 1995.

Katzenstein, Peter. "International Relations and Domestic Structures: Foreign Economic Policies of Advanced Industrial States." *International Organization* 30, no. 1 (1976): 1–45.

Keck, Margaret E., and Kathryn Sikkink. *Activists beyond Borders: Advocacy Networks in International Politics*. Ithaca, NY: Cornell University Press, 1998.

Kegley, Charles W. *The Domestic Sources of American Foreign Policy: Insights and Evidence*. New York: St. Martins Press, 1987.

Kegley, Charles W., Eugene R. Wittkopf, and James M. Scott. *American Foreign Policy: Patterns and Process*. 6th ed. Belmont: Wadsworth/Thomson Learning, 2003.

Keleman, Michele. "Taylor War Crimes Trial Worries West Africa." *NPR News*. 6 April 2006.

Kiernan, Ben. "The Demography of Genocide in Southeast Asia." *Critical Asian Studies* 35, no. 4 (2003): 585–97.

———. *Genocide and Democracy in Cambodia: The Khmer Rouge, the United Nations, and the International Community*. New Haven, CT: Yale University Southeast Asia Studies, 1993.

———. "The US Bombardment of Cambodia, 1969–1973." *Vietnam Generation* 1, no. 1 (1989): 4–41.

King, Henry T., and Theodore C. Theofrastous. "From Nuremberg to Rome: A Step Backward for US Foreign Policy." *Case Western Reserve Journal of International Law* 31, no. 1 (1999): 47–106.

Kirsch, Philip, and Darryl Robinson. "Reaching Agreement at the Rome Conference." In *The Rome Statute for an International Criminal Court: A Commentary*, edited by Antonio Cassese. New York: Oxford University Press, 2002.

Klotz, Audie, and Cecelia Lynch. *Strategies for Research in Constructivist International Relations*. Armonk, NY: M.E. Sharpe, 2007.

Koh, Harold Hongju. "The Obama Administration and International Law." Address by Harold Hongju Koh to the American Society of International Law. 15 March 2010.

Kramer, Reed. "A Casualty of the Cold War's End." CSIS Africa Notes. July 1995.

Kraul, Chris. "Colombia Hands Ex-Paramilitary Leader over to U.S." *Los Angeles Times*, 6 March 2009.

Kritz, Neil J. *Transitional Justice: How Emerging Democracies Reckon with Former Regimes*. 3 vols. Washington, DC: United States Institute of Peace Press, 1995.

Kyriakou, Niko. "Cambodia Steps Closer to Justice." *Asia Times Online*, 31 March 2005.

Lambourne, Wendy. "Transitional Justice and Peacebuilding after Mass Violence." *International Journal of Transitional Justice* 3, no. 1 (2009): 28–48.

Le Monde. "Hun Sen Interviewed on Cease-Fire, Peace Talks." 22 May 1991.

LeBlanc, Lawrence J. *The United States and the Genocide Convention*. Durham, NC: Duke University Press, 1991.

Lehrer, Jim. "Liberia's New President." *Newshour with Jim Lehrer*. Transcript of interview. 23 March 2006.

Leigh, Monroe. "The United States and the Statute of Rome." *American Journal of International Law* 95, no. 1 (2001): 124–31.

Levy, Gilat, and Ronny Razin. "It Takes Two: An Explanation for the Democratic Peace." *Journal of the European Economic Association* 2, no. 2 (2004): 1–29.

Lewis, Paul. "Rwanda Agrees to a U.N. War-Crimes Tribunal." *New York Times*, 9 August 1994.

Lietzau, William K. "The United States and the International Criminal Court: Concerns from a US Military Perspective." *Law and Contemporary Problems* 64, (2001): 119–40.

Lundy, Patricia, and Mark McGovern. "Whose Justice? Rethinking Transitional Justice from the Bottom Up." *Journal of Law and Society* 35, no. 2 (2008): 265–92.

Mahoney, James. "Path Dependence in Historical Sociology." *Theory and Society* 29, no. 4 (2000): 507–48.

Mahony, Chris. "Judd Gregg's War against Liberia's Charles Taylor." *Fair Observer*, May 30, 2012.

Mamdani, Mahmood. "Reconciliation without Justice." *Southern African Review of Books* 46 (1996): 3–5.

Mani, R. "Dilemmas of Expanding Transitional Justice, or Forging the Nexus between Transitional Justice and Development." *International Journal of Transitional Justice* 2, no. 3 (2008): 253–65.

Mannon, Travis. "Committee to Interrogate Extradited Paramilitaries Leaders in US." *Colombia Reports*, 16 August 2011.

———. "Extradited Paramilitaries Should Serve Sentence in Colombia: OAS." *Colombia Reports*, 21 October 2011.

Maseri, Sergio Gómez. "EU y el mundo deben apoyar con vigor y cuanto antes la desmovilización de los grupos paramilitares." *El Tiempo*, 16 December 2004.

McAdams, James. *Transitional Justice and the Rule of Law in New Democracies.* Notre Dame, IN: University of Notre Dame Press, 1997.

McElroy, Robert. *Morality and American Foreign Policy: The Role of Ethics in International Affairs.* Princeton, NJ: Princeton University Press, 1992.

McEvoy, Kieran, and Lorna McGregor. *Transitional Justice from Below: Grassroots Activism and the Struggle for Change.* Portland, OR: Hart, 2008.

Mearsheimer, John J. *The Tragedy of Great Power Politics.* New York: Norton, 2001.

Meierhenrich, Jens. *The Legacies of Law: Long-Run Consequences of Legal Development in South Africa, 1652–2000.* Cambridge: Cambridge University Press, 2010.

Merwe, Hugo van der, Victoria Baxter, and Audrey R. Chapman. *Assessing the Impact of Transitional Justice: Challenges for Empirical Research.* Washington, DC: US Institute of Peace, 2009.

Mey, Elyda. "Cambodian Diaspora Communities in Transitional Justice." International Center for Transitional Justice. March 2008.

Mills, C. Wright. *The Power Elite.* London: Oxford University Press, 1956.

Milošević Indictment. "Prosecutor V. Milošević (It-01-51-I), Indictment." 22 November 2001.

Ministry of Foreign Affairs. "Point de press." 14 January 2000.

Moon, Bruce. "The State in Foreign and Domestic Policy." In *Foreign Policy Analysis: Continuity and Change in Its Second Generation,* edited by Laura Neack, Jeanne Hey, and Patrick Haney. Englewood Cliffs, NJ: Prentice Hall, 1995.

Morris, Madeline H. "Trials of Concurrent Jurisdiction: The Case of Rwanda." *Duke Journal of Comparative and International Law* 7 (1996): 349.

Morris, Virginia, and Michael Scharf. *An Insider's Guide to the International Criminal Tribunal for the Former Yugoslavia.* Vol. 1. Irvington-on-Hudson: Transnational Publishers, 1995.

Muck, William, and Eric Wiebelhaus-Brahm. "Patterns of Transitional Justice Assistance among the International Community." Sixth European Consortium for Political Research General Conference. Reykjavik. 25 August 2011.

Mundis, Daryl. "United States of America and International Justice: Has Lady Liberty Lost Her Way, the Editorial Comments on the USA and the ICC." *Journal of International Criminal Justice* 2, no. 1 (2004): 2–10.

Nagy, Rosemary. "Transitional Justice as Global Project: Critical Reflections." *Third World Quarterly* 29, no. 2 (2008): 275–89.

Nesiah, Vasuki. "Gender and Truth Commission Mandates." International Center for Transitional Justice. 2006.

New York Times. "Colombia's Capitulation." 6 July 2005.

———. "Senator George Mcgovern Calls for International Force to Overthrow Khmer Rouge Government." 22 August 1978.

Ni Aolain, Fionnuala, Christine Bell, and Colm Campbell. "The Battle for Transitional Justice: Hegemony, Iraq, and International Law." In *Judges, Transition, and Human Rights Culture: Essays in Honour of Stephen Livingstone*, edited by John Morison, Kieran McEvoy, and Gordon Anthony. New York: Oxford University Press, 2007.

Nye, Joseph. *Soft Power: The Means to Success in the World*. New York: Public Affairs, 2004.

O'Donnell, Guillermo, and Philippe C. Schmitter. *Transitions from Authoritarian Rule. Tentative Conclusions about Uncertain Democracies*. Baltimore: Johns Hopkins University Press, 1986.

Olsen, Tricia D., Leigh A. Payne, and Andrew G. Reiter. *Transitional Justice in Balance: Comparing Processes, Weighing Efficacy*. Washinton, DC: United States Institute of Peace, 2010.

Open Society Justice Initiative. "Corruption Allegations at Khmer Rouge Court Must Be Investigated Thoroughly." Press release. 14 February 2007.

Orbovich, Cynthia, and Richard Molnar. "Modeling Foreign Policy Advisory Processes." In *Political Psychology and Foreign Policy*, edited by Eric Singer and Valerie Hudson. Boulder, CO: Westview, 1992.

Orentlicher, Diane F. "Independent Study on Best Practices, Including Recommendations, to Assist States in Strengthening Their Domestic Capacity to Combat All Aspects of Impunity." UN Doc. E/CN.4/2004/88. 27 February 2004.

———. "Settling Accounts: The Duty to Prosecute Human Rights Violations of a Prior Regime." *Yale Law Journal* 100, no. 8 (1991): 2537–2615.

———. "Unilateral Multilateralism: United States Policy toward the International Criminal Court." *Cornell International Law Journal* 36 (2003–4): 415–33.

———. "Updated Set of Principles for the Protection and Promotion of Human Rights through Action to Combat Impunity." UN Doc. E/CN.4/2005/102/Add.1. 8 February 2005.

Orford, A. "Commissioning the Truth." *Columbia Journal of Gender and Law* 15 (2006): 851–83.

Osiel, Mark. *Mass Atrocity, Collective Memory, and the Law*. New Brunswick, NJ: Transaction Publishers, 1997.

OSJI. "Recent Developments at the Extraordinary Chambers in the Courts of Cambodia." June 2011.

Ottaway, David B. "Shultz Sees Liberian Doe, Cites 'Genuine Progress.'" *Washington Post*, 15 January 1987.

Pardo, Rodrigo. "Changes in the Andean Region and Foreign Policy Alternatives for Colombia." Peace Initiatives and Colombia's Armed Conflict. Woodrow Wilson Center and Fundación Ideas Para La Paz, September 2009.

Parker, Tom. "Prosecuting Saddam: The Coalition Provisional Authority and the Evolution of the Iraqi Special Tribunal." *Cornell International Law Journal* 38 (2005): 899–909.

Patel, Ana Cutter, Pablo de Greiff, and Lars Waldorf, eds. *Disarming the Past: Transitional Justice and Ex-Combatants*. New York: Social Science Research Council, 2010.

Payne, Richard J., and Eddie Ganaway. "The Influence of Black Americans on US Policy towards Southern Africa." *African Affairs* 79 (1980): 567–85.

PBS. "Ambassador Pierre-Richard Prosper of the Office of War Crimes Issues Discusses War Tribunals with Host Daljit Dhaliwal." *Wide Angle*, 25 August 2002.

Peelo, Moira, and Keith Soothill. "The Place of Public Narratives in Reproducing Social Order." *Theoretical Criminology* 4, no. 2 (2000): 131–48.

Perriello, Tom, and Marieke Wierda. "The Special Court for Sierra Leone under Scrutiny." International Center for Transitional Justice, March 2006.

Peskin, Victor. *International Justice in Rwanda and the Balkans: Virtual Trials and the Struggle for State Cooperation*. New York: Cambridge University Press, 2008.

Phnom Penh Post. "The American Role in Putting Together a KR Trial Deal." 28 April–11 May 2000.

———. "Pm-Unsg Talks Agree: More Talks." 18 February–2 March 2000.

———. "Sen. John Kerry Urges U.S. to Help Fund ECCC." 27 May 2008.

———. "U.S. Special Adviser Assessing Khmer Rouge Court." 27 May 2008.

"Position Statement on Security, Reconciliation and Peace in Liberia, Presented to the Authority of Ecowas and the Government of the Federal Republic of Nigeria." 15 March 2002.

Power, Samantha. "Bystanders to Genocide." *Atlantic*, September 2001.

———. *"A Problem from Hell": America and the Age of Genocide*. New York: Harper Perennial, 2002.

Presidencia de la República. "Proceso de paz con Las Autodefensas." Oficina Alto Comisionado para la Paz informe ejecutivo. December 2006.

Prosper, Pierre-Richard. "Address at the Peace Palace in the Hague." Press release. US Ambassador for War Crimes Issues. 19 December 2001.

———. "War Crimes in the 21st Century." Press release. US Ambassador for War Crimes Issues. 26 October 2004.

Putnam, R. "Diplomacy and Domestic Politics: The Logic of Two-Level Games." *International Organization* 42, no. 3 (1988): 427–60.

Ramcharan, B. G. *The International Conference on the Former Yugoslavia: Official Papers*. Boston: Kluwer, 1997.

Rapp, Stephen J. "Remarks by Ambassador-at-Large for War Crimes Issues at Question and Answer Session at the Forum Hosted by the Women of Ateneo." Makati, Philippines. 10 May 2011.

———. "Remarks by the Ambassador-at-Large for War Crimes Issues on International Justice and the Use of Force." International Humanitarian Law Dialogs. Chautauqua, NY. 30 August 2010.

Ratner, Steven, and J. S. Abrams. "Striving for Justice: Accountability and the Crimes of the Khmer Rouge." A Study for the United States Department of State under the Cambodian Genocide Justice Act. 1995.

Rawson, D. "Coping with Chaos while Acting Justly: Lessons from Rwanda." In *Effective Strategies for Protecting Human Rights*, edited by David Barnhizer. Burlington, VT: Dartmouth, 2001.

Reisman, Taegin. "Appeals Chamber Upholds Taylor's Jail Sentence." *International Justice Monitor*, 26 September 2013.

Rempe, D. M. "The Past as Prologue? A History of US Counterinsurgency Policy in Colombia, 1958–66." US Army War College, Strategic Studies Institute. 2002.

Reuters. "Japan Announces 2.5 Billion Yen in Fresh Cambodian Aid." 11 January 2000.

———. "US Official Optimistic about Cambodia Trial Talks." 9 March 2000.

Risse-Kappen, Thomas. "Public Opinion, Domestic Structure and Foreign Policy in Liberal Democracies." *World Politics* 43 (1991): 491–517.

Ronayne, Peter. *Never Again? The United States and the Prevention and Punishment of Genocide since the Holocaust*. Lanham, MD: Rowman & Littlefield, 2001.

Ropp, Steve C., Thomas Risse-Kappen, and Kathryn Sikkink. *The Power of Human Rights: International Norms and Domestic Change*. Cambridge: Cambridge University Press, 1999.

Rosenau, James N. *Domestic Sources of Foreign Policy*. New York: Free Press; London: Collier-Macmillan, 1967.

Rwanda Letter to UN. "Letter Dated 28 September 1994 from the Permanent Representative of Rwanda to the United Nations Addressed to the President of the Security Council." UN Document S/1994/1115. 1994.

Sadat, Leila Nadya, and S. Richard Carden. "The New International Criminal Court: An Uneasy Revolution." *Georgetown Law Journal* 88 (2000): 381–474.

Savelsberg, Joachim J., and Ryan D. King. *American Memories: Atrocities and the Law*. New York: Russell Sage Foundation, 2011.

Schabas, William A. "International War Crimes Tribunals and the United States." *Diplomatic History* 35, no. 5 (2011): 769–86.

———. "Victor's Justice: Selecting Situations at the International Criminal Court." *John Marshall Law Review* 43 (2009): 535–52.

———. "United States Hostility to the International Criminal Court: It's All about the Security Council." *European Journal of International Law* 14, no. 4 (2004): 701–20.

Scharf, Michael P. "Is It International Enough? A Critique of the Iraqi Special Tribunal in Light of the Goals of International Justice." *Journal of International Criminal Justice* 2 (2004): 330–37.

———. "The United States and the International Criminal Court: A Recommendation for the Bush Administration." *ILSA Journal of International and Comparative Law* 7 (2001): 385–89.

Scharf, Michael P., and Ahran Kang. "Errors and Missteps: Key Lessons the Iraqi Special Tribunal Can Learn from the ICTY, ICTR, and SCSL." *Cornell International Law Journal* 38 (2005): 911–47.

Scheffer, David J. *All the Missing Souls: A Personal History of the War Crimes Tribunals.* Princeton, NJ: Princeton University Press, 2011.

———. "The Negotiating History of the ECCC's Personal Jurisdiction." *Cambodia Tribunal Monitor,* 22 May 2011.

———. "Staying the Course with the International Criminal Court." *Cornell International Law Journal* 35 (2002): 47–100.

———. "Why the Cambodia Tribunal Matters to the International Community." http://www.cambodiatribunal.org/commentary/40.html.

Schelling, Thomas C. *The Strategy of Conflict.* Cambridge: Harvard University Press, 1960.

Sciolino, Elaine. "U.S. Names Figures It Wants Charged with War Crimes." *New York Times,* 17 December 1992.

SCSL Judgement. "Prosecutor v. Charles Ghankay Taylor." Trial Chamber II, Special Court for Sierra Leone. 26 April 2012.

Semana. "Los paras perdieron su disfraz." 7 May 2004.

Semple, Kirk, and Somini Sengupta. "Pushing Peace in Africa, Bush Tells Liberian President to Quit." *New York Times,* 26 June 2003.

Senior Subcommission on International Operations of the Commission on Foreign Relations. "Is a U.N. International Criminal Court in the U.S. National Interest?" 105th Cong. 23 July 1998.

Sewall, Sarah B., and Carl Kaysen. *The United States and the International Criminal Court: National Security and International Law.* Lanham, MD: Rowman & Littlefield, 2000.

Shawcross, William. *Sideshow: Kissinger, Nixon and the Destruction of Cambodia.* New York: Simon and Schuster, 1979.

Shirlow, Peter, and Kieran McEvoy. *Beyond the Wire: Former Prisoners and Conflict Transformation in Northern Ireland.* Ann Arbor, MI: Pluto Press, 2008.

Shklar, Judith *Legalism: Law, Morals and Political Trials.* Cambridge: Harvard University Press, 1986.

Sieff, Michelle. "A 'Special Court.'" Global Policy Forum, 2001.

Sikkink, Kathryn. *The Justice Cascade: How Human Rights Prosecutions Are Changing World Politics.* Norton, 2011.

Sirleaf, Ellen Johnson. "Annual Message to the Legislature." President of the Republic of Liberia. 25 January 2010.

———. "The Challenges of Post-war Reconstruction: The Liberian Experience." Event at Chatham House. President of the Republic of Liberia. 13 June 2011.

Slaughter, Anne-Marie. *The Idea That Is America: Keeping Faith with Our Values in a Dangerous World.* New York: Basic Books, 2007.

Smith, Karen Elizabeth, and Margot Light. *Ethics and Foreign Policy.* New York: Cambridge University Press, 2001.

Snyder, Glen Herald, and Paul Diesing. *Conflict among Nations: Bargaining, Decision Making, and System Structure in International Crises.* Princeton, NJ: Princeton University Press, 1977.

South China Morning Post. "Compromise Offered on Trial Judges." 12 January 2000.

———. "Hun Sen's Trial Offer Puts UN on the Spot." 13 January 2000.

Spiropoulos, J. "Draft Code of Offences against the Peace and Security of Mankind, Report by Special Rapporteur." UN Doc. A/CN.4/25. *Extract from the Yearbook of the International Law Commission* 2 (1950).

Sprout, Harold, and Margaret Sprout. *Man-Milieu Relationship Hypotheses in the Context of International Politics.* Princeton, NJ: Princeton University Press, 1956.

Sriram, Chandra Lekha. "Justice as Peace? Liberal Peacebuilding and Strategies of Transitional Justice." *Global Society* 21, no. 4 (2007): 579–91.

Sriram, Chandra Lekha, and Johanna Herman. "DDR and Transitional Justice: Bridging the Divide?" *Conflict, Security & Development* 9, no. 4 (2009): 455–74.

Stanford University. "United Self-Defense Forces of Colombia." Mapping Militant Organizations. 2012.

Stanton, Gregory. "Seeking Justice in Cambodia." Genocide Watch. Statute for the Special Court for Sierra Leone. No date.

Stone, Jeremy. *Every Man Should Try: Adventures of a Public Interest Activist.* New York: Public Affairs, 1999.

Sunstein, Cass. *Free Markets and Social Justice.* New York: Oxford University Press, 1997.

Swiss Peace/FDFA. "Dealing with the Past: Conceptual Framework." 2006.

Taylor, Telford. *The Anatomy of the Nuremberg Trials: A Personal Memoir.* Alfred A. Knopf, 1992.

Teitel, Ruti G. *Transitional Justice.* New York: Oxford University Press, 2000.

Tejan-Cole, Abdul. "A Big Man in a Small Cell: Charles Taylor and the Special Court for Sierra Leone." In *Prosecuting Heads of State*, edited by Ellen L. Lutz and Caitlin Reiger. New York: Cambridge University Press, 2009.

Thoms, Oskar N. T., James Ron, and Roland Paris. "State-Level Effects of Transitional Justice: What Do We Know?" *International Journal of Transitional Justice* 4 (2010): 329–54.

Timberg, Craig. "Liberian President Backs Bid to Move Taylor Trial to Hague." *Washington Post*, 31 March 2006.

———. "A Warlord's Exile Divides His Hosts: Liberian Ex-President Charles Taylor Doing Business as Usual in Nigeria." *Washington Post*, 9 October 2005.

Tocqueville, Alexis de. *Democracy in America*. Trans. Henry Reeve. 2nd ed. 2 vols. London: Saunders and Otley, 1836.

Tran, Mark, and Hella Pick. "UN to Set up Commission to Investigate Atrocities in Former Yugoslavia; Europeans Dilute US Call for War Crimes Tribunal." *Guardian*, 7 October 1992.

TRC Consolidated Final Report (Unedited), Volume II. 29 June 2009.

"Act That Established the Truth and Reconciliation Commission (TRC) of Liberia." Enacted by the National Transitional Legislative Assembly. 12 May 2005.

TRC press release. 11 December 2009.

UC Berkeley School of Law. "Truth behind Bars: Colombian Paramilitary Leaders in US Custody." International Human Rights Law Clinic. February 2010.

UN Commission on Human Rights. "Situation of Human Rights in Cambodia: Report of the Special Representative of the Secretary-General for Human Rights in Cambodia, Thomas Hammarberg, Submitted in Accordance with Commission Resolution 1997/49." 20 February 1998.

———. "The Situation of Human Rights in the Territory of the Former Yugoslavia." CHR Res. 1992/S-2/1. 1992.

UN Convention on the Prevention and Punishment of the Crime of Genocide. 1948.

UN Diplomatic Conference of Plenipotentiaries on the Establishment of an International Criminal Court. UN Document a/Conf.183/C.1/L.70; a/Conf.183/C.1/L.90; a/Conf.183/Sr.9. 1998.

UN General Assembly Resolution 57/228. "Khmer Rouge Trials." 22 May 2003.

UN General Assembly Resolution 177 (II). 21 November 1947.

UN High Commissioner for Refugees. "2008 Global Trends: Refugees, Asylum-Seekers, Returnees, Internally Displaced and Stateless Persons." 16 June 2009.

UN, "Non-paper on Khmer Rouge Trial." 5 January 2000.

UN Press Statement by Legal Counsel Hans Corell. "Negotiations between the UN and Cambodia Regarding the Establishment of the Court to Try Khmer Rouge Leaders." 8 February 2002.

UN Report of the Group of Experts for Cambodia Established Pursuant to General Assembly Resolution 52/135. 18 February 1999.

UN Report of the Secretary-General on the Khmer Rouge Trials. UN Doc. A/57/761.

UN Report of the Secretary-General to the UN Security Council. "The Rule of Law and Transitional Justice in Conflict and Post-conflict Societies." S/2004/616. 23 August 2004.

UN Secretary-General Briefing to the Security Council on Visit to Southeast Asia. 29 February 2000.

UN Security Council Resolution 780. "Requesting the Establishment of a Commission of Experts in the Former Yugoslavia." 6 October 1992.

UN Security Council Resolution 1315. 14 August 2000.

UN Security Council Resolution 1593. 31 March 2005.

UN Security Council Resolution 1638. 11 November 2005.

UN Security Council Resolution 1970. "Peace and Security in Africa." 26 February 2011.

US Cambodia Democracy and Accountability Act. 2003.

US Cambodian Genocide Justice Act. 22 U.S.C. 2656. 1994.

US Congress. "Is a U.N. International Criminal Court in the U.S. National Interest?" Senior Subcommission on International Operations of the Commission on Foreign Relations. 105th Cong. 23 July 1998.

US Congressional Record. Proceedings and Debates of the 106th Congress, May 24, 2000 to June 12, 2000, vol. 146, pt. 7. 2000.

US Department of Treasury. "Treasury Takes Action against FARC/AUC Narco-Terrorist Leaders in Continued Effort to Halt Narcotics Trafficking." Press release. 19 February 2004.

US Embassy in Cambodia. "The ECCC and OSJI." 15 March 2007.

———. "Friends of the ECCC or RGC?" 16 March 2007.

———. "Press Statement: Visit of Deputy Secretary of State John D. Negroponte to Cambodia." 16 September 2008.

US Fact Sheet. "The International Criminal Court." Bureau of Political-Military Affairs. 2 August 2002.

US Foreign Operations and Related Programs Appropriations Act. 2009.

US Government Accountability Office (GAO). "Plan Colombia: Drug Reduction Goals Were Not Fully Met, but Security Has Improved; U.S. Agencies Need More Detailed Plans for Reducing Assistance." Report to the Honorable Joseph R. Biden, Jr., Chairman, Committee on Foreign Relations, U.S. Senate. October 2008.

US H.Amdt. 480. "An Amendment to H.R. 2601 [109th Cong.]: Foreign Relations Authorization Act, Fiscal Years 2006 and 2007." 20 July 2005.

US H.Congr. Res. 127. "Calling on the Government of the Federal Republic of Nigeria to Transfer Charles Ghankay Taylor, Former President of the Republic of Liberia, to the Special Court for Sierra Leone to Be Tried for War Crimes, Crimes against Humanity, and Other Serious Violations of International Humanitarian Law." 5 May 2005.

US House of Representatives. "Confronting War Crimes in Africa." Hearing before the Subcommittee on Africa, Committee on International Relations. 24 June 2004.

———. "HR 5114, Amendment Deleted Language Which Prohibited Any Assistance for the Khmer Rouge and Non-Communist Resistance Forces in Cambodia." 27 June 1990.

———. "Human Rights in Cambodia." 26 July 1977.

US House of Representatives. "The Impact of Liberia's Election on West Africa." Hearing before the Subcommittee on Africa, Global Human Rights and International Operations, Committee on International Relations. 8 February 2006.

———. "US Policy toward Liberia." Hearing before the Subcommittee on Africa, Committee on International Relations. 2 October 2003.

———. "Sudan: Losing Ground on Peace?" Hearing before the Subcommittee on Africa, Committee on International Relations, 1 November 2005.

US Letter to President Uribe. from Senator Lugar. 22 May 2005.

US Letter to President Uribe from Several Democratic Senators. 3 June 2005.

US Letter to President Uribe Organized by Rep. Tom Lantos, Ranking Member of House International Relations Committee. 23 September 2003.

US Letter from the Permanent Representative of the United States of America to the United Nations Addressed to the Secretary-General. UN Document S/25575. 5 April 1993.

US Public Law 99-83. US International Security and Development Cooperation Act, 1985.

US Public Law 100-690. 102 Stat. 4267. 1988.

US Public Law 108-199. Consolidated Appropriations Act, 2004. 23 January 2004.

US Public Law 109-102. Foreign Operations, Export Financing, and Related Programs Appropriations Act, 2006. 14 November 2005.

US Public Papers of the Presidents. "Meeting with Samuel K. Doe, Head of State of Liberia." *Weekly Compilation of Presidential Documents.* 17 August 1982.

US State Department. "American Foreign Policy and the International Criminal Court." Press release, Marc Grossman, Under Sec'y for Political Affairs. 6 May 2002.

———. "Clinton Proclamation Regarding Sierra Leone." 11 October 2000.

———. "Country Reports: Colombia." 1997.

———. "Daily Press Briefing." 1 February 2005.

———. "Daily Press Briefing." 5 May 2005.

———. "Determination and Certification of the Colombian Government and Armed Forces with Respect to Human Rights Related Conditions." 11 September 2009.

———. "Determination and Certification of the Colombian Government and Armed Forces with Respect to Human Rights Related Conditions." 15 September 2010.

———. "Domestic and International Law," in History of the Department of State During the Clinton Presidency (1993–2001).

———. "International Criminal Court: Letter to United Nations Secretary General Kofi Annan." Press release, John R. Bolton, Under Sec'y of State for Arms Control and International Sec. 6 May 2002.

———. "Issues Update." Press release, Pierre-Richard Prosper, US Ambassador for War Crimes Issues. 6 May 2002.

———. "Memorandum of Justification Concerning Human Rights Conditions with Respect to Assistance for the Colombian Armed Forces." 8 September 2009.

US State Department. "Memorandum of Justification Concerning Human Rights Conditions with Respect to Assistance for the Colombian Armed Forces." Foreign Operations, and Related Programs Appropriations Act. 2 September 2010.

———. Secretary of State Hillary Clinton, Address to Joint Session of Liberian National Legislature. 13 August 2009.

———. "State Dept. on Sierra Leone Court Upholding Taylor Conviction." 26 September 2013.

———. "Statement on U.S. Funding for Trial of Charles Taylor." 25 November 2010.

———. "The Verdict in the Charles Taylor Trial at the Special Court for Sierra Leone." 26 April, 2012.

US Denounces 'Climate of Impunity' in Democratic Republic of Congo," 7 July 2003.

US v. Diego Vecino. "Superseding Indictment." No. 05-00967 (S.D.N.Y.) (3 March 2009).

US v. Rendon-Herrera et al. "Superseding Indictment." No. 04-962 (S.D.N.Y.) (16 April 2009).

US White House. "Press Briefing." 5 May 2005.

———. "Statement by the President." Office of the Press Secretary. 11 October 2000.

USAID. "Overseas Loans and Grants, Obligations and Loan Authorizations July 1, 1945–September 30, 2001." No date.

———. "USAID-Colombia Fact Sheet." April 2010.

———. "USAID-Colombia Fact Sheet on the Justice Reform and Modernization Program." October 2008.

USUN. "Resolution to Establish an International Tribunal for the Prosecution of Certain Persons Responsible for Serious Violations of International Humanitarian Law in the Territory of Cambodia During the Period 15 April 1975–7 January 1979." 28 April 1998.

———. "Rwanda: Bringing the Guilty to Justice." Cable 02491. 15 June 1994.

Vasquez, J. A., and C. Elman. Realism and the Balancing of Power: A New Debate. Upper Saddle River, NJ: Prentice Hall, 2003.

Vicuna, Francisco Orrego. "International Criminal Court and the In and Out Club." Journal of International Criminal Justice 2, no. 1 (2004): 35–37.

Vieira, Constanza. "US Supervision of Colombian Paramilitary Demobilization Becomes Evident." Antiwar.com. 19 August 2006.

Wald, Patricia M. "Is the United States' Opposition to the ICC Intractable?" Journal of International Criminal Justice 2, no. 1 (2004): 19–25.

Waldorf, Lars. "Mass Justice for Mass Atrocity: Rethinking Local Justice as Transitional Justice." Temple Law Review 79, no. 1 (2006): 1–87.

Waugaman, Adele. "The United States in Darfur: Trapped by 'Genocide.'" *International Justice Tribune*, November 21, 2005.

Wedgwood, Ruth. "Fiddling in Rome: America and the International Criminal Court." *Foreign Affairs* 77, no. 6 (1998): 20–24.

———. "The International Criminal Court: An American View." *European Journal of International Law* 10, no. 93 (1999).

Wells-Dang, Andrew. "Republican Group Meddles in Cambodia." *Asia Times Online*, 16 April 2004.

Wierda, Marieke, and Anthony Triolo. "Resources." In *International Prosecutors*, edited by Stephan Parmentier Luc Reydams, Cedric Ryngaert, and Jan Wouters. New York: Oxford University Press, 2011.

Willis, James F. *Prologue to Nuremberg: The Politics and Diplomacy of Punishing War Criminals of the First World War*. Westport, CT: Greenwood Press, 1982.

Winn, Peter A. "Legal Ritual." *Law and Critique* 2, no. 2 (1991): 207–32.

Wohlforth, William C. "Realism and Foreign Policy." In *Foreign Policy: Theories, Actors, Cases*, edited by Steve Smith, Amelia Hadfield, and Tim Dunne. New York: Oxford University Press, 2012.

Wood, William. "The Peace Process in Colombia with the Autodefensas Unidas De Colombia-AUC." Woodrow Wilson Center seminar. 28 June 2004.

———. "U.S. Policy in Colombia: Current and Future Challenges." Woodrow Wilson Center. 14 June 2005.

Woodrow Wilson Center and Fundación Ideas Para La Paz. "Peace Initiatives and Colombia's Armed Conflict." September 2009.

Woolsey, Theodore S. "Retaliation and Punishment." *Proceedings of the American Society of International Law* 62 (1915): 62–69.

Yalta Memorandum. "Memorandum to President Roosevelt from the Secretaries of State and War and the Attorney General." 22 January 1945.

Zacklin, Ralph. "Some Major Problems in the Drafting of the ICTY Statute." *Journal of International Criminal Justice* 2, no. 2 (2004): 361–67.

Zalaquett, José. "Confronting Human Rights Violations Committed by Former Governments: Principles Applicable and Political Constraints." In *State Crimes: Punishment or Pardon. Papers and Report of the Conference, November 4–6, 1988, Wye Center, MD*. Queenstown, MD: Justice and Society Program of the Aspen Institute, 1989.

Zolo, Danilo. "Iraqi Special Tribunal: Back to the Nuremberg Paradigm." *Journal of International Criminal Justice* 2 (2004): 313–29.

INDEX

Page numbers followed by *t* and *f* indicate tables and figures, respectively. Numbers n indicate notes.

local NGOs, 155, 160
Lomé Accords, 90
London Agreement, 34–35
London Conference, 35
Lugar, Richard, 130
LURD, 90, 119n90

MacArthur, Douglas, 34–35
Mahony, Chris, 166
Malinowski, Tom, 178
Management Sciences for
    Development, Inc. (MSD),
    136–137, 148n76; interviews,
    169, 172
Mancuso, Salvatore, 128–129, 141
Massalay, Salif, 166
McCloskey, Peter, 51n51
McConnell, Mitch, 70
McGovern, George, 56
McHenry, Donald, 176
media interviews, 160, 170
media relations, 115n13
Melia, Tom, 178
Mendez, Juan, 178
Metzger, Macdonald, 167
military support, 124
Millares, Daniel, 173
Milošević, Slobodan, 37
Mladić, Ratko, 37
MODEL Party, 119n90
Morgenthau, Henry, Jr., 33–34
Morocco, 5t
"Moscow Declaration," 33
Muse, Toby, 175
Muskie, Edmund, 79n16

Nagy, Rosemary, 22
narcotrafficking, 129, 144n12, 145n25
National Commission for
    Reparations and Reconciliation
    (CNRR) (Colombia), 131,
    142; establishment of, 134;
    international assistance to, 135,
    136t; interviews, 170, 172–173, 175;
    priorities, 134; USAID support
    for, 134–137, 135t
National Endowment for Democracy,
    161, 162
national interest, 11
National Land Fund (Colombia), 136

National Liberation Army (ELN)
    (Colombia), 124, 143n2, 181
National Patriotic Front of Liberia
    (NPFL), 88, 120n120, 180
National Security Council (US),
    89, 176
Natsios, Andrew, 177
Nazism, 32, 47
Neak Luong, Cambodia, 77n2
Negroponte, John, 72
Netherlands: assistance to ECCC, 71,
    71t; assistance to transitional
    justice, 7n3, 155; support for
    CNRR, 135, 136t; support for
    SCSL, 102
New York Times, 131
NGOs: international, 155, 183;
    interviews, 160–161, 164–165, 170,
    175; local, 155, 183–185
Nigeria, 93–94, 97–98; asylum for
    Charles Taylor, 94, 116n46; and
    CPA, 120n103
Nixon, Richard, 179
Nol, Lon, 77n2
Noriega, Roger, 128–129
Norman, Hinga, 102–103
North Atlantic Treaty Organization
    (NATO), 46
Northwestern University, 107
NPFL. see National Patriotic Front of
    Liberia
Nuremberg tribunal, 3, 20–21, 34–35

Obama, Barack, 44–45, 154
Obasanjo, Olusegun, 94, 96–97
Office for Vulnerable Populations
    (USAID), 134
Office of Cambodian Genocide
    Investigations (US), 60, 80n27
Office of Global Criminal Justice
    (Office of War Crimes Issues)
    (US), 19, 39, 91, 154
Office of Legal Affairs (OLA)
    (UN), 64
Office of Overseas Prosecutorial
    Development Assistance and
    Training (OPDAT) (US), 19,
    131–132
Office of Strategic Services (OSS)
    (US), 33

Voeten, Erik, 178
Vong, Ton, 162

war crimes: accountability for, 39;
    international consensus on, 35;
    trials after WWII for, 31–32
war crimes ambassadors, 19–20
war on terrorism, 84n81, 126
Warren, Mary Lee, 129
Washington Office on Latin America,
    170, 174
Watson, Diane, 95, 97
whistleblower culture, 74
Wiedemann, Kent, 65, 161
Wilhelm II, 31
Williams, Abiodun, 168
Williamson, Clint, 44, 72, 74, 176, 180
Wilson, Richard, 178

Wilson, Woodrow, 31, 33–34
Women NGO Secretariat of
    Liberia, 165
Woodrow Wilson Center, 170, 174
Wood, William, 128
Woolsey, Theodore S., 48n1
World Bank, 170, 173

Yale University: Cambodian Genocide
    Program (CGP), 60–61, 70, 84n77
Yalta conference, 34
Yalta Memorandum, 34
Yarsiah, James, 168
Yugoslavia. *see* Former Yugoslavia

Zacklin, Ralph, 64
Zamora, Angelica, 174
Zoellick, Robert, 43